W9-COD-660

Actuarial Statistics with

R

Theory and Case Studies

Guojun Gan, PhD, FSA   Emiliano A. Valdez, PhD, FSA

ACTEX Learning

Requests for permission should be addressed to
    ACTEX Learning
    4 Bridge Street
    New Hartford CT 06057

Manufactured in the United States of America

10 9 8 7 6 5 4 3 2 1

Cover design by Jeff Melaragno
Cover photo by Brandon Hill. Website: www.brandonhill.photography

    Library of Congress Control Number: 2018907085

ISBN: 978-1-63588-548-4

Contents

List of Figures

ix

List of Tables

Foreword

This timely book offers the reader a thorough introduction and overview of the topic of statistics, with applications in actuarial science, mathematical finance and quantitative risk management. The text contains sections on supervised learning, unsupervised learning, time-series models and simulation. These topics, related to both traditional and modern methods in data analytics are deemed important for today's actuaries according to the International Actuarial Association and the profession at large. The authors have brought together in one volume a unique and inspiring survey of these topics. The breadth of the coverage provides an almost full-scale picture of statistics that is applicable in actuarial, financial and quantitative risk management contexts.

One of the great merits of this book is that the presentation is far from encyclopedic. In the treatment of the different topics, several chapters contain the necessary theoretical background, immediately followed by many case studies as practical illustrations. The case studies are relevant, timely and trigger a reader's curiosity to learn more. They also cover a broad spectrum of highly relevant issues in insurance practice and will enable the reader to immediately apply what they learned to a practical situation. This pedagogical approach of blending theory with case studies using R makes this book unique in the area of statistics and at the same time relevant to both students and practitioners. The appendix offering an introduction to R provides a useful addition that helps to make the book self-contained and comprehensive. The mathematical skills required to be able to read the book are at a reasonable level. It assumes knowledge in probability and inference; a one-year course in mathematical statistics is sufficient.

The actuarial community is fortunate to have Guojun Gan and Emiliano Valdez write this significant book for the actuarial profession and the financial community. Dr. Valdez has built up a worldwide reputation over the years and Dr. Gan is quickly gaining momentum as a recognized expert in data mining and data analytics. Both authors are colleagues at the University of Connecticut, which offers an outstanding actuarial program. I have had the pleasure to work with Dr. Valdez on some research-related projects. During our collaborations and accompanying discussions, I saw firsthand Dr. Valdez's strong commitment to improving and expanding the knowledge base for the actuarial profession. This book is a testament to his commitment. Both authors deserve praise and congratulations for this remarkable work!

Jan Dhaene

Prof. Dr. Jan Dhaene holds a Ph.D. in Actuarial Science from KU Leuven (Belgium) and is a full professor with the Actuarial Research Group of the Department of Accountancy, Finance and Insurance at the Faculty of Business and Economics of KU Leuven. He is a member of the Institute of Actuaries of Belgium.

He is the head of the Insurance Research Centre (Actuarial Research Group) at KU Leuven. He is the co-author of several books on actuarial science and has authored over 120 scientific papers in refereed journals. He is an Associate Editor of Insurance: Mathematics & Economics, a member of the editorial board of ASTIN Bulletin, Advisory Editor of the Journal of Computational and Applied Mathematics, and the Editor-in-Chief of the Iranian Journal of Risk and Insurance.

Preface

This book is written primarily for actuarial students and practitioners who wish to learn the basic fundamentals and applications of statistical and simulation models using R programming. We assume that readers have studied probability at the level of (Ross, 2012a). We also assume that readers come to it with some knowledge of mathematical statistics (e.g., descriptive statistics, hypothesis testing, and confidence intervals), finance (e.g., risk-free interest rate, stocks, and returns), linear algebra (e.g., matrix operations), and calculus. We do not assume any prior programming experience.

In this textbook, we use a series of case studies to introduce the applications of classical supervised learning, unsupervised learning, time series, and simulation models. The content covers several topics on data analytics that have been prescribed by the International Actuarial Association. In particular, it has been designed to cover the learning objectives for the Statistics for Risk Modeling (SRM) Exam established by the Society of Actuaries. Some materials from this textbook also cover parts of the syllabus for the Modern Actuarial Statistics (MAS-I and MAS-II) Exams of the Casualty Actuarial Society. The treatment in this textbook differs from existing books in the following ways. First, this textbook teaches the steps of how to implement models in R at an elementary level. Second, this book gives students the opportunity to recognize the power of applied statistics and R programming by exposing them to real world problems. Finally, this book uses the case study method that helps better connect theory to practice and bridge the gap between academia and the workforce (Barkley et al., 2014).

During the past two decades, the rapid advancement of information technology has led to an explosive increase of data in various fields. Beyond all doubt, we are living in the era of *big data*; the term *big data* was coined to describe the enormous amount of data captured by enterprises in our world. According to a report (Manyika et al., 2011) published by McKinsey & Company, an American multinational management consulting firm, big data is the "the Next Frontier for Innovation, Competition, and Productivity." Big data has also attracted significant attention from many national governments including the US government.

In March 2012, the Obama Administration announced more than $200 million in investment to launch the "Big Data Research and Development Initiative."

Big data is affecting almost all industries, including the insurance industry (Ferris et al., 2014). Actuaries generally have excellent business acumen, but many do not get the proper training in order to code in high-level programming languages such as Java, C++, C#, and R. As coding and programming are essential to conduct analysis for large datasets, we have written this textbook to teach R programming to undergraduate students who intend to pursue a career in actuarial science, finance, or quantitative risk management. At the same time, this textbook aims to teach students topics in applied statistics including supervised learning, unsupervised learning, and time series models. Although this book does not deal directly with big data, it helps students develop the skills that are necessary for big data analysis.

Among the many high-level programming languages, we have chosen to teach R to students for the following reasons. First, R is an open source programming language and software environment designed for data analysis and visualization. Students can use R free of charge. Second, R contains many packages that make the language versatile and because of this versatility, R has become very popular and is useful both in academia and in the professional world. Third, R is easy to learn compared to other high-level programming languages such as C++ and Java. Finally, R is one of the top five tools used for big data mining and analysis according to a survey conducted by KDNuggets in 2012 (Chen et al., 2014, Section 5.4).

This book can serve several purposes. First, this book can be used as a primary textbook for a course taken by students to study the SRM Exam or a similar one. Second, this book is useful for students and practitioners to learn R programming and its applications in actuarial science, finance, and quantitative risk management. Third, this book is also suitable as a supplementary book used by instructors for courses related to statistical data analysis. Finally, the uniqueness of the case study approach used by this book provides significant promise to recommend it as a reference for advanced actuarial exams and online modules requiring R programming.

This book would not have been made possible without the assistance of several people. First, we would like to extend our appreciation to the following reviewers whose comments helped to significantly improve the quality of this book: Mary Pat Campbell, Runhuan Feng, Louise Francis, Yuanying Michelle Guan, Emma Ran Li, Nicole Radziwill, Peng Shi, and Xiaofei Susan Wang. We would like to thank the students at the University of Connecticut who used and commented on earlier versions of this book. Our special thanks also go to Michal Pesta and the participants of the Workshop on Advanced Statistical Methods hosted by the Czech Society of Actuaries and Charles University in Prague on June 25-26, 2018; many materials presented by Professor Valdez at that workshop were derived from this textbook. We are also very grateful to Garrett Doherty, who checked the final layout and shepherded the book through production, Brandon Hill, who took the cover pictures, and Jeff Melaragno, who designed the book cover. Last but not certainly the least, our warm-hearted thanks go to Stephen Camilli of ACTEX Learning, whose continued support and constant communication helped facilitate the completion of this book.

Guojun Gan and Emiliano A. Valdez
Storrs, Connecticut, USA
June 30, 2018

Access to R Code and Data Sets

As part of your purchase of this book, you may also access the R code and data sets mentioned within the book. To access these, navigate to the Product Supplements section of the publisher's website, `www.actexmadriver.com`. If you have any issues accessing this material, please contact the publisher at `support@actexmadriver.com`.

Part I

Supervised Learning

Chapter 1

Simple Linear Regression

Linear regression is an approach that uses linear functions to model the relationship between a scalar **dependent variable** and one or more independent variables. The **independent variables** are also referred to as the **explanatory variables** or **covariates**. In this chapter, we introduce simple linear regression models, which involve only one independent variable.

1.1 Scatter Plots and Regression

The goal of linear regression is to use a linear function to approximate the relationship between the dependent variable and independent variables. The resulting linear regression model can be used to understand this relationship or to predict values of the dependent variable given values of the independent variables. In some situations, a theory may be available to specify how the dependent variable varies as independent variables change. In many other situations, no theories exist to specify the relationship between the dependent variable and independent variables. In the latter situations, we can use data to figure out the relationship and an important step is to graph the data appropriately.

To build simple linear regression models with a dataset that involves one dependent variable and one independent variable, we can start with a scatter plot at the beginning of an analysis. Let X and Y denote the independent variable and the dependent variable, respectively. The dataset contains n observed values (x_1, y_1), (x_2, y_2), ..., (x_n, y_n) of (X, Y). A scatter plot is a graphical tool used to examine the relationship between the two variables X and Y. From a scatter plot of X and Y, we get a first look at how Y varies as X changes.

Figure 1.1 shows scatter plots of two synthetic datasets. The scatter plot in Figure 1.1(a) of the first dataset shows that there is a strong linear relationship

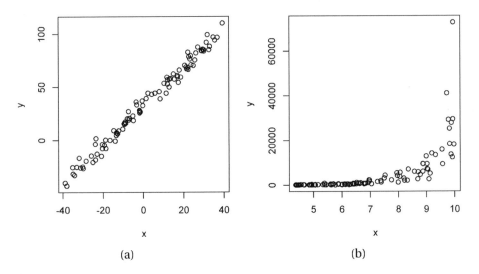

(a)   (b)

Figure 1.1: *Scatter plots of two synthetic datasets.*

between X and Y. From the scatter plot shown in Figure 1.1(b), we see that the two variables of the second dataset have a nonlinear relationship. The scatter plot is clearly a useful device to gain a visual understanding of the relationship between two variables. From the scatter plots, we can also see the ranges of the variables. For example, the independent variable of the first dataset ranges from -40 to 40. The dependent variable of the second dataset ranges from 0 to about 80000. It should be noted that a nonlinear relationship as shown in Figure 1.1(b) can be converted a linear relationship by transformation.

We can quantify the strength of the linear relationship between two variables using a **correlation** statistic. The **ordinary** or **Pearson correlation** coefficient between two variables is defined as

$$r = \text{Corr}(x, y) = \frac{1}{(n-1)s_x s_y} \sum_{i=1}^{n} (x_i - \bar{x})(y_i - \bar{y}), \tag{1.1}$$

where $\bar{x}$ and s_x are the sample mean and the **sample standard deviation** of $\{x_1, x_2, \ldots, x_n\}$, respectively, and $\bar{y}$ and s_y are defined similarly. The sample mean and the sample standard deviation of $\{x_1, x_2, \ldots, x_n\}$ are defined as

$$\bar{x} = \frac{1}{n} \sum_{i=1}^{n} x_i \tag{1.2}$$

and

$$s_x = \sqrt{\frac{1}{n-1} \sum_{i=1}^{n} (x_i - \bar{x})^2}, \tag{1.3}$$

respectively.

The correlation coefficient r ranges from -1 to 1. If $r > 0$, the variables are said to be positively correlated. If $r < 0$, the variables are said to be negatively correlated. If $|r|$ is close to 1, then the variables are strongly correlated. For example, the correlation coefficients of the two variables for the datasets shown in Figure 1.1(a) and Figure 1.1(b) are 0.9929 and 0.6521, respectively.

Exercise 1.1. Let r be the ordinary correlation coefficient between $\{x_1, x_2, \ldots, x_n\}$ and $\{y_1, y_2, \ldots, y_n\}$. For $i = 1, 2, \ldots, n$, let

$$z_i = ax_i + b,$$

where a and b are constants.

(a) Show that $s_z = |a| s_x$.

(b) For $a \neq 0$, show that $\mathrm{Corr}(z, y) = \dfrac{a}{|a|} \cdot r$.

(c) For $a = 0$, what can you conclude about the ordinary correlation coefficient between z and y?

Exercise 1.2. Consider the following dataset:

i	1	2	3	4	5
x_i	-0.6	0.2	-0.8	1.6	0.3
y_i	1.1	-2.5	-5.6	-0.1	0.8

(a) Calculate the sample means and the sample standard deviations of x and y.

(b) Calculate the ordinary correlation coefficient of x and y.

1.2 Simple Linear Regression Model

Let X and Y denote the independent variable and the dependent variable, respectively. Let n be the sample size. For $i = 1, 2, \ldots, n$, let (x_i, y_i) be the observed values of (X, Y) in the ith case. Then the simple linear regression model is specified as follows (Frees, 2009; Olive, 2017):

$$y_i = \beta_0 + \beta_1 x_i + \epsilon_i, \quad i = 1, 2, \ldots, n, \tag{1.4}$$

where β_0 and β_1 are parameters and ϵ_i is a random variable representing the error for the ith case. Suppressing the subscript i, the simple linear regression model can be written compactly as follows:

$$y = \beta_0 + \beta_1 x + \epsilon.$$

The parameters β_0 and β_1 are referred to the **intercept** and the **slope** parameters, respectively. The values of the two parameters are unknown and must be estimated from the data. The errors $\epsilon_1, \epsilon_2, \ldots, \epsilon_n$ depend on the unknown parameters and thus are not observable quantities.

In the simple linear regression model, we make the following assumptions:

(a) $x_1, x_2, \ldots, x_n$ are nonstochastic variables.
(b) $y_1, y_2, \ldots, y_n$ are independent random variables.
(c) $\text{Var}(y_i) = \sigma^2$.

The above assumptions are referred to as the observables representation sampling assumptions (Frees, 2009). They are equivalent to the following set of error representation sampling assumptions:

(a) $x_1, x_2, \ldots, x_n$ are nonstochastic variables.
(b) $\epsilon_1, \epsilon_2, \ldots, \epsilon_n$ are independent random variables.
(c) $E[\epsilon_i] = 0$ and $\text{Var}(\epsilon_i) = \sigma^2$ for each $i = 1, 2, \ldots, n$.

The second assumption means that the value of the error in one case gives no information about the value of the error in another case. The last assumption means that the scatter plot of the errors ϵ_i versus the observed values x_i of the independent variable X is a null scatter plot that has no pattern.

For the purpose of obtaining tests and confidence statements with small samples, we often make the following additional normality assumption:

(d) $\epsilon_1, \epsilon_2, \ldots, \epsilon_n$ are normally distributed.

The above normality assumption is much stronger than what we need in some situations. If the errors are determined to follow a different distribution, then the linear regression model might not be appropriate for the data.

1.3 Ordinary Least Squares Estimation

The simple linear regression model has two parameters, denoted by the Greek letters β_0 and β_1. These parameters are unknown quantities. Estimates of the parameters are computable functions of the data and are usually denoted by putting a hat over the corresponding Greek letters, e.g., $\hat{\beta}_0$ is the estimate of the parameter β_0.

The method of least squares is a widely used method for obtaining estimates of the parameters in a linear regression model. In the **method of least squares**, the regression coefficients are determined by minimizing the following objective function:

$$SS(\beta_0, \beta_1) = \sum_{i=1}^{n} [y_i - (\beta_0 + \beta_1 x_i)]^2, \tag{1.5}$$

which represents the sum of squared deviations for the regression line.

The optimization problem can be solved analytically by using basic calculus. To find the parameter values that minimize the sum of squared deviations, we differentiate the objective function with respect to β_0 and β_1 and set the derivatives to zero:

$$\frac{\partial SS(\beta_0, \beta_1)}{\partial \beta_0} = -2 \sum_{i=1}^{n} [y_i - (\beta_0 + \beta_1 x_i)] = 0, \tag{1.6a}$$

$$\frac{\partial SS(\beta_0, \beta_1)}{\partial \beta_1} = -2 \sum_{i=1}^{n} [y_i - (\beta_0 + \beta_1 x_i)] x_i = 0. \tag{1.6b}$$

Equations (1.6) are called the normal equations of the simple linear regression model.

Solving the normal equations gives the following estimated regression coefficients:

$$\hat{\beta}_1 = r \frac{s_y}{s_x}, \quad \hat{\beta}_0 = \bar{y} - \hat{\beta}_1 \bar{x}, \tag{1.7}$$

where

- $\bar{x}$ is the sample mean of $x_1, x_2, \ldots, x_n$.
- s_x is the sample standard deviation of $x_1, x_2, \ldots, x_n$.
- $\bar{y}$ is the sample mean of $y_1, y_2, \ldots, y_n$.
- s_y is the sample standard deviation of $y_1, y_2, \ldots, y_n$.
- r is the Pearson correlation coefficient defined in Equation (1.1).

The $\hat{\beta}_0$ and the $\hat{\beta}_1$ in Equation (1.7) are referred to as the least squares intercept and slope estimates, respectively. The fitted regression line is

$$\hat{y} = \hat{\beta}_0 + \hat{\beta}_1 x.$$

The fitted value for the ith case is given by

$$\hat{y}_i = \hat{\beta}_0 + \hat{\beta}_1 x_i. \tag{1.8}$$

The observed residual for the ith case is given by the following equation:

$$e_i = y_i - \hat{y}_i = y_i - (\hat{\beta}_0 + \hat{\beta}_1 x_i). \tag{1.9}$$

Like the parameters β_0 and β_1, the variance σ^2 is also an unknown quantity and needs to be estimated from the data. Under the assumption that $E[\epsilon_i] = 0$ and $\text{Var}(\epsilon_i) = \sigma^2$, we can estimate σ^2 from the **mean square error** (MSE):

$$s^2 = \frac{1}{n-2} \sum_{i=1}^{n} e_i^2, \tag{1.10}$$

where e_i is defined in Equation (1.9). The square root $s = \sqrt{s^2}$ is referred to as the residual standard deviation.

Exercise 1.3. Show that the least squares estimate $\hat{\beta}_1$ given in Equation (1.7) can also be expressed as

$$\hat{\beta}_1 = \frac{S_{xy}}{SS_x} = r\sqrt{\frac{SS_y}{SS_x}}, \tag{1.11}$$

where

$$SS_x = \sum_{i=1}^{n} (x_i - \bar{x})^2,$$

$$SS_y = \sum_{i=1}^{n} (y_i - \bar{y})^2,$$

and

$$S_{xy} = \sum_{i=1}^{n} (x_i - \bar{x})(y_i - \bar{y}).$$

Exercise 1.4. Consider the dataset given in Exercise 1.2 and the linear regression model $y_i = \beta_0 + \beta_1 x_i + \epsilon_i$. Calculate the ordinary least squares estimates $\hat{\beta}_0$ and $\hat{\beta}_1$.

1.4 Model Evaluation

Once we fit a basic linear regression model, we need to justify the quality of the fit of the regression model. To measure the fit of linear regression models, we can use the coefficient of **determination**, which is also referred to as R-**squared**. The coefficient of determination is denoted by R^2. Note that R^2 is a symbol and does not mean the square of R.

To define R^2, we first introduce the decomposition of variability. The total deviation of the dependent variable can be written as

$$y_i - \bar{y} = (y_i - \hat{y}_i) + (\hat{y}_i - \bar{y}), \tag{1.12}$$

where $y_i - \hat{y}_i$ is the unexplained deviation and $\hat{y}_i - \bar{y}$ is the deviation explained by the model. Under the method of least squares, we can show that

$$\sum_{i=1}^{n}(y_i - \bar{y})^2 = \sum_{i=1}^{n}(y_i - \hat{y}_i)^2 + \sum_{i=1}^{n}(\hat{y}_i - \bar{y})^2, \tag{1.13}$$

where $\hat{y}_i$ is the fitted value at point i and is defined in Equation (1.8).

The term on the left hand side of Equation (1.13) is referred to as the **total sum of squares** and is the total variation without the knowledge of x. We write

$$SST = \sum_{i=1}^{n}(y_i - \bar{y})^2. \tag{1.14}$$

The first term on the right hand side of Equation (1.13) is referred to as the **error sum of squares** and represents the total variation remaining after the introduction of x. We write

$$SSE = \sum_{i=1}^{n}(y_i - \hat{y}_i)^2. \tag{1.15}$$

The second term on the right hand side of Equation (1.13) is called the **regression sum of squares** and represents the total variation explained by the model. We write

$$SSR = \sum_{i=1}^{n}(\hat{y}_i - \bar{y})^2. \tag{1.16}$$

The coefficient of determination is defined as

$$R^2 = 1 - \frac{SSE}{SST}. \tag{1.17}$$

The above definition can be applied for general regression models, where $SSE + SSR = SST$ might not hold. For linear regression models, we can also define the R^2 as follows:

$$R^2 = \frac{SSR}{SST}. \tag{1.18}$$

The R^2 can be interpreted as the proportion of variability explained by the regression model. It takes values from 0 to 1. The higher the R^2, the better the fit of the model.

Another goodness-of-fit statistic is the **root mean squared error (RMSE)**, which is defined as

$$s = \sqrt{\frac{1}{n-2} \sum_{i=1}^{n} e_i^2},$$ (1.19)

which is the square root of the MSE defined in Equation (1.10). The RMSE is also referred to as the **residual standard error**. The MSE is an estimator of σ^2 mentioned in the assumptions of the regression model. The residual standard error is the size of a typical deviation of the response from the regression model.

The sources of variability can be summarized in a table called the **ANOVA (analysis of variance) table** as shown in Table 1.1. In Table 1.1, SSR, SSE, and SST are defined in Equations (1.16), (1.15), (1.14), respectively. The symbols MSR and MSE denote the regression mean square and the mean squared error, respectively. These mean squares are calculated by dividing the corresponding sum of squares by their degrees of freedom, that is,

$$MSR = \frac{SSR}{1} = SSR$$ (1.20)

and

$$MSE = \frac{SSE}{n-2} = s^2.$$ (1.21)

Source	Sum of Squares	Degrees of Freedom	Mean Square
Regression	SSR	1	MSR
Error	SSE	$n-2$	MSE
Total	SST	$n-1$	

Table 1.1: *The ANOVA table.*

The number of **degrees of freedom** is the number of values in the final calculation of a statistic that are free to vary. We can think of degrees of freedom of a statistic as the number of independent pieces of information available to estimate the statistic. For example, the following n values

$$y_1 - \bar{y}, y_2 - \bar{y}, \ldots, y_n - \bar{y}$$

are used to calculate SST. However, the n values satisfy the following equation

$$\sum_{i=1}^{n} (y_i - \bar{y}) = 0.$$

When $n-1$ of the n values are determined, the remaining one value is determined. Hence the degrees of freedom of SST is $n-1$. Similarly, the following n values

$$\hat{y}_1 - \bar{y}, \hat{y}_2 - \bar{y}, \ldots, \hat{y}_n - \bar{y}$$

are used to calculate SSR. However, the n values satisfy the following equations

$$\frac{\hat{y}_i - \bar{y}}{\hat{y}_j - \bar{y}} = \frac{x_i - \bar{x}}{x_j - \bar{x}}, \quad i, j = 1, 2, \ldots, n.$$

When any one of the n values is determined, the remaining $n-1$ values can be determined. Hence the degrees of freedom of SSR is 1.

Exercise 1.5. For $i = 1, 2, \ldots, n$, let $\hat{y}_i = \hat{\beta}_0 + \hat{\beta}_1 x_i$ be the fitted value at point i. Show that

(a)
$$\sum_{i=1}^{n} (y_i - \hat{y}_i)(\hat{y}_i - \bar{y}) = 0.$$

(b)
$$\sum_{i=1}^{n} (y_i - \bar{y})^2 = \sum_{i=1}^{n} (y_i - \hat{y}_i)^2 + \sum_{i=1}^{n} (\hat{y}_i - \bar{y})^2.$$

Exercise 1.6. Let r be the Pearson correlation coefficient between $\{x_i\}$ and $\{y_i\}$ that is defined in Equation (1.1). Let R^2 be the coefficient of determination from the simple linear regression model that is defined in Equation (1.17). Show that

$$r = \sqrt{R^2}.$$

Exercise 1.7. Consider the dataset given in Exercise 1.2.

(a) Construct the ANOVA table as shown in Table 1.1 for the linear regression model $y_i = \beta_0 + \beta_1 x_i + \epsilon_i$.

(b) Calculate the R^2 from the ANOVA table.

1.5   Statistical Inference

Once we have built a model, we can conduct hypothesis tests and predict new outcomes. In particular, we can conduct hypothesis tests to assess the importance of a variable and calculate confidence intervals of the regression coefficients. We can predict the outcome of a new input and calculate the prediction intervals of the outcome.

Statistical inference requires some assumptions. We assumed that the errors $\{e_i\}$ are independent and identically distributed. In addition, we also assumed that $\{e_i\}$ are normally distributed. Under such assumptions, the estimated standard deviation, also referred to as the **standard error**, of the slope estimate $\hat{\beta}_1$ is given by

$$se(\hat{\beta}_1) = \frac{s}{s_x\sqrt{n-1}}, \tag{1.22}$$

where s and s_x are the residual standard error and the sample standard deviation of x, respectively. In addition, the t-ratio defined as

$$t(\hat{\beta}_1) = \frac{\hat{\beta}_1 - d}{se(\hat{\beta}_1)} \tag{1.23}$$

can be shown to follow the t-distribution with $n-2$ degrees of freedom. In Equation (1.23), d is a hypothesized value of the slope parameter β_1.

To assess whether the explanatory variable is significant, we can investigate whether $\beta_1 = 0$ using the t-test. For example, we can formulate the following hypothesis test

$$H_0 : \beta_1 = 0 \text{ versus } H_a : \beta_1 \neq 0,$$

where H_0 is the **null hypothesis** and H_a is the **alternative hypothesis**. We reject H_0 in favor of H_a if

$$|t(\hat{\beta}_1)| > t_{n-2,1-\alpha/2},$$

where $t(\hat{\beta}_1)$ is the t-ratio defined in Equation (1.23) with $d = 0$ and $t_{n-2,1-\alpha/2}$ is the critical value that represents the $(1-\alpha/2)$th quantile of the t-distribution with $n-2$ degrees of freedom.

Table 1.2 presents some common **hypothesis tests** and the corresponding procedures to make decisions.

Instead of comparing the t-ratios to the critical values, we can construct p-**values** and compare them to given significance levels. The procedure for calculating p-values of various hypotheses is summarized in Table 1.3. How the p-values are interpreted is given in Table 1.4.

Hypothesis testing focuses on a single conclusion of statistical significance. We can use **confidence intervals** to provide a range of plausible values of an

Hypothesis Test	Reject H_0 in favor of H_a if
$H_0 : \beta = d$ versus $H_a : \beta > d$	$t(\hat{\beta}) > t_{n-2,1-\alpha}$
$H_0 : \beta = d$ versus $H_a : \beta < d$	$t(\hat{\beta}) < -t_{n-2,1-\alpha}$
$H_0 : \beta = d$ versus $H_a : \beta \neq d$	$|t(\hat{\beta})| > t_{n-2,1-\alpha/2}$

Table 1.2: *Some hypothesis tests and the corresponding decision-making procedures.*

Hypothesis Test	p-value
$H_0 : \beta = d$ versus $H_a : \beta > d$	$P(t(\hat{\beta}) < t_{n-2})$
$H_0 : \beta = d$ versus $H_a : \beta < d$	$P(t(\hat{\beta}) > t_{n-2})$
$H_0 : \beta = d$ versus $H_a : \beta \neq d$	$P(|t(\hat{\beta})| < |t_{n-2}|)$

Table 1.3: *Some hypothesis tests and the corresponding p-values. In the table, t_{n-2} is a random variable following a t-distribution with $n - 2$ degrees of freedom.*

estimate. Given a significance level α, a $100(1 - \alpha)\%$ confidence interval for the slope estimate $\hat{\beta}$ is given by

$$(\hat{\beta} - t_{n-2,1-\alpha/2} \cdot se(\hat{\beta}), \hat{\beta} + t_{n-2,1-\alpha/2} \cdot se(\hat{\beta})). \tag{1.24}$$

We can also calculate confidence intervals for new outcomes. Let x_* be a new value of the explanatory variable. Then the predicted value of y is

$$\hat{y}_* = \hat{\beta}_0 + \hat{\beta}_1 x_*.$$

The standard error of the this prediction at x_* is given by

$$se(\hat{y}_*) = s\sqrt{1 + \frac{1}{n} + \frac{(x_* - \bar{x})^2}{(n-1)s_x^2}}. \tag{1.25}$$

A $100(1 - \alpha)\%$ confidence interval of the prediction, also referred to as **prediction interval**, is given by

$$(\hat{y}_* - t_{n-2,1-\alpha/2} \cdot se(\hat{y}_*), \hat{y}_* + t_{n-2,1-\alpha/2} \cdot se(\hat{y}_*)). \tag{1.26}$$

p-value Range	Meaning
$[0, 0.01]$	Strong presumption against H_0
$[0.1, 1]$	Low presumption against H_0

Table 1.4: *Interpretation of p-values.*

1.6   Residual Analysis

Under the assumptions of the basic linear regression model, the deviations (i.e., ϵ_i) are identically and independently distributed and normally distributed. If these assumptions are satisfied, then the residuals of the fitted model should contain little or no information.

The purpose of residual analysis is to check if there are any patterns that can be observed from the residuals. In general, there are five common types of patterns:

(a) Lack of independence. The deviations $\{\epsilon_1, \epsilon_2, \ldots, \epsilon_n\}$ have some relationships and are not independent.

(b) Heteroscedasticity. The variability $\text{Var}(\epsilon_i)$ is not constant and varies by observation.

(c) Relationships between deviations and explanatory variables. If an explanatory variable helps explain the deviation ϵ, then the variable should be used to build a better model.

(d) Non-normal distributions. If the distribution of the deviation departs seriously from normality, then the inference procedures based on normality are not valid any more.

(e) Unusual points. An unusual point may have a large effect on the regression model.

There are two types of unusual points: outliers and high leverage points. To quantify whether an observation is an unusual point, let us first define standardized residuals and leverages. The **leverage** for the ith observation is defined as

$$h_{ii} = \frac{1}{n} + \frac{(x_i - \bar{x})^2}{(n-1)s_x^2}. \tag{1.27}$$

The standardized residual of the ith observation is defined as

$$\frac{e_i}{s\sqrt{1 - h_{ii}}} = \frac{y_i - \hat{y}_i}{s\sqrt{1 - h_{ii}}}. \tag{1.28}$$

An observation is said to be an **outlier** if the absolute value of its standardized residual is larger than 2, that is,

$$\frac{|e_i|}{s\sqrt{1 - h_{ii}}} > 2.$$

An observation is said to be a **high leverage point** if its leverage is larger than $6/n$, that is,

$$h_{ii} > \frac{6}{n}.$$

It is worth noting that an observation can be an outlier and a high leverage point simultaneously.

There are several ways to deal with unusual points. If an observation is a severe unusual point, we can remove it before fitting a linear regression model. Otherwise, we can fit a linear regression model by including the point.

1.7 Summary

In this chapter, we introduced the simple linear regression model, which involves only one independent variable. In particular, we introduced the method of least squares for estimating parameters, goodness-of-fit measures, and residual analysis. For more information about the simple linear regression model, readers are referred to (Bingham and Fry, 2010), (James et al., 2013), (Weisberg, 2013), (Faraway, 2014), and (Olive, 2017). For a brief description of the history of linear regression and its applications, readers are referred to (Frees, 2009, Chapter 1).

1.8 End-of-Chapter Exercises

Exercise 1.8. For $i = 1, 2, \ldots, n$, let w_i be defined as

$$w_i = \frac{x_i - \bar{x}}{(n-1)s_x^2}.$$

Show that

(a) The sum of $w_1, w_2, \ldots, w_n$ is zero, i.e.,

$$\sum_{i=1}^{n} w_i = 0.$$

(b) The sum of $w_1 x_1, w_2 x_2, \ldots, w_n x_n$ is one, i.e.,

$$\sum_{i=1}^{n} w_i x_i = 1.$$

(c) The least squares estimate $\hat{\beta}_1$ can be expressed as

$$\hat{\beta}_1 = \sum_{i=1}^{n} w_i y_i. \tag{1.29}$$

Exercise 1.9. Let $\hat{\beta}_1$ be the least squares estimate of the parameter β_1 in the simple linear regression model. Show that

(a)
$$E[\hat{\beta}_1] = \beta_1.$$

(b)
$$\text{Var}(\hat{\beta}_1) = \frac{\sigma^2}{s_x^2(n-1)}.$$

Exercise 1.10. For $i = 1, 2, \ldots, n$, let u_i be defined as

$$u_i = \frac{1}{n} - \frac{(x_i - \bar{x})\bar{x}}{(n-1)s_x^2}.$$

Show that

(a) The sum of $u_1, u_2, \ldots, u_n$ is one, i.e.,

$$\sum_{i=1}^{n} u_i = 1.$$

(b) The sum of $u_1 x_1, u_2 x_1, \ldots, u_n x_n$ is zero, i.e.,

$$\sum_{i=1}^{n} u_i x_i = 0.$$

(c) The least squares estimate $\hat{\beta}_0$ can be expressed as

$$\hat{\beta}_0 = \sum_{i=1}^{n} u_i y_i.$$

Exercise 1.11. Let $\hat{\beta}_0$ be the least squares estimate of the parameter β_0 in the simple linear regression model. Show that

(a)
$$E[\hat{\beta}_0] = \beta_0.$$

(b)
$$\text{Var}(\hat{\beta}_0) = \left(\frac{1}{n} + \frac{\bar{x}^2}{(n-1)s_x^2}\right)\sigma^2.$$

Exercise 1.12. Let $\hat{\beta}_0$ and $\hat{\beta}_1$ be the least squares estimates of the parameters β_0 and β_1 in the simple linear regression model, respectively. Show that

$$\text{Cov}(\hat{\beta}_0, \hat{\beta}_1) = -\frac{\bar{x}}{(n-1)s_x^2}\sigma^2,$$

where $\text{Cov}(\hat{\beta}_0, \hat{\beta}_1)$ denotes the covariance between $\hat{\beta}_0$ and $\hat{\beta}_1$.

Exercise 1.13. Let x_* be a value of the explanatory variable. Let $\hat{\mu}_*$ be the estimate of the mean $\mu_* = E[y|x_*]$ and let $\hat{y}_*$ be the prediction of the response variable at x_*. Show that

(a)
$$\text{Var}(\hat{\mu}_*) = \left(\frac{1}{n} + \frac{(x_* - \bar{x})^2}{(n-1)s_x^2} \right)\sigma^2.$$

(b)
$$\text{Var}(\hat{y}_*) = \left(1 + \frac{1}{n} + \frac{(x_* - \bar{x})^2}{(n-1)s_x^2} \right)\sigma^2.$$

Exercise 1.14. Let e_i be the residual at the i point, i.e.,

$$e_i = y_i - (\hat{\beta}_0 + \hat{\beta}_1 x_i).$$

Show that
$$\text{Var}(e_i) = (1 - h_{ii})\sigma^2,$$

where h_{ii} is defined in Equation (1.27).

Exercise 1.15. Consider the following linear regression model without the intercept:
$$y_i = \beta_1 x_i + \epsilon_i, \quad i = 1, 2, \dots, n,$$

where $\epsilon_1, \epsilon_2, \dots, \epsilon_n$ are independent and identically distributed with mean 0 and variance σ^2.

(a) Use the least squares method to derive an expression for the estimate $\hat{\beta}_1$ of the slope parameter β_1.

(b) Find an expression of the variance of $\hat{\beta}_1$.

Chapter 2

Case Study: Implementing the Capital Asset Pricing Model

The capital asset pricing model (CAPM) is a widely used model in finance that is used to price an individual stock or portfolio. In this case study, we illustrate how to implement the CAPM using a simple linear regression model. In particular, readers will be able to do the following in R:

- summarize and visualize data
- build simple linear regression models
- use the method of least squares to estimate regression parameters
- calculate and interpret the coefficient of determination (R^2) and the mean squared error
- create and interpret the ANOVA table
- calculate confidence intervals of regression coefficients
- calculate prediction intervals
- understand the numbers in the model summary produced by R
- identify outliers and high leverage points

2.1 Problem Description

Sharpe (1964) and Lintner (1965) developed the capital asset pricing model (**CAPM**), which can be used to price an individual stock or portfolio. Under the CAPM model, all investors are assumed to be rational and risk-averse, have homogeneous expectations, be broadly diversified across a range of investments, and be able to borrow and lend money freely at the same risk-free rate. In such a

19

market, the expected return of a stock can be expressed as

$$E[R] = R_f + \beta(E[R_m] - R_f), \tag{2.1}$$

where R is the return on the stock, R_m is the return on the market portfolio, R_f is the return on the risk-free asset, and β is a parameter that can be interpreted as a measure of the riskiness of the stock. In the CAPM, β is determined by

$$\beta = \frac{\text{Cov}(R, R_m)}{\text{Var}(R_m)} = \rho(R, R_m)\frac{\sqrt{\text{Var}(R)}}{\sqrt{\text{Var}(R_m)}}, \tag{2.2}$$

where $\text{Cov}(R, R_m)$ denotes the covariance between R and R_m, $\rho(R, R_m)$ denotes the correlation between R and R_m, $\text{Var}(R)$ and $\text{Var}(R_m)$ denote the variances of R and R_m, respectively.

To implement the CAPM, we can fit a basic (or single) linear regression model of a stock's excess return on the market-portfolio's excess return as follows

$$R_i - R_{f,i} = \alpha + \beta(R_{m,i} - R_{f,i}) + \epsilon_i, \quad i = 1, 2, \ldots, n, \tag{2.3}$$

where R_i is the realized return on the stock in period i, $R_{m,i}$ is the realized return on the stock in period i, $R_{f,i}$ is the realized return on the risk-free asset in period i, n is the number of data points, and ϵ_i is random noise.

Under the assumptions of the CAPM, the regression coefficients (α, β) estimated from Equation (2.3) are such that α is zero and β is the same as in the CAPM model given in Equation (2.1). In the subsequent sections, we illustrate the implementation of the CAPM by estimating the β of Manulife Financial's stock. Manulife Financial is one of the largest insurance companies with its corporate headquarter in Toronto, Canada. In our implementation, we use the S&P 500 index as a proxy for the market-portfolio and the 3-month US treasury rate as the risk-free rate.

2.2 Data Description

To estimate the β of Manulife Financial's stock, we follow standard practice in the securities industry and use monthly prices. We downloaded historical monthly data from Yahoo Finance[1]. The symbols of Manulife Financial's stock, the S&P 500 index, and the 3-month treasury rate are MFC, ^GSPC, and ^IRX, respectively.

Since we downloaded the data from the same source, the formats of the files are the same. All the data files contain the following seven columns: Date,

---

[1]http://finance.yahoo.com/

Open, High, Low, Close, Volume, and Adj Close. Since the data is monthly data, the Date column contains the dates of the first business days of the available months. The Open, High, Low, and Close columns contain the open, the highest, the lowest, and the close prices of the corresponding months, respectively. The Volume column contains the number of transactions for the months. The Adj Close column contains the close price adjusted for dividends. We use the prices from the Adj Close column for our estimation.

The price data of the three securities was saved as three CSV (Comma-Separated Values) files named as MFC.csv, sp500.csv, and irx.csv, respectively. Although the three files have the same format, they contain a different number of data points. The file MFC.csv contains prices for 192 days, with one observation from each month, from September 24, 1999 to August 3, 2015. The file sp500.csv contains prices for 788 days from January 3, 1950 to August 3, 2015. The file irx.csv contains prices for 308 days from January 4, 1990 to August 3, 2015.

2.3 Loading the Data into R

Since the data was saved into CSV files, we can use the function read.csv to load the data into R. Suppose that the data files are in the current working directory. Then we can read the data as follows:

```
> mfc <- read.csv('MFC.csv',stringsAsFactors=FALSE)
> sp500 <- read.csv('sp500.csv',stringsAsFactors=FALSE)
> irx <- read.csv('irx.csv',stringsAsFactors=FALSE)
> head(mfc)
          Date  Open  High   Low Close  Volume Adj.Close
1 2015-08-03 17.74 18.00 14.26 15.76 2708000  15.76000
2 2015-07-01 18.76 18.91 17.08 17.73 1899400  17.59599
3 2015-06-01 18.30 19.61 18.04 18.59 2290100  18.44949
4 2015-05-01 18.18 19.34 18.07 18.35 1795600  18.21131
5 2015-04-01 16.97 18.58 16.79 18.21 1697600  17.93680
6 2015-03-02 17.48 17.73 16.57 17.01 2081400  16.75480
> dim(mfc)
[1] 192    7
> dim(sp500)
[1] 788    7
> dim(irx)
[1] 308    7
```

In the above code, we used the function head to display the first several rows of the data frame. Actually, this function can be used to display the first several elements of a vector and the first several rows of a matrix. From the first several rows of the stock price data, we see that the prices are in reverse chronological order.

Exercise 2.1. Suppose that we read the file MFC.csv using the following command

```
1 mfc <- read.csv('MFC.csv')
```

What is the return value of the following call?

```
1 mode(mfc$Date)
```

Exercise 2.2. Let mfc be the data frame created by

```
1 mfc <- read.csv('MFC.csv', stringsAsFactors=FALSE)
```

Look at the help of the function as.Date and convert the vector of strings mfc$Date to a vector of date objects in R.

Now we have the raw price data of the three securities in the R workspace. Suppose that we want to use 10 years of monthly returns from January 2005 to December 2014 to estimate the β of Manulife Financial's stock. We need to extract the price data and calculate the returns for the stock and the S&P 500 index. Since the monthly prices are obtained from the first business days of the months, we can use the next month's price as this month's end price. Then we can extract the price data and calculate the returns as follows:

```
 1 > ind <- seq(from=127,to=8,by=-1)
 2 > mfcReturn <- mfc$Adj.Close[ind] / mfc$Adj.Close[ind+1]
   - 1
 3 > sp500Return <- sp500$Adj.Close[ind] / sp500$Adj.Close[
   ind+1] - 1
 4 > rfRate <- irx$Adj.Close[ind+1] / 1200
 5 > dat10y <- data.frame(mfc=mfcReturn - rfRate, sp500=
   sp500Return - rfRate)
 6 > head(dat10y)
 7            mfc           sp500
 8 1   0.062016836   0.016885013
 9 2   0.030516898  -0.021359322
10 3  -0.045465272  -0.022376915
```

```
11 4   0.006420319   0.027587880
12 5   0.038077092  -0.002544381
13 6   0.049531119   0.033418287
14 > tail(dat10y)
15               mfc          sp500
16 115 -0.004217211   0.037640295
17 116 -0.046100286  -0.015528837
18 117 -0.014556400   0.023190627
19 118  0.056440711   0.024531089
20 119 -0.040707677  -0.004192755
21 120 -0.157704995  -0.031071639
```

In the above code, we first created a vector of indices named ind in order to extract the data we wanted for our analysis. The vector contains a sequence of decreasing integers so that we can change the order of the prices to a chronological order. Then we calculated the monthly returns for the stock and the index. We also calculated the risk-free rates from the 3-month US treasury rates by dividing them by 12×100 because these treasury rates are annualized percentages. In Line 5 of the above output, we calculated the excess monthly returns of the stock and the index and put them into a data frame named dat10y.

In Line 14 of the above output, we used the function tail to display the last several rows of the data frame. Similar to the function head, the function tail is a useful function for checking data in R.

2.4 Data Visualization and Summarization

We now have the excess returns on the stock and the index in the R workspace. We are ready to examine the data before fitting a regression model. We need to make sure the data satisfies the assumptions of linear regression models.

To get an impression of the distribution of each variable, we plot **histograms** of the two variables as follows:

```
1 par(mfrow=c(1,2))
2 hist(dat10y$mfc, breaks=20)
3 hist(dat10y$sp500, breaks=20)
```

The resulting histograms are shown in Figure 2.1. The histograms show that both variables are approximately normally distributed.

Instead of plotting histograms, we can also calculate the summary statistics to investigate the distribution of an individual variable in isolation of the other. Common summary statistics include the minimum, the maximum, the mean,

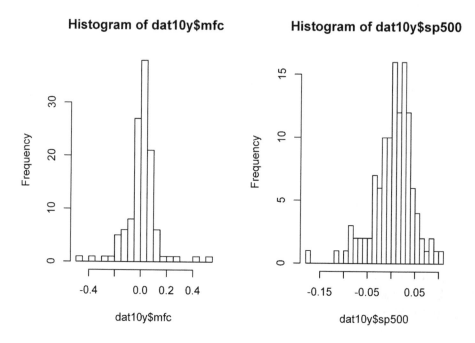

Figure 2.1: *Histograms of the excess returns on Manulife Financial's stock and the S&P 500 index.*

and the percentiles. To get the summary statistics of the variables, we use the function summary as follows:

```
> summary(dat10y)
      mfc                    sp500
 Min.    :-0.453189    Min.    :-0.170175
 1st Qu.:-0.025397     1st Qu.:-0.016219
 Median : 0.014469     Median : 0.008698
 Mean    : 0.005639    Mean    : 0.004129
 3rd Qu.: 0.051921     3rd Qu.: 0.028892
 Max.    : 0.526619    Max.    : 0.107715
```

The output of the function summary gives us an overview of the statistical properties of the data. From these summary statistics, we observe a wide range of excess returns on both Manulife Financial's stock and the S&P500 index, but more so with the excess returns on Manulife Financial's stock. For example, for Manulife Financial's stock, the maximum excess return is 52.7% and the minimum excess return is -45.3%. Furthermore, since the mean is less than the median, both variables are slightly skewed to the left.

Histograms and summary statistics are useful to examine the distribution of an individual variable in isolation of the other. Since linear regression is used to model the linear relationship between variables, we can use **scatter plots** to visualize the relationship between the two variables. To produce a scatter plot of the excess returns on the stock and those on the index, we proceed as follows:

```
with(dat10y, plot(sp500, mfc))
```

In the above code, we used the function `with`, which applies an expression to a dataset. The above command is equivalent to the following command:

```
plot(dat10y$sp500, dat10y$mfc)
```

The resulting scatter plot is shown in Figure 2.2. The scatter plot shows a positive linear relationship.

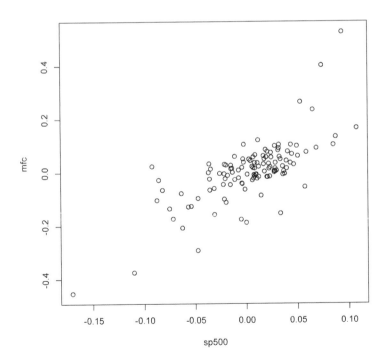

Figure 2.2: *A scatter plot of the excess returns on Manulife Financial's stock and those on the S&P 500 index.*

To calculate the correlation coefficient between the excess returns, we proceed as follows:

```
1 > with(dat10y, cor(mfc, sp500))
2 [1] 0.725671
```

The correlation coefficient of the excess returns turns out to be about 0.73, which indicates that the excess returns on the stock are positively correlated to those on the index. In this case, when the excess return on the index is high, the excess return on the stock is also high, and vice versa.

Exercise 2.3. The sample mean and the sample standard deviation of $\{x_1, x_2, \ldots, x_n\}$ are defined in Equation (1.2) and Equation (1.3), respectively.

(a) Write an R function called `calculateStd(x)` to calculate the sample standard deviation of the vector x. What is the return of the following call?

```
1 calculateStd(dat10y$mfc)
```

(b) Write an R function called `calculateCorr(x,y)` to calculate the Pearson correlation coefficient of the two vectors x and y. What is the return of the following call:

```
1 calculateCorr(dat10y$mfc, dat10y$sp500)
```

2.5 Fitting a Basic Linear Regression Model

According to our analysis in the previous section, the excess returns on the stock seem to be normally distributed and have a strong positive linear relationship with those of the index. In this section, we fit a linear regression model to the data by using the method of least squares to estimate the regression coefficients.

To fit a regression line to the data in R, we use the function lm as follows:

```
1 > fit <- lm(mfc ~ sp500, data=dat10y)
2 > summary(fit)
3
4 Call:
```

```
 5 lm(formula = mfc ~ sp500, data = dat10y)
 6
 7 Residuals:
 8      Min        1Q    Median        3Q       Max
 9 -0.21652  -0.04091  -0.00232   0.04084   0.34572
10
11 Coefficients:
12               Estimate  Std. Error  t value  Pr(>|t|)
13 (Intercept)  -0.002436    0.007262   -0.335     0.738
14 sp500         1.955416    0.170676   11.457    <2e-16 ***
15 ---
16 Signif. codes:  0 '***' 0.001 '**' 0.01 '*' 0.05 '.' 0.1
      ' ' 1
17
18 Residual standard error: 0.07917 on 118 degrees of
      freedom
19 Multiple R-squared:  0.5266,    Adjusted R-squared:  0.5226
20 F-statistic: 131.3 on 1 and 118 DF,   p-value: < 2.2e-16
```

From Line 1 of the above output, we see that the function lm takes two arguments. The first argument is a formula. The variable on the left hand side of the symbol ~ is the dependent variable y; the variable on the right hand side of the symbol is the independent variable x. Table 2.1 gives some common names of regression variables. The second argument specifies the data set. We saved the fitting result to an object named fit and then used the function summary to show the summary of the fitted regression model.

Variable y	Variable x
Dependent variable	Independent variable
Response	Treatment
Output	Input
Endogenous variable	Exogenous variable
Predicted variable	Predictor variable
Regressand	Regressor

Table 2.1: *Common names of regression variables.*

The model summary contains the formula used to fit the model, summary statistics of the residuals, the regression coefficients, and other useful information. From the model summary, we get the intercept and slope estimates:

$$\hat{\alpha} = -0.002436, \quad \hat{\beta} = 1.955416. \qquad (2.4)$$

We can also plot the fitted regression line and the data in the same figure using the function `abline` as follows:

```
with(dat10y, plot(sp500, mfc))
abline(fit)
```

The resulting plot is shown in Figure 2.3, from which we see that the data points surround the fitted regression line.

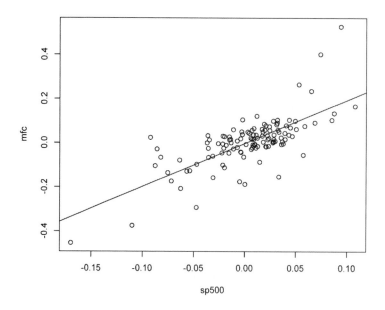

Figure 2.3: *A scatter plot of sp500 and mfc with the fitted regression line.*

Exercise 2.4. Use the formulas given in Equation (1.7) and write a piece of R code to calculate the estimated regression coefficients $\hat{\alpha}$ and $\hat{\beta}$. Compare your results to the estimates shown in the model summary. You can use the R built-in functions `cor`, `sd`, and `mean` to calculate the correlation coefficient, the sample standard deviation, and the sample mean, respectively.

Exercise 2.5. Let x and y be the two vectors obtained from the following R code:

```
x <- dat10y$sp500
y <- dat10y$mfc
```

(a) Write R code to compute the following sum:

$$\sum_{i=1}^{n} w_i y_i, \tag{2.5}$$

where n is the length of the vector x and

$$w_i = \frac{x_i - \bar{x}}{s_x^2(n-1)}.$$

Here $\bar{x}$ and s_x denote the sample mean and the sample standard deviation of x, respectively.

(b) Does the value of the sum in Equation (2.5) equal to the slope estimate $\hat{\beta}$ given in Equation (2.4)?

2.6 Model Evaluation

Once we fit a basic linear regression model, we need to justify the quality of the fit of the regression model. To measure the fit of linear regression models, we can use the **coefficient of determination**, which is also referred to as R-**squared**.

Exercise 2.6. The fitted values $\{\hat{y}_i\}$ can be extracted from the R object produced by lm as follows:

```
1  fit  <-  lm(mfc  ~  sp500,  data=dat10y)
2  haty  <-  fit$fitted.values
```

(a) Write R code to calculate SST, SSE, and SSR defined in Equations (1.14), (1.15), and (1.16), respectively.

(b) Calculate $SSE + SSR - SST$. Is it equal to zero?

(c) Calculate the following sum

$$\sum_{i=1}^{n} (y_i - \hat{y}_i)(\hat{y}_i - \bar{y}).$$

Is it equal to zero?

The R^2 of the linear regression model can be found in the model summary. For the model we just fitted, the R^2 is 0.5266. The R^2 shows that the basic linear regression model explains more than half of the total variability of the dependent variable.

Exercise 2.7. Suppose that we save the summary of the model into a variable as follows:

```
fit <- lm(mfc ~ sp500, data=dat10y)
fitsummary <- summary(fit)
```

(a) The R object fitsummary is a list. The estimated regression coefficients are stored in the object coefficients of the list. Use list operations to extract the estimated regression coefficients $\hat{\alpha}$ and $\hat{\beta}$ from the list fitsummary.

(b) Use the formula in Equation (1.17) and write R code to calculate the R^2.

In R, we can produce the ANOVA table using the function anova as follows:

```
> anova(fit)
Analysis of Variance Table

Response: mfc
          Df   Sum Sq Mean Sq F value    Pr(>F)
sp500      1  0.82277 0.82277  131.26 < 2.2e-16 ***
Residuals 118  0.73966 0.00627
---
Signif. codes:  0 '***' 0.001 '**' 0.01 '*' 0.05 '.' 0.1
    ' ' 1
```

The ANOVA table produced by R does not show the total sum of squares. However, we can derive the total sum of squares by the following formula

$$SST = SSR + SSE.$$

Exercise 2.8. Given the following ANOVA table produced by R:

```
            Df   Sum Sq  Mean Sq  F value     Pr(>F)
sp500        1  0.82277  0.82277   131.26  < 2.2e-16 ***
Residuals  118  0.73966  0.00627
```

Calculate the R^2 and the residual standard error s.

2.7 Residual Analysis

In this section, we examine the residuals to check if there are any unusual points. To find high leverage points, we can proceed as follows:

```
> barx <- with(dat10y, mean(sp500))
> sx <- with(dat10y, sd(sp500))
> n <- dim(dat10y)[1]
> h <- 1/n + (dat10y$sp500 - barx)^2 / ( (n-1) * sx^2 )
> indh <- h > 6/n
> HighLeveragePoints <- dat10y[indh,]
> HighLeveragePoints
            mfc          sp500
44    0.02373827  -0.09219977
45   -0.45318935  -0.17017452
49   -0.37464108  -0.11011453
81    0.16592281   0.10771471
> h[indh]
[1] 0.05145677 0.14952613 0.06898800 0.05819836
```

From the above R output, we see that there are four high leverage points. We can label the high leverage points in the scatter plot using the following piece of code:

```
with(dat10y, plot(sp500, mfc))
abline(fit)
for(i in 1:dim(HighLeveragePoints)[1] ) {
  p <- HighLeveragePoints[i,]
  text(p$sp500, p$mfc, labels=rownames(p), pos=3)
}
```

The resulting plot is shown in Figure 2.4. Since the leverages for the observations 44, 45, 49, and 81 are close to $6/120 = 0.05$, they are not severe high leverage

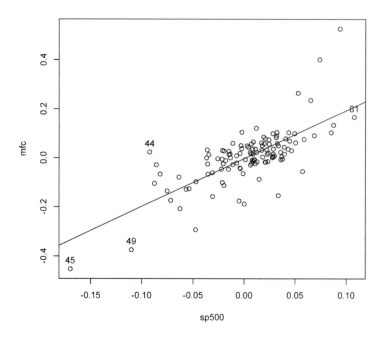

Figure 2.4: *Four high leverage points with labels above them.*

points. Here we call a point a severe high leverage point if its leverage is much larger than the average.

Now let us look at the standardized residuals to see if there are any severe outliers. To calculate the standardized residuals and identify outliers, we proceed as follows:

```
1 > e <- fit$residuals
2 > s <- sqrt( sum(e^2) / (n-2) )
3 > sr <- e / (s * sqrt(1-h) )
4 > indsr <- abs(sr) > 2
5 > Outliers <- dat10y[indsr,]
6 > sr[indsr]
7       44           49           51           52           53
             54           55           58           67           82
8   2.677566  -2.053673   4.469910   2.083716  -2.353886
        3.320130  -2.751849  -2.099776  -2.518124  -2.074143
```

We identified ten outliers. We can label these outliers in the scatter plot using the following code:

```
1 with(dat10y, plot(sp500, mfc))
2 abline(fit)
3 for(i in 1:dim(Outliers)[1] ) {
4   p <- Outliers[i,]
5   text(p$sp500, p$mfc, labels=rownames(p), pos=4)
6 }
```

The resulting graph is shown in Figure 2.5. From the figure, we see that most of the identified outliers are not severe outliers. Observations 51 and 54 might have a large effect on the regression model.

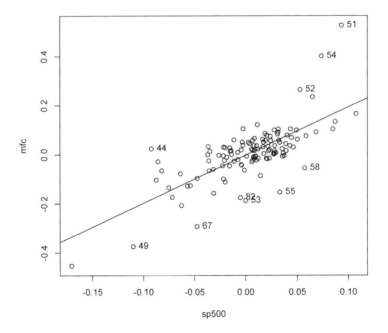

Figure 2.5: *Ten outliers with labels in their right-hand sides.*

From our above analysis, observations 45, 51, and 54 seem to be severe unusual points. We can remove them and fit a new linear regression model as follows:

```
1 > dat10yb <- dat10y[-c(45,51,54),]
2 > fitb <- lm(mfc ~ sp500, data=dat10yb)
```

```
 3 > summary(fitb)
 4
 5 Call:
 6 lm(formula = mfc ~ sp500, data = dat10yb)
 7
 8 Residuals:
 9      Min        1Q      Median        3Q        Max
10 -0.214103  -0.031488   0.002582   0.040869   0.187241
11
12 Coefficients:
13               Estimate Std. Error t value Pr(>|t|)
14 (Intercept)  -0.004871   0.006189  -0.787    0.433
15 sp500         1.550670   0.160483   9.663   <2e-16 ***
16 ---
17 Signif. codes:  0 '***' 0.001 '**' 0.01 '*' 0.05 '.' 0.1
       ' ' 1
18
19 Residual standard error: 0.06653 on 115 degrees of
       freedom
20 Multiple R-squared:  0.4481,   Adjusted R-squared:  0.4433
21 F-statistic: 93.36 on 1 and 115 DF,  p-value: < 2.2e-16
```

Comparing the R^2 from our first model, we see that the R^2 of the new model reduced to 0.4481. Since the three observations we removed are at both ends of the x-axis, deleting them from the data set makes the model worse. We can keep the original model because its R^2 is higher.

Exercise 2.9. Suppose that dat22 is a data frame created by the following R code[2]:

```
1 x <- c(1.5, 1.7, 2, 2.2, 2.5, 2.5, 2.7, 2.9, 3, 3.5, 3.4,
         9.5, 9.5, 3.8, 4.2, 4.3, 4.6, 4, 5.1, 5.1, 5.2, 5.5)
2 y <- c(3, 2.5, 3.5, 3, 3.1, 3.6, 3.2, 3.9, 4, 4, 8, 8,
         2.5, 4.2, 4.1, 4.8, 4.2, 5.1, 5.1, 5.1, 4.8, 5.3)
3 dat22 <- data.frame(x=x, y=y)
```

    (a) Fit a linear regression model to this data set using x as the explanatory variable and y as the dependent variable.

    (b) Calculate the leverages for all the observations and identify which observations are high leverage points.

---

[2]This data set was obtained from (Frees, 2009, p. 43).

(c) Calculate the standardized residuals for all the observations and identify which observations are outliers.

2.8 Statistical Inference

To assess whether the explanatory variable (i.e., the excess returns on the S&P 500 index) is significant, we can investigate whether $\beta = 0$ using the t-test. We can calculate the t-ratio and compare it with the critical value $t_{n-2,1-\alpha/2}$ as follows:

```
 1 > beta <- fit$coefficients[2]
 2 > n <- dim(dat10y)[1]
 3 > s <- sqrt( sum(fit$residuals^2) / (n-2) )
 4 > sx <- sd(dat10y$sp500)
 5 > sebeta <- s / (sx * sqrt(n-1) )
 6 > d <- 0
 7 > tratio <- (beta - d) / sebeta
 8 > alpha <- 0.05
 9 > tratio
10    sp500
11 11.45687
12 > qt(1-alpha/2, n-2)
13 [1] 1.980272
```

Since the t-ratio is larger than the critical value, we reject the null hypothesis H_0 at the significance level of 5%. In the above code, we used the function qt to calculate the critical value $t_{n-2,1-\alpha/2}$. The hypothesis test we just performed is just one of many hypothesis tests (see Table 1.2).

Exercise 2.10. Follow the procedures given in Table 1.2 and write R code to perform the following hypothesis tests:

(a) $H_0 : \beta = 2$ versus $H_a : \beta \neq 2$ at the significance level of 1%.

(b) $H_0 : \beta = 1.5$ versus $H_a : \beta < 1.5$ at the significance level of 5%.

Exercise 2.11. Write R code to calculate a 95% confidence interval for the slope estimate $\hat{\beta}$.

Exercise 2.12. Suppose that the excess return on the S&P 500 index is −10%. Write R code to calculate a 99% prediction interval of the excess return on Manulife Financial's stock.

2.9   Summary

In this chapter, we introduced how to implement the capital asset pricing model using basic linear regression models. The CAPM is a model for pricing an individual security or portfolio. For more information on the CAPM, readers are referred to (Campbell et al., 1996, Chapter 5) and (Cochrane, 2001, Chapter 9). Through this case study, we introduced how to build and analyze basic linear regression models using R. In particular, we introduced how to visualize data and check some assumptions of regression models, fit a basic linear regression model to a dataset, and evaluate the fitted model, among others.

2.10   End-of-Chapter Exercises

Exercise 2.13. Given the following R output of a regression model

```
Call:
lm(formula = Y ~ X, data = data4c)

Residuals:
     Min       1Q   Median       3Q      Max
-0.87482 -0.02201  0.01517  0.05316  0.28862

Coefficients:
            Estimate Std. Error t value Pr(>|t|)
(Intercept) -0.17469    0.04537   -3.85  0.00014 ***
X            1.01923    0.01012  100.73  < 2e-16 ***
---
Signif. codes:  0 '***' 0.001 '**' 0.01 '*' 0.05 '.' 0.1 ' ' 1

Residual standard error: 0.09373 on 353 degrees of freedom
Multiple R-squared:  0.9664,    Adjusted R-squared:  0.9663
F-statistic: 1.015e+04 on 1 and 353 DF,  p-value: < 2.2e-16
```

and

```
> qt(0.95,353)
[1] 1.649182
> qt(0.975,353)
[1] 1.966707
```

(a) What does -0.17469 mean?

(b) Is variable X significant? Why?

(c) What are the hypotheses associated with the t-value 100.73?

(d) What is the mean square error of this model?

(e) What is the sample standard deviation of the variable X?

(f) Suppose that the variable X has a change of 3. What is the expected change of Y?

(g) Suppose that the variable X has a change of 2. What is the 95% confidence interval of the expected change in Y?

(h) Test the following hypothesis at the 5% level of significance:

$$H_0 : \beta_1 = 1 \text{ versus } H_a : \beta_1 \neq 1$$

(i) Test the following hypothesis at the 5% level of significance:

$$H_0 : \beta_1 = 1 \text{ versus } H_a : \beta_1 > 1$$

Exercise 2.14. Summary statistics of the variables income (in thousands) and education (in years) are provided below:

```
> summary(income)
   Min. 1st Qu.  Median    Mean 3rd Qu.    Max.
  0.611   4.106   5.930   6.798   8.187  25.880
> sd(income)
[1] 4.245922
> summary(education)
   Min. 1st Qu.  Median    Mean 3rd Qu.    Max.
  6.380   8.445  10.540  10.740  12.650  15.970
> sd(education)
[1] 2.728444
```

The regression model

$$\text{income} = \beta_0 + \beta_1 \text{education} + \epsilon$$

was fitted to the data summarized above. The fitted regression line is shown in Figure 2.6.

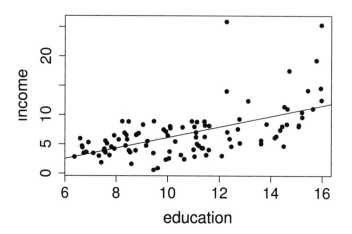

Figure 2.6: *The linear regression model fitted to the data.*

The ANOVA table from the fit and additional R outputs are given below:

```
> anova(fit)
Analysis of Variance Table

Response: income
            Df  Sum Sq Mean Sq F value    Pr(>F)
education    1  607.42  607.42   50.06 2.079e-10 ***
Residuals  100 1213.39   12.13
---
Signif. codes:  0 '***' 0.001 '**' 0.01 '*' 0.05 '.' 0.1 ' ' 1

> qt(.95,100)
[1] 1.660234
> qt(.975,100)
[1] 1.983972
```

(a) How many observations were used to fit the model?

(b) Calculate the coefficient of determination and interpret this value.

(c) Calculate the correlation coefficient of income and education.

(d) Compute the least squares estimate of the slope of the regression line and verbally interpret this estimate.

(e) Calculate the standard error of $\hat{\beta}_1$.

(f) Test the following hypothesis at the 5% level of significance:

$$H_0 : \beta_1 = 0.5 \text{ versus } H_a : \beta_1 \neq 0.5$$

(g) Suppose that education was expressed in months instead of years. How will this scaling affect the least squares estimate of β_1? Justify.

Chapter 3

Multiple Linear Regression Models

In this chapter, we introduce multiple linear regression models, which generalize the simple linear regression model by allowing for more than one independent variable. In particular, we discuss several aspects related to multiple linear regression models, including the method of least squares estimation, some inference, and regression diagnostics.

3.1   Scatter Plot Matrix

In Section 1.1, we introduced scatter plots, which are used to visualize the relationship between the dependent variable and the independent variable. When there is more than one independent variable, we need to look at several scatter plots. In this section, we introduce the **scatter plot matrix** that provides a convenient way to organize several scatter plots.

Figure 3.1 shows a scatter plot matrix of a synthetic dataset with three variables: X_1, X_2, and Y. From the figure, we see that a scatter plot matrix is a 2-dimensional array of scatter plots except for the diagonal. The axes are labeled by the variable names on the diagonal. For example, the variable Y appears on the horizontal axes of all the scatter plots in the rightmost column and on the vertical axes of all the scatter plots in the bottom row.

Each scatter plot in a scatter plot matrix shows the relationship between the variable on the vertical axis and the variable on the horizontal axis. For example, the scatter plot of X_1 and X_2 in the top row and the second column of the scatter plot matrix in Figure 3.1 visualizes the relationship between X_1 and X_2. The scatter plot of X_1 and X_2 shows that X_1 and X_2 have a positive relationship.

41

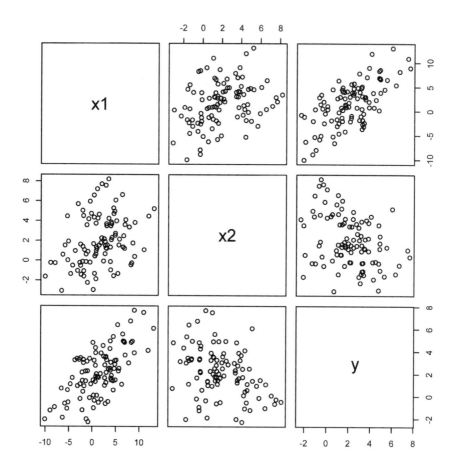

Figure 3.1: *A scatter plot matrix created from a synthetic dataset with two independent variables.*

The scatter plot of X_1 and Y shows that when X_1 increases, Y also increases on average. However, the scatter plot of X_2 and Y shows that the two variables have a negative relationship.

A scatter plot matrix helps us to see the marginal relationships between the dependent variable and each of the independent variables. However, the marginal relationships are not sufficient for us to understand the joint relationship between the dependent variable and more than one independent variable simultaneously. **Added variable plots**, also called **partial regression plots**, are useful to see the joint effect of multiple independent variables.

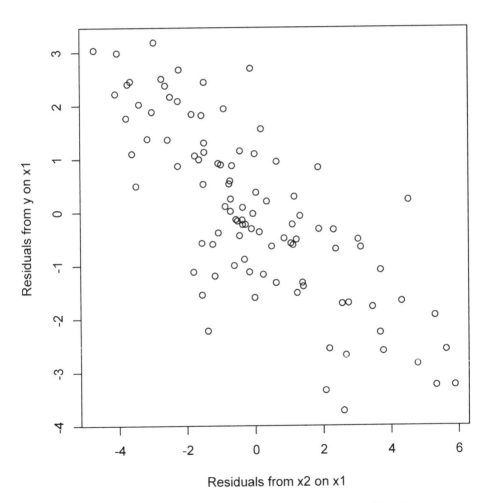

Figure 3.2: *An added variable plot for X_2 adjusted for X_1.*

Suppose that a dataset has k independent variables X_1, X_2, ..., X_k, which may be correlated. To see the effect of adding X_j to the model that includes X_1, ..., X_{j-1}, X_{j+1}, ..., X_k, we create an added variable plot as follows:

(a) Compute the residuals of regressing the dependent variable against the independent variables X_1, ..., X_{j-1}, X_{j+1}, ..., X_k;

(b) Compute the residuals from regressing X_j against X_1, ..., X_{j-1}, X_{j+1}, ..., X_k;

(c) Plot the residuals from (a) against the residuals from (b).

Figure 3.2 shows the added variable plot that summarized the relationship between Y and X_2 adjusting for X_1. Comparing Figure 3.2 with the scatter plot of Y and X_2 in Figure 3.1, we see that the former shows a stronger relationship than does the later. This means that the two variables X_1 and X_2 act jointly to explain the dependent variable.

3.2   Independent Variables and Regressors

There are several types of potential independent variables: **continuous, ordinal**, and **nominal**. A **continuous variable** has continuous measurements such as the weight of a person. An ordinal variable has discrete but ordered measurements such as the letter grade of a student. Nominal variables are also referred to as **categorical variables** and have discrete measurements that do not have a natural order, e.g., the gender of a person. All these types of potential independent variables can be useful for building a multiple linear regression model.

To build a multiple linear regression model, we first create a set of **regressors** from the set of potential independent variables. Regressors take numerical values and can be used in regression directly. A multiple linear regression model might include the following regressors (Weisberg, 2013):

Intercept An intercept is a regressor that is always equal to 1. An intercept is usually included in a multiple linear regression model. Dropping the intercept in a multiple linear regression model forces the regression plane through the origin and may lead to inaccurate models.

Independent variable A regressor can be equal to an independent variable if the independent variable is binary or has continuous measurements. This is the simplest type of regressor.

Transformations of independent variables Sometimes we transform the independent variables to different scales to create accurate regression models.

For example, we may standardize an independent variable if it has a different magnitude than other independent variables. We will discuss some transformation methods in Section 3.7.

Polynomials Sometimes the dependent variable and the independent variables have a nonlinear relationship. In such cases, we can accommodate the nonlinear relationship in the multiple linear regression model by including polynomial regressors of the independent variables.

Splines Using splines is similar to using polynomials except that we use a linear combination of different basis functions for splines. The basis functions have useful properties that can model local behavior better than polynomials.

Principal components Sometimes we have a large number of independent variables that might be related. In such cases, we can use a few principal components of these independent variables as regressors.

Combinations of independent variables Combining independent variables can also be useful in regression models. Products of regressors are often used in multiple linear regression models to allow for joint effects of the regressors.

Dummy variables A categorical variable, called a **factor**, takes on one of a fixed number of possible values. Since categorical variables are different from continuous variables, we cannot use them directly in regression models. To incorporate categorical independent variables in a regression model, we convert them to **dummy variables**, which are regressors that often take values of 0 and 1.

Converting a categorical variable to dummy variables can be done as follows. Let $(x_1, x_2, \ldots, x_n)$ be the observations of a categorical variable, which takes m distinct values: $A_1, A_2, \ldots, A_m$. Then we convert the categorical variable to $m-1$ binary dummy variables as follows:

$$z_{ij} = \begin{cases} 1, & \text{if } x_i = A_j, \\ 0, & \text{if } x_i \neq A_j, \end{cases} \quad i = 1, 2, \ldots, n. \tag{3.1}$$

We only need $m-1$ binary dummy variables to represent all the information contained in a categorical variable with m distinct values. The reason is that knowing the values of the $m-1$ binary dummy variables allows us to determine the value of the categorical variable exactly.

Exercise 3.1. Convert the following categorical variables into binary dummy variables:

x_1	x_2
A	G
B	G
A	J
C	G
E	J

3.3 Multiple Linear Regression Model

Let Y be the dependent variable and X_1, X_2, ..., X_k be the regressors, which are created from a set of independent variables. Let y_i be the observed value of the dependent variable in the ith case. Let $(x_{i1}, x_{i2}, ..., x_{ik})$ be the observed values of the regressors in the ith case. Then the multiple linear regression model is specified as follows (Frees, 2009; Olive, 2017):

$$y_i = \beta_0 + \beta_1 x_{i1} + \cdots + \beta_k x_{ik} + \epsilon_i, \tag{3.2}$$

where β_0, β_1, ..., β_k are unknown parameters to be estimated. We can also write the multiple linear regression model in matrix form as follows:

$$y_i = \boldsymbol{\beta}' \mathbf{x}_i + \epsilon_i,$$

where $\boldsymbol{\beta} = (\beta_0, \beta_1, ..., \beta_k)'$ and $\mathbf{x}_i = (1, x_{i1}, x_{i2}, ..., x_{ik})'$. The superscript $'$ denotes matrix transpose. When $k = 1$, we get the simple linear regression model discussed in Chapter 1.

The multiple linear regression model can be written in matrix form as follows:

$$\mathbf{y} = \mathbf{X}\boldsymbol{\beta} + \boldsymbol{\epsilon}, \tag{3.3}$$

where $\mathbf{X}$ and $\mathbf{y}$ denote a matrix and a vector defined as follows:

$$\mathbf{X} = \begin{pmatrix} \mathbf{x}_1' \\ \mathbf{x}_2' \\ \vdots \\ \mathbf{x}_n' \end{pmatrix} = \begin{pmatrix} 1 & x_{11} & x_{12} & \cdots & x_{1k} \\ 1 & x_{21} & x_{22} & \cdots & x_{2k} \\ \vdots & \vdots & \vdots & \ddots & \vdots \\ 1 & x_{n1} & x_{n2} & \cdots & x_{nk} \end{pmatrix}, \quad \mathbf{y} = \begin{pmatrix} y_1 \\ y_2 \\ \vdots \\ y_n \end{pmatrix}, \text{ and } \boldsymbol{\epsilon} = \begin{pmatrix} \epsilon_1 \\ \epsilon_2 \\ \vdots \\ \epsilon_n \end{pmatrix}. \tag{3.4}$$

The matrix $\mathbf{X}$ defined above is also called the **design matrix** of the regression model.

Under a multiple linear regression model, we assume that:

(a) $x_{i1}, x_{i2}, \ldots, x_{ik}$ are nonstochastic variables;
(b) $\text{Var}(y_i) = \sigma^2$;
(c) $y_1, y_2, \ldots, y_n$ are independent random variables;

Note that the above set of assumptions is equivalent to the following set of assumptions:

(a) $x_{i1}, x_{i2}, \ldots, x_{ik}$ are nonstochastic variables;
(b) $E[\epsilon_i] = 0$ and $\text{Var}(\epsilon_i) = \sigma^2$;
(c) $\epsilon_1, \epsilon_2, \ldots, \epsilon_n$ are independent random variables;

The first set of assumptions is referred to as the set of **observables representation sampling assumptions** and the second set of assumptions is referred to as the **error representation sampling assumptions**.

For the purpose of obtaining tests and confidence statements with small samples, we often make the following normality assumption:

(d) $\epsilon_1, \epsilon_2, \ldots, \epsilon_n$ are normally distributed.

The above normality assumption is a strong assumption. If we think that the errors follow a different distribution, then the linear regression model might not be appropriate for the data.

3.4 Ordinary Least of Squares Estimation

The multiple linear regression model contains $k + 1$ parameters, denoted by the Greek letters β_0, β_1, ..., β_k. These parameters are unknown quantities, which must be estimated from the data. Estimates of the parameters are computable functions of the data and are usually denoted by putting a hat over the corresponding Greek letters, e.g., $\hat{\beta}_0$ is the estimate of the parameter β_0.

The method of least squares can be used to obtain estimates of the parameters in a multiple linear regression model. In the **method of least squares**, the regression coefficients are determined by minimizing the following objective function:

$$SS(\boldsymbol{\beta}) = \sum_{i=1}^{n} \left(y_i - \boldsymbol{\beta}'\mathbf{x}_i \right)^2, \tag{3.5}$$

which represents the sum of squared deviations for the regression plane. We can also write the above objective function in matrix form as follows:

$$SS(\boldsymbol{\beta}) = \boldsymbol{\epsilon}'\boldsymbol{\epsilon} = (\mathbf{y} - \mathbf{X}\boldsymbol{\beta})'(\mathbf{y} - \mathbf{X}\boldsymbol{\beta}), \tag{3.6}$$

where $\mathbf{X}$, $\mathbf{y}$, and $\boldsymbol{\epsilon}$ are defined in Equation (3.4).

Minimizing the objective function given in Equation (3.6) can be done analytically by setting the derivatives of $SS(\boldsymbol{\beta})$ with respect to $\boldsymbol{\beta}$ to zeros:

$$\frac{\partial SS(\boldsymbol{\beta})}{\partial \boldsymbol{\beta}} = 2\mathbf{X}'\mathbf{X}\boldsymbol{\beta} - 2\mathbf{X}'\mathbf{y} = \mathbf{0}, \tag{3.7}$$

which gives the following estimates of the parameters:

$$\hat{\boldsymbol{\beta}} = (\mathbf{X}'\mathbf{X})^{-1}\mathbf{X}'\mathbf{y}. \tag{3.8}$$

Given the estimated parameters, we calculate the fitted value for the ith case as follows:

$$\hat{y}_i = \hat{\boldsymbol{\beta}}'\mathbf{x}_i. \tag{3.9}$$

In matrix form, the vector of fitted values for all the n cases can be expressed as

$$\hat{\mathbf{y}} = \mathbf{X}\boldsymbol{\beta} = \mathbf{X}(\mathbf{X}'\mathbf{X})^{-1}\mathbf{X}'\mathbf{y} = \mathbf{H}\mathbf{y}, \tag{3.10}$$

where $\mathbf{H}$ is defined as

$$\mathbf{H} = \mathbf{X}(\mathbf{X}'\mathbf{X})^{-1}\mathbf{X}'. \tag{3.11}$$

The matrix $\mathbf{H}$ defined above is called the **hat matrix** or the **projection matrix**. From Equation (3.10), we see that the hat matrix projects the vector of dependent variable values onto the vector of fitted values.

The observed residual vector is defined as

$$\mathbf{e} = \mathbf{y} - \hat{\mathbf{y}} = \mathbf{y} - \mathbf{X}\hat{\boldsymbol{\beta}}, \tag{3.12}$$

where $\mathbf{e}' = (e_1, e_2, \ldots, e_n)$.

The prediction of the dependent variable at a new point $\mathbf{x}_* = (1, x_{*,1}, x_{*,2}, \ldots, x_{*,k})'$ is calculated similarly as

$$\hat{y}_* = \hat{\boldsymbol{\beta}}'\mathbf{x}_*.$$

Exercise 3.2. Let $\mathbf{X}$ be the design matrix for a multiple linear regression model with n samples and k regressors, which include the intercept. Let $\mathbf{H}$ be the hat matrix defined in Equation (3.11).

(a) Show that $(I - \mathbf{H})\mathbf{X} = \mathbf{0}$, where I is an $n \times n$ identity matrix and $\mathbf{0}$ is an $n \times n$ zero matrix.

(b) Show that

$$(I - \mathbf{H})\begin{pmatrix} 1 \\ 1 \\ \vdots \\ 1 \end{pmatrix} = \begin{pmatrix} 0 \\ 0 \\ \vdots \\ 0 \end{pmatrix}.$$

(c) Show that

$$\sum_{i=1}^{n} \hat{y}_i = n\bar{y}.$$

3.5 Model Evaluation

In Section 1.4, we introduced two goodness-of-fit measures, R^2 and the residual standard error, for evaluating the simple linear regression model. We can also use these goodness-of-fit measures to evaluate multiple linear regression models.

The measure R^2 is defined similarly as in Section 1.4, i.e.,

$$R^2 = 1 - \frac{SSE}{SST} = \frac{SSR}{SST}, \tag{3.13}$$

where

$$SSE = \sum_{i=1}^{n}(y_i - \hat{y}_i)^2 = \sum_{i=1}^{n}(y_i - \hat{\boldsymbol{\beta}}'\mathbf{x}_i)^2 = (\mathbf{y} - \mathbf{X}\hat{\boldsymbol{\beta}})'(\mathbf{y} - \mathbf{X}\hat{\boldsymbol{\beta}}), \tag{3.14}$$

$$SSR = \sum_{i=1}^{n}(\hat{y}_i - \bar{y})^2 \tag{3.15}$$

and

$$SST = \sum_{i=1}^{n}(y_i - \bar{y})^2. \tag{3.16}$$

The R^2 takes on values from 0 to 1 and can be interpreted as the proportion of variability explained by the regression model. The higher the R^2, the better the fit of the model.

The **residual standard deviation** is defined as follows:

$$s = \sqrt{\frac{1}{n - (k + 1)} \sum_{i=1}^{n}(y_i - \hat{y}_i)^2}, \tag{3.17}$$

where $\hat{y}_i$ is the fitted value in the ith case, i.e.,

$$\hat{y}_i = \hat{\boldsymbol{\beta}}' \mathbf{x}_i.$$

The square of the residual standard deviation, s^2, is called the **mean square error (MSE)**.

The sources of variability can be summarized in the **ANOVA (analysis of variance)** table shown in Table 3.1. In Table 3.1, SSR, SSE, and SST are defined in Equations (3.15), (3.14), (3.16), respectively. The symbols MSR and MSE denote the regression mean square and the mean squared error, respectively. These mean squares are calculated by dividing the corresponding sum of squares by its degrees of freedom, that is,

$$MSR = \frac{SSR}{k} \tag{3.18}$$

and

$$MSE = \frac{SSE}{n - (k+1)} = s^2. \tag{3.19}$$

Source	Sum of Squares	Degrees of Freedom	Mean Square
Regression	SSR	k	MSR
Error	SSE	$n - (k+1)$	MSE
Total	SST	$n - 1$	

Table 3.1: *The ANOVA table for the multiple linear regression model with k regressors.*

One problem of R^2 is that it always increases when more variables are used in a linear regression model. If we use the R^2 as a criterion to select the best linear regression model, then the model that uses all variables will be selected. To circumvent this problem, we use the **adjusted** R^2, which is the coefficient of determination adjusted for degrees of freedom that is defined by

$$R_a^2 = 1 - \frac{SSE \times (n-1)}{SST \times (n - (k+1))} = 1 - \frac{MSE}{s_y^2} = 1 - \frac{s^2}{s_y^2}, \tag{3.20}$$

where s_y is the sample standard deviation of $\{y_i\}$.

The R_a^2 imposes a penalty for the complexity of the linear regression model by considering k in its definition. As a result, the R_a^2 does not necessarily increase as k increases. Indeed, if insignificant variables are introduced to a regression model, then the R_a^2 is likely to decrease.

Exercise 3.3. Let SSR and SST be defined in Equations (3.15) and (3.16), respectively. Show that

$$SSR = \hat{\mathbf{y}}'\hat{\mathbf{y}} - n\bar{y}^2$$

and

$$SST = \mathbf{y}'\mathbf{y} - n\bar{y}^2.$$

Exercise 3.4. Let $\hat{y}_i$ be the fitted value of the dependent variable from the multiple linear regression model that is defined in Equation (3.9). Show that

(a)

$$\sum_{i=1}^{n}(y_i - \hat{y}_i)(\hat{y}_i - \bar{y}) = 0.$$

(b)

$$\sum_{i=1}^{n}(y_i - \bar{y})(\hat{y}_i - \bar{y}) = SSR.$$

(c)

$$SSE + SSR = SST,$$

where SSE, SSR, and SST are defined in Equations (3.14), (3.15), and (3.16), respectively.

Exercise 3.5. Let $r(\mathbf{y}, \hat{\mathbf{y}})$ denote the Pearson correlation coefficient between $\mathbf{y}$ and $\hat{\mathbf{y}}$, where $\mathbf{y}$ is the vector of dependent variable values and $\hat{\mathbf{y}}$ is the vector of the corresponding fitted values. Show that

$$r(\mathbf{y}, \hat{\mathbf{y}}) = \sqrt{R^2},$$

where R^2 is defined in Equation (3.13).

3.6 Statistical Inference

Under the assumptions given in Section 3.3, it can be shown that for each $j = 0, 1, \ldots, k$, the regression coefficient $\hat{\beta}_j$ is normally distributed and its standard deviation is given by

$$se(\hat{\beta}_j) = s\sqrt{\text{the } (j+1)\text{th diagonal element of } (\mathbf{X}'\mathbf{X})^{-1}}, \qquad (3.21)$$

where s is the residual standard error defined in Equation (3.17). Under the null hypothesis $\beta_j = d$ and the above assumptions, it can be shown that the sampling distribution of the t-ratio

$$t(\hat{\beta}_j) = \frac{\hat{\beta}_j - d}{se(\hat{\beta}_j)} \tag{3.22}$$

is a t-distribution with $df = n - (k+1)$ degrees of freedom.

Hypothesis Test	Reject H_0 in favor of H_a if
$H_0 : \beta_j = d,\ H_a : \beta_j > d$	$t(\hat{\beta}_j) > t_{n-(k+1),1-\alpha}$
$H_0 : \beta_j = d,\ H_a : \beta_j < d$	$t(\hat{\beta}_j) < -t_{n-(k+1),1-\alpha}$
$H_0 : \beta_j = d,\ H_a : \beta_j \neq d$	$|t(\hat{\beta}_j)| > t_{n-(k+1),1-\alpha/2}$

Table 3.2: *Some hypothesis tests and the corresponding decision-making procedures. In the table, α is the significance level and $t_{n-(k+1),1-\alpha}$, called the critical t-value, is the $(1 - \alpha)$th percentile from the t-distribution with $n - (k+1)$ degrees of freedom.*

Using the t-ratios, we can conduct tests of the null hypothesis for a single regression coefficient. Table 3.2 shows some common hypothesis tests and the corresponding decision-making procedures.

We can also conduct **general linear hypotheses**, which involve a set of regression coefficients. Let $\boldsymbol{\beta} = (\beta_0, \beta_1, \ldots, \beta_k)'$ be the regression coefficients of the multiple linear regression model, where k is the number of regressors, which might include the binary dummy variables. Under the general linear hypothesis, the null hypothesis H_0 is specified as follows:

$$\mathbf{C}\boldsymbol{\beta} = \mathbf{d}, \tag{3.23}$$

where $\mathbf{C}$ is a $p \times (k+1)$ matrix and $\mathbf{d}$ is a $p \times 1$ vector specified by the user.

For example, if we want to investigate the importance of a single regression coefficient, say β_j, we can express this coefficient as follows:

$$\mathbf{C}\boldsymbol{\beta} = (0, \cdots, 0, 1, 0, \cdots, 0) \begin{pmatrix} \beta_0 \\ \beta_1 \\ \vdots \\ \beta_k \end{pmatrix} = \beta_j.$$

If we want to test equality of two regression coefficients, say β_1 and β_2, we can express the equality as follows:

$$\mathbf{C}\boldsymbol{\beta} = (0, 1, -1, 0, \cdots, 0) \begin{pmatrix} \beta_0 \\ \beta_1 \\ \vdots \\ \beta_k \end{pmatrix} = \beta_1 - \beta_2 = 0.$$

Under the general linear hypothesis, the null hypothesis

$$H_0 : \mathbf{C}\boldsymbol{\beta} = \mathbf{d}$$

is tested against the alternative hypothesis

$$H_a : \mathbf{C}\boldsymbol{\beta} \neq \mathbf{d}.$$

To perform the general linear hypothesis, we calculate the following statistic:

$$F\text{-ratio} = \frac{(\mathbf{Cb} - \mathbf{d})' \left(\mathbf{C}(\mathbf{X'X})^{-1}\mathbf{C'} \right)^{-1} (\mathbf{Cb} - \mathbf{d})}{p \cdot s_{full}^2}, \tag{3.24}$$

where $\mathbf{b}$ is the estimates of regression coefficients, p is the number of independent constraints in the null hypothesis, s_{full} is the residual standard error of the full model, and $\mathbf{X}$ is the design matrix defined as

$$\mathbf{X} = \begin{pmatrix} 1 & x_{11} & x_{12} & \cdots & x_{1k} \\ 1 & x_{21} & x_{22} & \cdots & x_{2k} \\ \vdots & \vdots & \vdots & \ddots & \vdots \\ 1 & x_{n1} & x_{n2} & \cdots & x_{nk} \end{pmatrix}.$$

The F-**ratio** defined in Equation (3.24) follows an F-**distribution** with numerator degrees of freedom $df_1 = p$ and denominator degrees of freedom $df_2 = n - (k+1)$.

The procedure for testing the general linear hypothesis is given below (Frees, 2009):

(a) Fit the full regression model (i.e., the regression model that uses all the explanatory variables) and get the mean squared error, s_{full}^2.

(b) Specify the null hypothesis in matrix form and calculate the F-ratio defined in Equation (3.24).

(c) Choose a significance level α and calculate the F-value, which is the $(1 - \alpha)$th percentile, $F_{p,n-k-1,1-\alpha}$, from the F-distribution with $df_1 = p$ and $df_2 = n - (k+1)$.

(d) Reject the null hypothesis in favor of the alternative if the F-ratio is larger than the F-value.

Exercise 3.6. Let $\mathbf{Y} = (Y_1, Y_2, \ldots, Y_n)^T$ be a vector of n random variables. Let A be an $n \times n$ matrix and $\mathbf{Z} = A\mathbf{Y}$. Show that

$$\text{Var}(\mathbf{Z}) = A\,\text{Var}(\mathbf{Y})\,A',$$

where Var(**Y**) is defined as

$$\text{Var}(\mathbf{Y}) = \begin{pmatrix} \text{Var}(Y_1) & \text{Cov}(Y_1, Y_2) & \cdots & \text{Cov}(Y_1, Y_n) \\ \text{Cov}(Y_2, Y_1) & \text{Var}(Y_2) & \cdots & \text{Cov}(Y_2, Y_n) \\ \vdots & \vdots & \ddots & \vdots \\ \text{Cov}(Y_n, Y_1) & \text{Cov}(Y_n, Y_2) & \cdots & \text{Var}(Y_n) \end{pmatrix}$$

and Var(**Z**) is defined similarly.

Exercise 3.7. Consider the linear regression model

$$\mathbf{y} = \mathbf{X}\boldsymbol{\beta} + \boldsymbol{\epsilon},$$

where $\epsilon_1, \epsilon_2, \ldots, \epsilon_n$ are independent random variables with common mean $E[\epsilon_i] = 0$ and common variance $\text{Var}(\epsilon_i) = \sigma^2$. Let $\hat{\boldsymbol{\beta}}$ be the vector of estimated parameters given in Equation (3.8). Show that

(a) $E[\hat{\boldsymbol{\beta}}] = \boldsymbol{\beta}$.

(b) $\text{Var}(\hat{\boldsymbol{\beta}}) = \sigma^2 (X'X)^{-1}$.

Exercise 3.8. Express the following null hypotheses in matrix form $\mathbf{C}\boldsymbol{\beta} = \mathbf{d}$ by finding the matrix $\mathbf{C}$ and the vector $\mathbf{d}$.

(a) $\sum_{j=0}^{k} z_j \beta_j = d$,

   where $z_0, z_1, \ldots, z_k, d$ are constants.

(b) $\beta_1 = \beta_2 = \cdots = \beta_k = 0$;

(c) $\beta_{m+1} = \beta_{m+2} = \cdots = \beta_k = 0$, where $m \leq k$ is an integer and k is the number of explanatory variables.

3.7 Transformations

Transformations are an important tool to extend the linear regression methodology to problems where the dependent variable and the independent variables are thought to have a nonlinear relationship. Transformations can be used to achieve a linear model in the transformed scale.

There are several methods for transforming variables. See (Weisberg, 2013, Chapter 8) for details. One commonly used method is the power transformation defined as

$$y^* = \begin{cases} \dfrac{y^\lambda - 1}{\lambda}, & \text{if } \lambda \neq 0, \\ \ln(y), & \text{if } \lambda = 0, \end{cases} \tag{3.25}$$

where λ is a parameter. The **logarithmic transformation** is a special case of the **power transformation**.

When there is only one independent variable, we can create a scatter plot between the dependent variable and the independent variable to select an appropriate transformation. With many independent variables, selecting a transformation is harder. However, there are two empirical rules that are useful in linear regression modeling (Weisberg, 2013):

The log rule When the values of a variable are positive and spread more than one order of magnitude, then the logarithmic transformation of the variable is often helpful.

The range rule When the values of a variable spread less than one order of magnitude, then any transformation of the variable is unlikely to be helpful.

3.8 Regression Diagnostics

Once we have fitted a preliminary linear regression model, we need to check whether there are any **influential points**. These points are the observations that potentially have a disproportionate effect on the overall fit.

Influential points include high leverage points and outliers. A **high leverage point** is an observation that has an unusual value for a set of explanatory variables. To quantify whether an observation is a high leverage point, we define the **leverage** for the observation as follows.

Let $\mathbf{H}$ be the hat matrix defined in Equation (3.11). Then we have

$$\hat{y}_i = h_{i1} y_1 + h_{i2} y_2 + \cdots + h_{ii} y_i + \cdots + h_{in} y_n \tag{3.26}$$

for $i = 1, 2, \ldots, n$. The ith diagonal element of $\mathbf{H}$, h_{ii}, is called the leverage for the ith observation. From the definition of $\mathbf{H}$, we have

$$h_{ii} = \mathbf{x}_i' \left(\mathbf{X}'\mathbf{X} \right)^{-1} \mathbf{x}_i, \tag{3.27}$$

where

$$\mathbf{x}_i = \begin{pmatrix} 1 \\ x_{i1} \\ \vdots \\ x_{ik} \end{pmatrix}.$$

From Equation (3.26), we can see that if an observation has a greater h_{ii}, then the ith response y_i has a greater effect on the ith fitted value $\hat{y}_i$. As a rule of thumb, we declare an observation to be a high leverage point if the leverage is greater than three times the average, i.e.,

$$h_{ii} > \frac{3(k+1)}{n}. \tag{3.28}$$

Once we identify high leverage points, we have several ways to deal with them:

(a) Remove the observation.
(b) Include the observation but comment on its effect.
(c) Use another variable to represent the information.
(d) Use a nonlinear transformation of an explanatory variable.

Cook's distance is a measure for quantifying the influence of a point on the fitted value. For the ith observation $\mathbf{x}_i$, the Cook's distance is defined as:

$$D_i = \frac{\sum_{j=1}^{n} (\hat{y}_j - \hat{y}_{j(i)})^2}{(k+1)s^2}, \tag{3.29}$$

where s is the residual standard error and $\hat{y}_{j(i)}$ is the value of the jth observation that is predicted by the regression model fitted without the ith observation. Using Equation (3.29) to calculate Cook's distances for all observations requires fitting many regression models. Fortunately, we can calculate Cook's distance with the following formula:

$$D_i = \left(\frac{e_i}{se(e_i)} \right)^2 \frac{h_{ii}}{(k+1)(1-h_{ii})}, \tag{3.30}$$

where $e_i = y_i - \hat{y}_i$ is the ith residual from the full model and $se(e_i)$ is the standard error of e_i that is defined by

$$se(e_i) = s\sqrt{1 - h_{ii}}. \tag{3.31}$$

It can be shown that Equation (3.29) and Equation (3.30) are equivalent. From Equation (3.30), we see that Cook's distance consists of two parts: the first part is the square of the ith standardized residual and the second part is the contribution of leverage. Hence Cook's distance can be used to identify both outliers and high leverage points.

To identify influential points with Cook's distance, we compare Cook's distance to an F-distribution with $df_1 = k+1$ and $df_2 = n-(k+1)$ degrees of freedom. If the Cook's distance of an observation exceeds the 95th percentile of the F-distribution, then the observation has substantial influence on the model.

Exercise 3.9. Let **H** be the hat matrix defined in Equation (3.11) and h_{ii} the leverage for the ith observation defined in Equation (3.28). Show that

(a) $\mathbf{H} = \mathbf{HH}$.

(b) $0 \le h_{ii} \le 1$.

Exercise 3.10. Let $\mathbf{e} = (e_1, e_2, \ldots, e_n)'$, where $e_i = y_i - \hat{y}_i$ is the residual for the ith case. Show that

(a) $\mathbf{e} = (I - \mathbf{H})\mathbf{y}$, where **H** is defined in Equation (3.11) and I is an $n \times n$ identify matrix.

(b) $\text{Var}(\mathbf{e}) = \sigma^2(I - \mathbf{H})$.

Exercise 3.11. The trace of a square matrix is defined to be the sum of the diagonal elements of the matrix. Mathematically, let C be an $n \times n$ matrix with element c_{ij} in its (i, j)-entry. Then the trace of C is defined as

$$\text{tr}(C) = \sum_{i=1}^{n} c_{ii}.$$

(a) Let A be an $m \times n$ matrix and B an $n \times m$ matrix. Show that $\text{tr}(AB) = \text{tr}(BA)$.

(b) Let **H** be the hat matrix defined in Equation (3.11). Show that $\text{tr}(\mathbf{H}) = k+1$.

Exercise 3.12. Consider the regression model

$$\hat{y} = b_0 + b_1 x_1 + b_2 x_2 + b_3 x_3.$$

Suppose that $h_{22} = 0.35$ and $\frac{e_2}{se(e_2)} = -3.5$. Calculate Cook's distance D_2.

3.9   Variable Selection

Let k be the number of explanatory variables. For each $i = 0, 1, \ldots, k$, we can build

$$\binom{k}{i}$$

different linear regression models using only i explanatory variables. Then we can build

$$\sum_{i=0}^{k} \binom{k}{i} = 2^k$$

different linear regression models in total. The total number 2^k can also be derived from the fact that each independent variable can be either present or absent in a linear regression model.

In this section, we introduce a **stepwise algorithm** to select a better model.

Algorithm 3.1: A forward stepwise regression algorithm.

Input: A response variable y and k potential explanatory variables x_1, x_2, ..., x_k

Output: A linear regression model

1 Consider all possible regression models using one explanatory variable. For each of the k models, calculate the R_a^2. Choose the model with the highest R_a^2;

2 Consider all possible regression models by adding a variable to the model from the previous step. For each of the models, calculate the R_a^2 and choose the model with the largest R_a^2. If this largest R_a^2 is higher than that of the model from the previous step, choose the model with the largest R_a^2. If the largest R_a^2 is lower than that of the model from the previous step, keep the model from the previous step;

3 Consider all possible regression models by removing a variable from the model from the previous step. For each of the models, calculate the R_a^2. If the largest R_a^2 is higher than that of the model from the previous step, choose the model with the largest R_a^2. If the largest R_a^2 is lower than that of the model from the previous step, keep the model from the previous step;

4 Repeat steps 2 and 3 until no variables can be added in step 2.

Algorithm 3.1 shows the steps involved in a stepwise regression algorithm based on the R_a^2. Instead of enumerating all the 2^k possible linear regression models, the algorithm searches through a smaller number of candidate models in order to find a better model.

Alternatively, it is possible to search for better models using the backward stepwise regression algorithm. In backward stepwise algorithm, we start with the full model (i.e., the model with all available explanatory variables) and keep removing variables one at a time based on the R_a^2 until no variables can be removed. This algorithm is not discussed further in this book.

3.10 Collinearity

Collinearity occurs when one explanatory variable can be approximated by a linear combination of other explanatory variables. When there is more than one explanatory variable, we need to consider collinearity. When collinearity exists, the matrix $\mathbf{X'X}$ is close to singular, that is, the inverse $\mathbf{X'X}$ does not exist. As a result, we will not be able to obtain reliable regression coefficients from Equation (3.8) and it will be difficult for us to detect the importance of a variable.

To detect collinearity, we use the **variance inflation factor** defined as

$$VIF_j = \frac{1}{1 - R_j^2}, \quad j = 1, 2, \ldots, k, \tag{3.32}$$

where R_j^2 is the R^2 of the regression using x_j as the response and $(x_1, x_2, \ldots, x_{j-1}, x_{j+1}, \ldots, x_k)$ as the explanatory variables.

If an explanatory variable is nearly a linear combination of the other explanatory variables, then the R^2 of the regression using the explanatory variable as response will be close to 1 and the variance inflation factor will be large. As a rule of thumb, if a variance inflation factor exceeds 10, then severe collinearity exists in the data set.

The standard error of the regression coefficient of a variable and the variance inflation factor of the variable have the following relationship:

$$se(\hat{\beta}_j) = \frac{s\sqrt{VIF_j}}{s_{x_j}\sqrt{n-1}}, \tag{3.33}$$

where s is the residual standard error defined in Equation (3.17) and s_{x_j} is the sample standard deviation of the jth variable x_j defined as follows:

$$s_{x_j} = \sqrt{\frac{1}{n-1} \sum_{i=1}^{n} (x_{ij} - \bar{x}_j)^2}. \tag{3.34}$$

From Equation (3.33), we can see that a larger variance inflation factor results in a larger standard error. Because of the relationship between standard errors and variance inflation factors, we use variance inflation factors rather than R_j^2 to measure collinearity.

3.11 Summary

In this chapter, we introduced multiple linear regression models that involve one or more independent variables. We also introduced other topics related to multiple linear regression modeling, such as the method of least squares for estimating parameters, goodness-of-fit measures that can be used to evaluate multiple linear regression models, statistical inference for one or more coefficients, and variable selection. For more information about multiple linear regression models, readers are referred to (Miller and Wichern, 1977), (Frees, 2009), (Freedman, 2009), (Weisberg, 2013), and (Olive, 2017).

3.12 End-of-Chapter Exercises

Exercise 3.13. Demonstrate how to convert each of the following to a linear regression model:

(a) $y_i = \left(\beta_0 + \beta_1 x_{i1} + \beta_2 x_{i2} + \epsilon_i\right)^{-2}$, $i = 1, 2, \ldots, n$, where $\epsilon_1, \epsilon_2, \ldots, \epsilon_n$ are independent with common mean 0 and common variance σ^2.

(b) $y_i = \beta_0 \exp(\beta_1 x_i + \epsilon_i)$, $i = 1, 2, \ldots, n$, where $\beta_0 > 0$ and $\epsilon_1, \epsilon_2, \ldots, \epsilon_n$ are independent with common mean 0 and common variance σ^2.

(c) $y_i = \beta_0 + \beta_1 x_i + \beta_2 x_i^2 + \epsilon_i$, $i = 1, 2, \ldots, n$, where $\epsilon_1, \epsilon_2, \ldots, \epsilon_n$ are independent with common mean 0. The variance of ϵ_i is $x_i^2 \sigma^2$ for $i = 1, 2, \ldots, n$.

Exercise 3.14. Consider the simple linear regression model introduced in Chapter 1:

$$y_i = \beta_0 + \beta_1 x_i + \epsilon_i, \quad i = 1, 2, \ldots, n$$

and answer the following questions.

(a) What is the design matrix $\mathbf{X}$ for the simple linear regression model?

(b) Calculate the product of the transpose of $\mathbf{X}$ and $\mathbf{X}$, i.e., $\mathbf{X'X}$.

(c) Calculate the inverse of the following 2×2 matrix

$$\begin{pmatrix} a & b \\ b & c \end{pmatrix}$$

by solving the following equation

$$\begin{pmatrix} a & b \\ b & c \end{pmatrix} \begin{pmatrix} e & f \\ f & g \end{pmatrix} = \begin{pmatrix} 1 & 0 \\ 0 & 1 \end{pmatrix}.$$

(d) Calculate the inverse of $\mathbf{X}'\mathbf{X}$ by using the result of part (c).

(e) Calculate $\hat{\beta}_0$ and $\hat{\beta}_1$ using the following matrix operation:

$$(\mathbf{X}'\mathbf{X})^{-1}\mathbf{X}'\mathbf{y}.$$

Exercise 3.15. You are to fit the following linear regression model

$$y_i = \beta_1 x_i + \beta_2 x_i^2 + \epsilon_i$$

to the following dataset

i	1	2	3	4	5
x_i	−1	1	0	1	−2
y_i	2	0	−2	2	11

(a) Calculate the design matrix $\mathbf{X}$.

(b) Calculate $(\mathbf{X}'\mathbf{X})^{-1}$.

(c) Calculate $\hat{\beta}_1$ and $\hat{\beta}_2$.

(d) Calculate SSR, SSE, and SST. Conclude that the relationship $SSR + SSE = SST$ does not hold when the model does not include the intercept.

Chapter 4

Case Study: Predicting Intraday Movements of a Bond Index using ETFs

In this case study, we build multiple linear regression models for predicting intraday changes of a bond index based on the intraday movements of some ETFs (exchange-traded funds). An ETF trades like a stock where we can observe its intraday prices. After working through this case study, readers will be able to

- Transform data
- Build multiple linear regression models
- Use the method of least squares to estimate regression parameters
- Interpret regression coefficients
- Understand and calculate the mean squared error, the residual standard error, and the adjusted R^2
- Select variables
- Understand and calculate leverage and Cook's distance
- Understand and measure collinearity
- Perform hypothesis tests and calculate confidence intervals for a single regression coefficient

4.1   Problem Description

The Merrill Lynch US High Yield Master II Index (H0A0) is a benchmark index for high yield corporate bonds. Since the H0A0 index is a measure of the broad high yield market, it has been commonly used for risk management and performance attribution.

One problem of the H0A0 index is that it is updated only at the end of the day. In other words, the value of this index does not change during regular trading hours. If financial managers want to monitor portfolios on an intraday basis using this index, then financial managers can use the price of the index from the previous business day. Since the market is moving during regular trading hours, using the index price from the previous business day to calculate the portfolio value is not accurate, especially when the market is moving fast.

Since ETFs are traded like stocks, we can see the prices of ETFs on an intraday basis. In this case study, we build a multiple linear regression model to predict the intraday movements of the H0A0 index based on some bond ETFs (exchange-traded funds).

4.2   Data Description

We downloaded the daily values of the H0A0 index from the website `https://research.stlouisfed.org/fred2`, but we could also have downloaded weekly, monthly, and quarterly data from this website. Since our goal is to predict the intraday movements of the index, using daily data is better as it contains more information. Since we want to build a model to predict the intraday movements of the index, we use the daily data from the most recent year as this is more relevant to the current economic situation.

Symbol	Description
JNK	SPDR Barclays High Yield Bond ETF
BNDX	Vanguard Total International Bond ETF
VGLT	Vanguard Long-Term Government Bond ETF
VCSH	Vanguard Short-Term Corporate Bond ETF
BSV	Vanguard Short-Term Bond ETF
BIV	Vanguard Intermediate-Term Bond ETF
VGSH	Vanguard Short-Term Government Bond ETF
SCHZ	Schwab US Aggregate Bond ETF
VCLT	Vanguard Long-Term Corporate Bond ETF
HYG	iShares iBoxx $ High Yield Corporate Bond

Table 4.1: *A list of bond ETFs.*

In order to build a model to predict intraday movements of the H0A0 index, we selected a number of bond ETFs from Yahoo Finance and downloaded their daily prices. These bond ETFs are liquid and their prices fluctuate frequently during regular trading hours. The list of selected bond ETFs is shown in Table 4.1. We also organized the adjusted close price data of these ETFs and the H0A0 index into a table and saved the table into a CSV file named etf.csv.

Suppose that the file etf.csv is in the current working directory. To read the price data into R, we use the following command:

```
etf <- read.csv('etf.csv', stringsAsFactors=FALSE)
> head(etf, n=3)
      Date    HOA0      JNK      BNDX      VGLT      VCSH
1 9/2/14 1081.96 39.12966 51.31715 70.77320 78.53454
2 9/3/14 1081.09 39.01580 51.30728 70.91896 78.57377
3 9/4/14 1079.53 38.88296 51.29742 70.25817 78.55415
       BSV      BIV      VGSH      SCHZ      VCLT
1 79.06859 82.21562 60.57863 50.86496 87.76689
2 79.06859 82.30294 60.57863 50.90421 87.83419
3 79.07847 82.07977 60.58857 50.84534 87.22850
       HYG
1 89.50342
2 89.27471
3 88.97929
```

Exercise 4.1. Suppose the price data of the H0A0 index and the ETFs are contained in the data frame etf.

(a) Compute descriptive statistics (i.e., minimum, maximum, mean, median, standard deviation, 25th percentile, and 75 percentile) of the H0A0 index and the ETFs.

(b) Comment on the distribution of the data based on these descriptive statistics.

4.3 Multiple Linear Regression

Let Q be the price of the H0A0 index and let P_j be the price of the jth ETF for $j = 1, 2, \ldots, k$, where k is the number of selected ETFs. Then we can build the following model:

$$Q = \beta_0 + \beta_1 P_1 + \beta_2 P_2 + \cdots + \beta_k P_k + \epsilon. \tag{4.1}$$

However, the price data do not satisfy some of the assumptions described above. For example, the prices of the H0A0 index are not independent because the price in one day is related to the price in the previous day.

Exercise 4.2. Write R code to produce a histogram of the H0A0 prices with 100 bins.

Another choice is to use the daily returns to build the model. We can compute the daily returns as follows:

```
 1 > etfLogPrice <- log(etf[, 2:12])
 2 > etfreturns <- apply(etfLogPrice, 2, diff) * 252
 3 > head(etfreturns, n=3)
 4              HOAO         JNK         BNDX         VGLT
 5 [1,]  -0.2027138  -0.7343548  -0.04845794   0.5184909
 6 [2,]  -0.3638956  -0.8594348  -0.04844760  -2.3590515
 7 [3,]  -0.5351338  -0.2460995   0.58086035  -0.8728767
 8              VCSH         BSV          BIV         VGSH
 9 [1,]   0.12586823  0.00000000   0.2675188  0.00000000
10 [2,]  -0.06292626  0.03146115  -0.6842677  0.04135000
11 [3,]   0.25165887  0.09433440   0.1786981  0.04135569
12              SCHZ        VCLT          HYG
13 [1,]   0.1943761   0.1931548  -0.6447707
14 [2,]  -0.2916179  -1.7437522  -0.8352789
15 [3,]   0.1458437  -0.6674914  -0.2970605
```

In the above R code, we first computed log prices using the function `log`. Then we used the functions `apply` and `diff` to calculate the daily returns as the differences of log prices. The difference of subsequent log prices is also approximately equal to the percent change in the price. For example, for the H0A0 index, we have

$$\ln\frac{Q_{i+1}}{Q_i} = \ln\left(1 + \frac{Q_{i+1} - Q_i}{Q_i}\right) \approx \frac{Q_{i+1} - Q_i}{Q_i}.$$

We also annualized the daily returns by multiplying the returns by 252, the number of trading days in a year.

We can plot the histograms of the daily returns of the H0A0 index using the following R code:

```
1 dev.new(width=5, height=4)
2 hist(etfreturns$HOAO, br=100)
```

The resulting histogram is shown in Figure 4.1, from which we see that the daily returns of the index are now more approximately normally distributed.

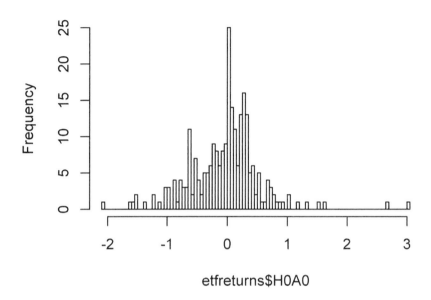

Figure 4.1: *A histogram of the daily returns of the H0A0 index.*

According to the above analysis, we will use daily returns to build the model:

$$y = \beta_0 + \beta_1 x_1 + \beta_2 x_2 + \cdots + \beta_k x_k + \epsilon, \tag{4.2}$$

where y, x_1, ..., x_k are the daily returns. Since we can observe the intraday movements of the ETFs, we can use the above model to predict the intraday movements of the H0A0 index. In the next section, we illustrate how to use R to estimate the parameters β_0, β_1, ..., β_k.

4.4 Fitting a Multiple Linear Regression Model

To fit a multiple linear regression model to the data, we use the function `lm` as follows:

```
> etfreturns <- data.frame(etfreturns)
```

```
> fith0a0 <- lm(H0A0 ~ ., data=etfreturns)
> summary(fith0a0)

Call:
lm(formula = H0A0 ~ ., data = etfreturns)

Residuals:
     Min       1Q    Median       3Q       Max
-1.42564  -0.21069  -0.00141   0.20464   2.01900

Coefficients:
              Estimate  Std. Error  t value  Pr(>|t|)
(Intercept)   0.00136     0.02748     0.049   0.96057
JNK           0.37515     0.10060     3.729   0.00024 ***
BNDX         -0.08135     0.06328    -1.286   0.19985
VGLT         -0.10687     0.04697    -2.275   0.02378 *
VCSH          0.23799     0.17160     1.387   0.16678
BSV          -0.32584     0.26918    -1.210   0.22730
BIV           0.19392     0.14859     1.305   0.19313
VGSH         -0.61291     0.29596    -2.071   0.03944 *
SCHZ          0.02867     0.13600     0.211   0.83319
VCLT          0.08937     0.04871     1.835   0.06780 .
HYG          -0.03378     0.09633    -0.351   0.72614
---
Signif. codes:  0 '***' 0.001 '**' 0.01 '*' 0.05 '.' 0.1
       ' ' 1

Residual standard error: 0.4298 on 239 degrees of freedom
Multiple R-squared:  0.4949,  Adjusted R-squared:  0.4738
F-statistic: 23.42 on 10 and 239 DF,  p-value: < 2.2e-16
```

In the function lm, the dot after the symbol ~ means that we want to use all variables in the model. In the model summary, we can see some descriptive statistics of the residuals, the regression coefficients, standard errors of the regression coefficients, etc. The R^2 of the model is 0.4949, which means that the model can only explain about half of the variability of the H0A0 returns.

The regression coefficients can be interpreted as follows. The intercept is the annualized daily return of the H0A0 index when the annualized daily returns of the ETFs are zero. The regression coefficient of JNK is 0.37515. This number means that the annualized daily return of the H0A0 index will increase by 0.037515 if the annualized daily return of JNK increases by 0.1, holding others constant. In addition, the regression coefficient of VGSH is −0.61291, which means the annualized daily return of the H0A0 index will decrease by −0.061291 if the annualized daily return of VGSH increases by 0.1, holding others constant.

Exercise 4.3. Let etfreturns be the data frame considered in this case study.

(a) What is the variable X created by the following R command?

```
1 X <- model.matrix(HOAO ~ ., data=etfreturns)
```

(b) Use the formula given in Equation (3.8) and write R code to calculate the regression coefficients $\hat{\beta}$. Do the values match the numbers shown in the model summary?

Exercise 4.4. Let fith0a0 be a multiple linear regression model fitted by the following command:

```
1 fith0a0 <- lm(HOAO ~ ., data=etfreturns)
```

Suppose that the intraday annualized daily returns of the ETFs are given in the following table:

ETF	Returns
JNK	-0.06
BNDX	0.02
VGLT	0.06
VCSH	0.01
BSV	0.01
BIV	0.02
VGSH	0.01
SCHZ	0.02
VCLT	-0.03
HYG	-0.04

Under this model, what is the predicted annualized daily return of the HOAO index?

One important assumption of the regression model is that the dependent variable should have constant variance. **Heteroscedasticity** occurs when the variance of the dependent variable varies by observation. A common procedure to detect heteroscedasticity is to plot the residuals against the fitted values from the regression model. If we see a pattern of non-constant variance in this graph, then there is presence of heteroscedasticity. Possible approaches to dealing with heteroscedasticity include transforming the variables or using weighted least squares (Faraway, 2005; Frees, 2009).

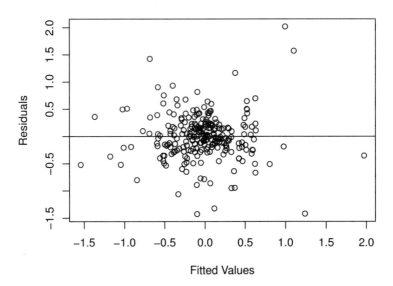

Figure 4.2: *A scatter plot of the residuals and the fitted values to detect heteroscedasticity.*

For our case study, we can plot the residuals versus the fitted values from the regression model as follows:

```
par(mar=c(4,4,1,1))
plot(fith0a0$fitted.values, fith0a0$residuals, xlab="
    Fitted Values", ylab="Residuals")
abline(0,0)
```

The resulting figure is shown in Figure 4.2, from which we do not detect heteroscedasticity.

4.5   Model Evaluation

To evaluate a multiple linear regression model, we can use the residual standard error, the R^2, and the R_a^2, which are commonly used goodness-of-fit measures.

The residual standard error, the R^2, and the adjusted R^2 (i.e., R_a^2) can be found in the model summary (see Section 4.4).

From the model summary produced by R, we see that the R^2 is 0.4949 and the R_a^2 is 0.4738. The value of the R^2 shows that the fitted multiple linear regression model explains about half of the total variation. The R_a^2 is lower than the R^2 due to the penalty of the model complexity.

Exercise 4.5. Let $\{\hat{y}_i\}$ be the fitted value of the following model:

```
1  fith0a0  <-  lm(HOA0  ~  .,  data=etfreturns)
```

Use the formula given in Equation (3.17) and write R code to calculate the residual standard deviation. Does the value match the residual standard error shown in the model summary?

Exercise 4.6. Consider the multiple linear regression model obtained by

```
1  fith0a0  <-  lm(HOA0  ~  .,  data=etfreturns)
```

Use the formulas given in Equations (3.13) and (3.20) and write R code to calculate the R^2 and the R_a^2. Do the values match the numbers in the model summary?

Exercise 4.7. Consider the multiple linear regression model obtained by

```
1  fith0a0  <-  lm(HOA0  ~  .,  data=etfreturns)
```

(a) Write R code to calculate the Pearson correlation coefficient between $\{y_i\}$ and $\{\hat{y}_i\}$.

(b) Is the square of the correlation coefficient equal to the R^2?

4.6 Model Selection

In the data set considered in this case study, we have 10 explanatory variables, each of which is a bond ETF. Then we can build $2^{10} = 1024$ different linear regression models. We have fitted a multiple linear regression model using all the 10

ETFs as explanatory variables. The model might not be the best model among the possible 1024 linear regression models in terms of the R_a^2. In this section, we use a **stepwise algorithm** to select a better model.

We can implement the forward stepwise regression algorithm in R as follows:

```
 1 k <- dim(etfreturns)[2] - 1
 2 indSelected <- c()
 3 indRemain <- c(1:k)
 4 vNames <- names(etfreturns)[2:11]
 5 dMaxRa2 <- 0
 6 # step 1
 7 jMax <- 0
 8 for( j in indRemain ) {
 9   strFormula <- as.formula( paste("HOAO ~ ", vNames[j]) )
10   fitTemp <- lm(strFormula, data = etfreturns)
11   fitTempSummary <- summary(fitTemp)
12   Ra2 <- fitTempSummary$adj.r.squared
13   if ( Ra2 > dMaxRa2 ) {
14     dMaxRa2 <- Ra2
15     jMax <- j
16   }
17 }
18 indSelected <- c(indSelected, jMax)
19 indRemain <- setdiff(indRemain, jMax)
20 while( length(indRemain) > 0 ) {
21   # step 2
22   jMax <- 0
23   for( j in indRemain ) {
24     strFormula <- as.formula( paste("HOAO ~ ", paste(
           vNames[c(indSelected, j)], collapse="+") ) )
25     fitTemp <- lm(strFormula, data = etfreturns)
26     fitTempSummary <- summary(fitTemp)
27     Ra2 <- fitTempSummary$adj.r.squared
28     if ( Ra2 > dMaxRa2 ) {
29       dMaxRa2 <- Ra2
30       jMax <- j
31     }
32   }
33   if( jMax > 0) {
34     indSelected <- c(indSelected, jMax)
35     indRemain <- setdiff(indRemain, jMax)
36   } else {
37     break
38   }
39   # step 3
```

```
40    jMax <- 0
41    for( j in indSelected ) {
42      strFormula <- as.formula( paste("H0A0 ~ ", paste(
           vNames[setdiff(indSelected, j)], collapse="+") )
           )
43      fitTemp <- lm(strFormula, data = etfreturns)
44      fitTempSummary <- summary(fitTemp)
45      Ra2 <- fitTempSummary$adj.r.squared
46      if ( Ra2 > dMaxRa2 ) {
47        dMaxRa2 <- Ra2
48        jMax <- j
49      }
50    }
51    if( jMax > 0) {
52      indSelected <- setdiff(indSelected, jMax)
53      indRemain <- c(indRemain, jMax)
54    }
55 }
56 indSelected
57 dMaxRa2
58 strFormula <- as.formula( paste("H0A0 ~ ", paste( vNames[
      indSelected], collapse="+") ) )
59 fitFinal <- lm(strFormula, data = etfreturns)
60 summary(fitFinal)
```

Executing the above R code gives the following output:

```
1 > indSelected
2 [1] 1 7 4 2 5
3 > dMaxRa2
4 [1] 0.4711413
5 > strFormula <- as.formula( paste("H0A0 ~ ", paste(
     vNames[indSelected], collapse="+") ) )
6 > fitFinal <- lm(strFormula, data = etfreturns)
7 > summary(fitFinal)
8
9 Call:
10 lm(formula = strFormula, data = etfreturns)
11
12 Residuals:
13     Min       1Q    Median       3Q       Max
14 -1.42877  -0.22593   0.01261   0.20510   2.20361
15
16 Coefficients:
17               Estimate Std. Error t value Pr(>|t|)
```

```
18 (Intercept)    -0.004911     0.027333    -0.180     0.8576
19 JNK             0.379553     0.029606    12.820     <2e-16  ***
20 VGSH           -0.507445     0.286996    -1.768     0.0783  .
21 VCSH            0.358403     0.162685     2.203     0.0285  *
22 BNDX           -0.072868     0.056965    -1.279     0.2021
23 BSV            -0.232502     0.220928    -1.052     0.2937
24 ---
25 Signif. codes:   0 '***' 0.001 '**' 0.01 '*' 0.05 '.' 0.1
         ' ' 1
26
27 Residual standard error: 0.4308 on 244 degrees of freedom
28 Multiple R-squared:   0.4818,   Adjusted R-squared:   0.4711
29 F-statistic: 45.37 on 5 and 244 DF,  p-value: < 2.2e-16
```

From the above output, we see that the best model found by the forward stepwise regression algorithm contains five variables. The R_a^2 is 0.4711. This model is not the best model in terms of R_a^2 because the full model has a higher R_a^2 than this model. In fact, the stepwise regression algorithm has the following drawbacks:

(a) The algorithm does not search all the 2^k possible linear regression models.
(b) The algorithm does not consider models with nonlinear combinations of explanatory variables.
(c) The algorithm does not take into account the user's special knowledge.

Exercise 4.8. The following R code produces a list that contains all the subsets of the set $\{1, 2, \ldots, k\}$:

```
1 listInd <- lapply(0:k, function(x) combn(k,x))
```

Using the above code, write a piece of R code to enumerate all the 2^{10} possible linear regression models and find the best model in terms of R_a^2.

4.7   Influential Points

We need to check whether there are any **influential points**, which potentially have a disproportionate effect on the overall fit.

Considering the full model, we can calculate the leverages as follows:

```
 1 > fit <- lm(HOAO ~ ., data = etfreturns)
 2 > X <- model.matrix(HOAO ~., data = etfreturns)
 3 > H <- X %*% solve( t(X) %*% X) %*% t(X)
 4 > leverages <- diag(H)
 5 > n <- nrow(etfreturns)
 6 > k <- 10
 7 > threshold <- 3 * (k+1) / n
 8 > subset(leverages, leverages > threshold)
 9       245
10 0.1666807
11 > plot(leverages, xlab="Observations", ylab="Leverages")
12 > lines( c(0,251), c(threshold, threshold) )
```

In the above code, we used the function model.matrix to create the design matrix **X** given in Equation (3.4) and then computed the matrix **H**. We used the function subset to get the observations whose leverages are greater than the threshold. We also plotted the leverages in a graph, which is shown in Figure 4.3. The horizontal line in the graph is the threshold. From the R output and Figure 4.3, we see that there is one high leverage point.

Exercise 4.9. Consider the full model obtained by the following R code:

```
1 fullModel <- lm(HOAO ~ ., data=etfreturns)
```

Write R code to verify the following equation

$$\bar{h} = \frac{1}{n} \sum_{i=1}^{n} h_{ii} = \frac{k+1}{n},$$

where h_{ii} is defined in Equation (3.27).

In this case study, we consider two approaches to handle the high leverage point we just found. For example, we compare the regression coefficients of the models with and without the high leverage point:

```
1 > fit1 <- lm(HOAO ~ ., data = etfreturns)
2 > fit2 <- lm(HOAO ~ ., data=etfreturns[-245,])
3 > cbind(fit1$coefficients, fit2$coefficients)
4                    [,1]            [,2]
5 (Intercept)   0.001360208   0.002407139
```

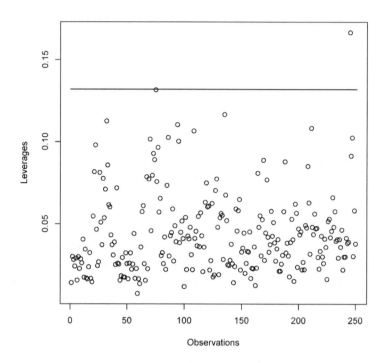

Figure 4.3: *Leverages for the observations.*

6	JNK	0.375145729	0.346869640
7	BNDX	-0.081344692	-0.087263631
8	VGLT	-0.106865881	-0.098866193
9	VCSH	0.237988509	0.215392283
10	BSV	-0.325836012	-0.367823984
11	BIV	0.193915979	0.204730776
12	VGSH	-0.612914959	-0.531318001
13	SCHZ	0.028674306	0.025695792
14	VCLT	0.089368369	0.076446240
15	HYG	-0.033780705	-0.008032117

From the above output, we see that this high leverage point affected many of the regression coefficients significantly. For example, the coefficient of JNK changed from 0.375 to 0.347. Comparing the high leverage point with the summary statistics of the data set, we found that the response at the high leverage point is the minimum of all the responses in the data set. However, the ETF returns at the high leverage point are not the extreme values. From this analysis, we suspect that the high leverage point is unusual and is not representative of the population. We can remove this point before fitting the linear regression model.

We can use Cook's distances to identify influential points. For the full model, we can calculate the Cook's distances using Equation (3.29) as follows:

```
1 > fit <- lm(HOAO ~ ., data = etfreturns)
2 > yhat <- fit$fitted.values
3 > n <- nrow(etfreturns)
4 > k <- 10
5 > e <- fit$residuals
6 > s <- sqrt( sum(e^2) / (n - (k+1) ) )
7 > D <- vector(mode="numeric", length=n)
8 > names(D) <- 1:n
9 > for(i in 1:n) {
10 +   fiti <- lm(HOAO ~ ., data=etfreturns[-i,])
11 +   yhati <- predict(fiti, etfreturns)
12 +   D[i] <- sum( (yhat - yhati)^2 ) / ((k+1) * s^2)
13 + }
14 > tail(sort(D))
15         136            69        73        33        247
                          76
16 0.07760533 0.09089115 0.09725478 0.12473757 0.12638168
       0.17787528
17 > qf(0.95, k+1, n-(k+1))
18 [1] 1.828864
```

In the above code, we used a for loop to fit regression models to calculate $\hat{y}_{j(i)}$. We also sorted the Cook's distances in ascending order and displayed the six largest Cook's distances of the observations. Since all the Cook's distances are less than the 95th percentile of the F-distribution with $df_1 = 11$ and $df_2 = 239$ degrees of freedom, which is around 1.829, none of the observations have substantial influence on the model.

Exercise 4.10. Consider the full model and write R code to calculate Cook's distances of all observations using Equation (3.30). Identify the six largest Cook's distances.

4.8   Collinearity

To calculate the variance inflation factors for the ETFs, we can use the following
R code:

```
vif <- matrix(0, nrow=10, ncol=1)
rownames(vif) <- names(etfreturns)[2:11]
for(i in 2:11) {
    formxi <- as.formula( paste(names(etfreturns)[i], "~
        . - HOAO" ) )
    fitxi <- lm( formxi, data = etfreturns )
    r2 <- summary(fitxi)$r.square
    vif[i-1] <- 1 / (1 - r2)
}
vif
```

In the above code, we created the regression formulas dynamically by using the
function as.formula to specify the response variable. We also used - HOAO in
the formula to exclude the index from the regression model.

Executing the above code gives the following output:

```
> vif
[,1]
JNK   12.998972
BNDX   1.486067
VGLT  13.528079
VCSH   3.199701
BSV    6.236206
BIV   15.808830
VGSH   3.165912
SCHZ   6.407404
VCLT   7.793102
HYG   12.786272
```

From the variance inflation factors shown above, we see that severe collinearity
exists in the data set. For example, the ETFs JNK, VGLT, BIV, and HYG can be
approximated by a linear combination of the other ETFs. We can build simpler
models by getting rid of some variables that have high variance inflation factors.
For example, the ETF BIV has a high variance inflation factor, indicating that
BIV is approximately a linear combination of other ETFs. We can calculate the
variance inflation factors for all ETFs by excluding BIV. We continue this process
until no ETFs have high variance inflation factors. Then we can build a regression
model with the ETFs that do not have high variance inflation factors.

Exercise 4.11. Consider the full model obtained by the following R code:

```
1 fullModel <- lm(HOAO ~ ., data=etfreturns)
```

Use two approaches to calculate the standard errors of the regression coefficients of the ten ETFs. In the first approach, use the following equation

$$se(\hat{\beta}_j) = s\sqrt{\text{the } (j+1)\text{th diagonal element of } (\mathbf{X}'\mathbf{X})^{-1}}.$$

In the second approach, use Equation (3.33). Do you get the same standard errors?

4.9 Heteroscedasticity

Often included in model diagnostics for a linear regression model is an examination that the error term must exhibit constant variance. The term heteroscedasticity is used to refer to the case when the variance of the errors violate this constant variance assumption. When this assumption is violated, it could result in an unstable regression model including the possibility of biased estimated coefficients.

A common approach for detecting heteroscedasticity is done visually by graphing the so-called residual plot. This is a simple scatter plot of the fitted values against the residuals. The residuals used are typically the standardized residuals which are calculated by dividing the residuals with the estimated residual standard deviation.

Some patterns we look for are demonstrated in Figure 4.4. This figure exhibits four different patterns of relationships between the fitted values and residuals: constant variance (upper left), mild nonconstant variance (upper right), increasing variance (lower left) and a U-shaped liked pattern (lower right).

For the full model, we can use the following R code to produce the residual plot:

```
1 fitted.values <- fit$fitted.values
2 residuals <- fit$residuals
3 s <- summary(fitHOAO)[[6]]
4 stdresid <- residuals/s
5 plot(fitted.values,stdresid,xlab="Fitted Values",ylab="
    Standardized Residuals",pch=16)
6 abline(h=0)
```

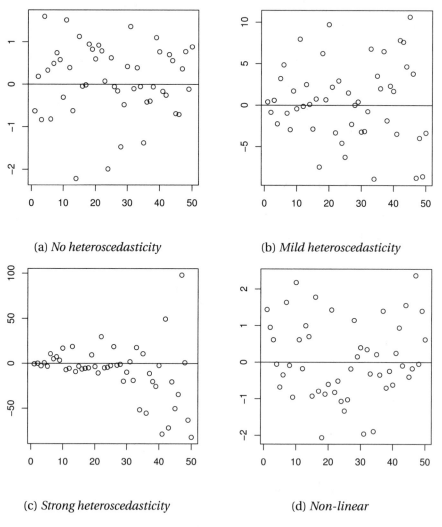

Figure 4.4: *Some patterns of heteroscedasticity.*

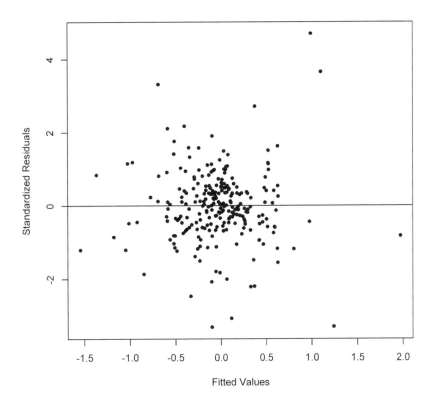

Figure 4.5: *The residual plot of the linear model.*

In Figure 4.5, we see a mild pattern of heteroscedastic residuals. Some approaches that have been suggested to handle heteroscedasticity include the following:

- Use of weighted least squares: The general idea is to give weights to the observations and then re-estimate the parameters with the usual least squares method.

- Transformation of the response variable: This is accomplished by re-defining the dependent variable y using Box-Cox transformations including a log transformation.

- Calculate more robust standard errors: This is beyond the scope of this book but see Chapter 5 of Frees (2010) for additional details.

4.10   Statistical Inference for a Single Regression Coefficient

In this section, we illustrate how to conduct hypothesis testing for a single regression coefficient. For example, to conduct the following hypothesis test

$$H_0 : \beta_5 = -0.5, \quad \beta_5 < -0.5$$

at the significance level 5% under the full model (i.e., the model that uses all ten ETFs as explanatory variables), we can proceed in R as follows:

```
 1 > fullModel <- lm(HOAO ~ ., data=etfreturns)
 2 > beta5 <- -0.5
 3 > b5 <- fullModel$coefficients[6]
 4 > s <- sqrt( sum(fullModel$residuals^2 ) / fullModel$df )
 5 > X <- model.matrix(HOAO ~ ., data=etfreturns)
 6 > seb5 <- s * sqrt( diag( solve(t(X) %*% X) )[6] )
 7 > tratio <- (b5 - beta5) / seb5
 8 > tratio
 9        BSV
10 0.6470102
11 > qt(1 - 0.05, df = fullModel$df )
12 [1] 1.651254
```

In the above R code, we illustrated how to calculate the t-ratio and the critical t-value. Since the t-ratio is less than the critical t-value, we fail to reject H_0 at the 5% significance level.

Exercise 4.12. Consider the full model obtained by the following R code:

```
1 fullModel <- lm(HOAO ~ ., data=etfreturns)
```

Do you agree or disagree with the statement that the HOAO index will increase 1% if the JNK ETF increases 1% and all other ETFs do not change?

4.11   Summary

In this chapter, we introduced how to use multiple linear regression models to predict the intraday movements of the HOAO index. The HOAO index is a high yield bond index whose price is only quoted at the end of the day. However, it is important to estimate the intraday prices of this index for the purpose of risk management and performance attribution.

In this case study, we explained how to fit a multiple linear regression model to a dataset and interpret the regression coefficients. Since multiple linear regression involves several explanatory variables, we needed to introduce the selection of explanatory variables, using a forward stepwise regression algorithm, in order to build better models. We also introduced how to identify and deal with influential points and collinearity. In addition, we performed important statistical inference for a single regression coefficient. For more information about multiple linear regression, readers are referred to (Frees, 2009, Chapters 4 and 5) and (Faraway, 2014).

4.12   End-of-Chapter Exercises

Exercise 4.13. Consider the following model for predicting the intraday returns of the H0A0 index with ETFs:

$$\text{H0A0} = \beta_0 + \beta_1 \text{JNK} + \beta_2 \text{BNDX} + \beta_3 \text{HYG} + \epsilon$$

and the following R output

```
1 > fit <- lm(H0A0 ~ JNK + BNDX + HYG, data=etfreturns)
2 > summary(fit)
3
4 Call:
5 lm(formula = H0A0 ~ JNK + BNDX + HYG, data = etfreturns)
6
7 Residuals:
8      Min       1Q    Median       3Q      Max
9 -1.49990 -0.22154  0.01883  0.21256  2.27704
10
11 Coefficients:
12              Estimate Std. Error t value Pr(>|t|)
13 (Intercept) -0.005499   0.027772  -0.198   0.8432
14 JNK          0.441199   0.098792   4.466 1.22e-05 ***
15 BNDX        -0.095008   0.052842  -1.798   0.0734 .
16 HYG         -0.034143   0.095360  -0.358   0.7206
17 ---
18 Signif. codes:  0 '***' 0.001 '**' 0.01 '*' 0.05 '.' 0.1
        ' ' 1
19
20 Residual standard error: 0.4371 on 246 degrees of freedom
21 Multiple R-squared:  0.4622,  Adjusted R-squared:  0.4556
```

```
22 F-statistic: 70.46 on 3 and 246 DF,   p-value: < 2.2e-16
```

You are also given the following output:

```
1 > pt(246, 0.95)
2 [1] 0.998311
3 > pt(246, 0.975)
4 [1] 0.998522
5 > pt(250, 0.95)
6 [1] 0.9983366
7 > pt(250, 0.975)
8 [1] 0.998545
```

(a) What does -0.005499 represent?

(b) Is the ETF JNK useful for predicting H0A0? Why?

(c) What are the hypotheses associated with the t-value 4.466?

(d) What is the mean square error of this model?

(e) What is the sample standard deviation of the variable Y?

(f) Suppose that the ETF returns are: JNK $= 0.01$, BNDX $= -0.05$, HYG $= 0.02$. What is the expected change of H0A0?

(g) Test the following hypothesis at the 5% level of significance:

$$H_0 : \beta_1 = 0.5 \text{ versus } H_a : \beta_1 \neq 0.5$$

(h) One number is missing in the following R output:

```
1 > X <- model.matrix(H0A0 ~ JNK + BNDX + HYG, data=
    etfreturns)
2 > round(solve( t(X) %*% X ), 5)
3              (Intercept)      JNK      BNDX       HYG
4 (Intercept)      0.00404  0.00108  -0.00033  -0.00086
5 JNK              0.00108        ?   0.00072  -0.04722
6 BNDX            -0.00033  0.00072   0.01461  -0.00042
7 HYG             -0.00086 -0.04722  -0.00042   0.04759
```

What is the value of that number?

Exercise 4.14. Consider the following summary of a linear regression model:

```
 1 Call:
 2 lm(formula = HOAO ~ JNK + BIV + HYG, data = etfreturns)
 3
 4 Residuals:
 5      Min       1Q    Median        3Q       Max
 6 -1.57066 -0.20500   0.01758   0.21895   2.26017
 7
 8 Coefficients:
 9              Estimate Std. Error t value Pr(>|t|)
10 (Intercept) -0.006775   0.027805  -0.244    0.808
11 JNK          0.428347   0.099625   4.300 2.47e-05 ***
12 BIV         -0.058059   0.038425  -1.511    0.132
13 HYG         -0.023355   0.095947  -0.243    0.808
14 ---
15 Signif. codes:  0 '***' 0.001 '**' 0.01 '*' 0.05 '.' 0.1
       ' ' 1
16
17 Residual standard error: 0.438 on 246 degrees of freedom
18 Multiple R-squared:  0.4601,    Adjusted R-squared:
       0.4535
19 F-statistic: 69.88 on 3 and 246 DF,  p-value: < 2.2e-16
```

The given values, the fitted values, and the leverages of the first six observations are given in the following table:

i	y_i	$\hat{y}_i$	h_{ii}
1	-0.2	-0.32	0.006396
2	-0.36	-0.32	0.011215
3	-0.54	-0.12	0.004587
4	0.06	-0.09	0.005337
5	-0.38	-0.47	0.014196
6	-0.8	-0.03	0.0097

Calculate the Cook's distances for the second and fourth observations.

Chapter 5

Case Study: Estimating Fair Market Values of Variable Annuities

In this case study, we introduce how to estimate the fair market values of the guarantees embedded in variable annuities using multiple linear regression models. Such regression models can approximate the time-consuming Monte Carlo simulation model, which is commonly used to calculate the fair market values of the guarantees. After working through this case study, readers will be able to

- Understand and create binary dummy variables
- Handle categorical explanatory variables in linear regression
- Calculate and understand various validation measures
- Evaluate the out-of-sample performance of models
- Calculate and understand F-ratio
- Conduct hypothesis testing for a set of regression coefficients

5.1   Problem Description

A variable annuity is an insurance contract between a policyholder and an insurance company. Under a variable annuity contract, the policyholder agrees to make one lump-sum or a series of purchase payments to the insurance company and the insurance company agrees to make benefit payments to the policyholder, beginning either immediately or at a future date. The premiums of the policyholder are invested in a basket of mutual funds provided by the insurance companies.

One important feature of variable annuities is that they come with guarantees. Common guarantees include guaranteed minimum death benefit (GMDB), guaranteed minimum withdrawal benefit (GMWB), guaranteed minimum income benefit (GMIB), and guaranteed minimum maturity benefit (GMMB). Because of these guarantee features, variable annuities have become popular around the world (IRI, 2011). However, these guarantees are financial guarantees and cannot be adequately addressed by traditional actuarial approaches (Hardy, 2003).

Dynamic hedging is a popular method to manage the financial risks associated with variable annuities and is adopted by many insurance companies. Dynamic hedging requires calculating the fair market values and Greeks (i.e., sensitivities) of the guarantees embedded in every variable annuity contract. Since the guarantees are complex, their fair market values cannot be calculated in closed form. Monte Carlo simulation is used in practice to calculate the fair market values of these guarantees.

One drawback of Monte Carlo simulation is that it is computationally intensive. Using Monte Carlo simulation to calculate the fair market values of a large portfolio of variable annuities may take hours or several days. One approach to addressing the computational problem is to build a mathematical model to replace the Monte Carlo simulation model (Gan, 2013; Gan and Lin, 2015). In this case study, we build a multiple linear regression model to estimate the fair market values of the guarantees. The regression model is much more computationally efficient than the underlying Monte Carlo simulation model.

5.2   Data Description

The dataset is obtained from the paper by Gan and Lin (2017). This dataset contains a portfolio of 10,000 variable annuity contracts and the fair market values of the guarantees embedded in these variable annuities. The explanatory variables that describe these variable annuities include policyholder information (e.g., age, gender) and contract information (e.g., product type, issue date, maturity date, fund values). The description of these explanatory variables is given in Table 5.1.

The variable annuity contracts in the portfolio were generated randomly by a computer program. The policyholders are allowed to allocate the purchase payments in 10 mutual funds. The fair market value of the guarantees is calculated by a simple Monte Carlo simulation model. See Gan (2015b) for further details.

Variable	Description
recordID	Record id
survivorShip	Proportion of the account value not lapsed
gender	Gender of the policyholder
prodType	Product type of the variable annuity
issueDate	Issue date of the contract
matDate	Maturity date of the contract
birthDate	Birth date of the policyholder
currentDate	Valuation date
age	Age of the policyholder
baseFee	Basic fees of the contract
riderFee	Guarantee fees
gmdbAmt	GMDB amount
dbRollUpRate	Interest rate for GMDB balance
gmwbAmt	GMWB amount
gmwbBalance	GMWB balance
wbRollUpRate	Interest rate for GMWB balance
wbWithdrawalRate	Maximum withdrawal rate
gmmbAmt	GMMB amount
mbRollUpRate	Interest rate for GMMB balance
withdrawal	Total withdrawal
ttm	Time to maturity in years
FundNum$i$	Fund number of the ith fund, $i = 1, 2, \ldots, 10$
FundValue$i$	Account value of the ith fund, $i = 1, 2, \ldots, 10$
FundFee$i$	Management fee of the ith fund, $i = 1, 2, \ldots, 10$

Table 5.1: *Variables used to describe a variable annuity contract.*

5.3   Loading the Data into R

Variable annuity contracts and the fair market values of the guarantees are saved in the files inforce10k.csv and fmv_seriatim.csv, respectively. We can load the data into R as follows:

```
> inforce <- read.csv("inforce10k.csv")
> fmv <- read.csv("fmv_seriatim.csv")
> names(inforce)
 [1] "recordID"       "survivorShip"   "gender"
 [4] "prodType"       "issueDate"      "matDate"
 [7] "birthDate"      "currentDate"    "age"
```

```
 7  [10]  "baseFee"            "riderFee"            "gmdbAmt"
 8  [13]  "dbRollUpRate"       "gmwbAmt"             "gmwbBalance"
 9  [16]  "wbRollUpRate"       "wbWithdrawalRate"    "gmmbAmt"
10  [19]  "mbRollUpRate"       "withdrawal"          "ttm"
11  [22]  "FundNum1"           "FundValue1"          "FundFee1"
12  [25]  "FundNum2"           "FundValue2"          "FundFee2"
13  [28]  "FundNum3"           "FundValue3"          "FundFee3"
14  [31]  "FundNum4"           "FundValue4"          "FundFee4"
15  [34]  "FundNum5"           "FundValue5"          "FundFee5"
16  [37]  "FundNum6"           "FundValue6"          "FundFee6"
17  [40]  "FundNum7"           "FundValue7"          "FundFee7"
18  [43]  "FundNum8"           "FundValue8"          "FundFee8"
19  [46]  "FundNum9"           "FundValue9"          "FundFee9"
20  [49]  "FundNum10"          "FundValue10"         "FundFee10"
21  > names(fmv)
22  [1]  "RecordID" "fmv"
```

From the above R output, we see that the contracts are described by many variables, which include age, gender, and fund information. The contracts and their corresponding fair market values are linked through the variable `RecordID`.

It is convenient to work on a data frame that contains both the contract information and the fair market values. We combine the two data frames as follows:

```
1  > inforce2 <- merge(inforce, fmv, by.x = "recordID", by.y
      = "RecordID")
```

In the above code, we used the function `merge` to combine the two data frames based on the record identifying keys. The function `merge` matches the fair market values and the contracts based on the identifying keys. Since the order of the identifying keys in the data frame `inforce` is different from that in the data frame `fmv`, we cannot use the function `cbind` to combine the two data frames without sorting the data.

5.4   Selecting Variables and Preparing Training Data

As we can see from the summary statistics (not shown here) of the variables, some variables (e.g., fund numbers, fund fees, survivorship) have identical values. We need to remove these variables before building regression models. See the exercise below.

Exercise 5.1. Why do we need to remove the variables with identical values before constructing regression models?

Since our goal is to build models to predict the fair market values of the guarantees, we also need to include the variables that affect the fair market value of the guarantees. These variables can be identified by looking at the actuarial valuation system for variable annuities or asking people who developed the valuation model. In the Monte Carlo simulation model used to calculate the fair market values, the following information from a variable annuity contract is used: gender, product type, issue date, maturity date, policyholder's age, GMDB amount, GMWB amount, GMWB balance, GMMB amount, amount of withdrawal, and fund values. In R, we can select these variables as follows:

```
1 > vNames <- c("recordID", "gender", "prodType", "
    issueDate", "matDate", "age", "gmdbAmt", "gmwbAmt", "
    gmwbBalance", "gmmbAmt", "withdrawal", paste("
    FundValue", 1:10, sep=""), "fmv")
2 > dat10k <- inforce2[,vNames]
```

In the above code, we created a vector of names of the variables that may potentially be important for predicting the fair market value and then we assigned the selected data to the data frame dat10k. Although recordID does not affect the fair market value of a variable annuity, we included it in the vector of names for reference purpose.

To build a multiple linear regression model to predict the fair market values and evaluate the model in terms of out-of-sample performance, we split the data set into two parts: a training dataset and a test dataset. The training dataset is used to estimate the parameters of the regression model. The test dataset is used to validate the regression model to make sure it is able to make accurate out-of-sample predictions.

We can select the training dataset randomly from the full dataset. In R, we can accomplish this by splitting the dataset as follows:

```
1 > set.seed(1)
2 > vInd <- sample(1:nrow(dat10k), size=1000)
3 > dat10kTrain <- dat10k[vInd,]
4 > dat10kTest <- dat10k[-vInd,]
```

In the above code, we split the data set into a training dataset with 1,000 observations and a test dataset with 9,000 observations. The function sample creates a vector of random integers from a given range. The function set.seed is used to make sure we can repeat our experiments. The statement set.seed(1) makes sure that we get the same vInd every time.

5.5   Categorical Variables

We notice that the variables used to describe a variable annuity contract contain two categorical variables: gender and product type. The categorical variables might be important to predict the fair market values. Initial investigation of the importance of these categorical variables can be done using **box plots**. A box plot is a statistical graphical tool for displaying groups of numerical data based on quantiles. For example, we can create box plots of the fair market values by levels of these categorical variables as follows:

```
> dev.new(width=4, height=4)
> plot(fmv ~ gender, data=dat10kTrain)
> plot(fmv ~ prodType, data=dat10kTrain)
```

In the above code, the function dev.new is used to specify the size of the plot. The resulting box plots are shown in Figure 5.1, from which we see that gender may have very little impact on the fair market values. We will confirm this when we fit the regression model. On the other hand, we see that product type has a big impact on the fair market values because we observe variation across the categories of the product type.

Since categorical variables are symbols, we cannot use them directly in regression models. We need to convert categorical variables to binary variables. In R, categorical variables are stored as factors (See Section A.7). If a factor has m levels, then it will be converted to $m - 1$ binary variables in the regression model. These binary variables are called **dummy variables**. To see the levels of the categorical variables, we can use the following command:

```
> summary(dat10kTrain[,c("gender", "prodType")])
 gender   prodType
 F:420    DBRP :186
 M:580    DBRU :207
          MB   :207
          WB   :205
          WBSU :195
```

From the output, we see that the variables gender and prodType have two and five levels, respectively. Hence these two variables will be converted to one and four dummy variables, respectively.

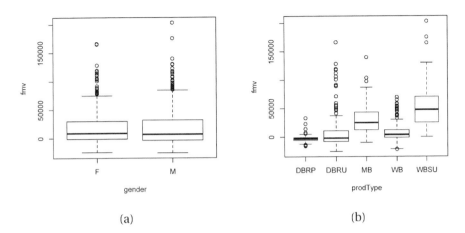

Figure 5.1: *Box plots of the fair market values. (a) Box plots by levels of gender. (b) Box plots by levels of product type.*

5.6 Building a Multiple Linear Regression Model

Since all the pre-selected variables in our dataset are used by the Monte Carlo simulation model to calculate the fair market values of the guarantees, we use all these variables to construct the multiple linear regression model.

It is straightforward to incorporate categorical independent variables into a multiple linear regression model in R. In the function lm, we can treat categorical variables just like numerical variables as follows:

```
> fit1 <- lm(fmv ~ . - recordID, data=dat10kTrain)
> summary(fit1)

Call:
lm(formula = fmv ~ . - recordID, data = dat10kTrain)

Residuals:
   Min     1Q  Median     3Q     Max
-51060  -8673   -2113   5490  127706

Coefficients:
                 Estimate  Std. Error  t value  Pr(>|t|)
(Intercept)    -1.501e+05   1.863e+04   -8.058  2.26e-15 ***
genderM        -1.169e+03   1.098e+03   -1.064   0.28742
prodTypeDBRU   -2.446e+03   2.120e+03   -1.154   0.24882
```

```
16  prodTypeMB     -2.357e+03   3.473e+03    -0.679   0.49747
17  prodTypeWB     -6.125e+03   3.314e+03    -1.849   0.06483  .
18  prodTypeWBSU   -2.977e+03   3.320e+03    -0.897   0.37019
19  issueDate       1.826e+00   5.666e-01     3.222   0.00132  **
20  matDate         1.426e+00   3.458e-01     4.124   4.03e-05 ***
21  age             3.195e+02   6.471e+01     4.937   9.34e-07 ***
22  gmdbAmt         1.001e-01   9.993e-03    10.020   < 2e-16  ***
23  gmwbAmt         9.595e+00   1.361e+00     7.053   3.32e-12 ***
24  gmwbBalance    -4.239e-01   9.387e-02    -4.516   7.07e-06 ***
25  gmmbAmt         2.230e-01   1.519e-02    14.681   < 2e-16  ***
26  withdrawal     -5.171e-01   8.424e-02    -6.138   1.21e-09 ***
27  FundValue1     -9.945e-02   1.222e-02    -8.135   1.25e-15 ***
28  FundValue2     -3.209e-02   1.095e-02    -2.929   0.00348  **
29  FundValue3     -9.828e-02   1.531e-02    -6.419   2.14e-10 ***
30  FundValue4     -1.676e-01   1.657e-02   -10.112   < 2e-16  ***
31  FundValue5     -1.359e-01   2.005e-02    -6.777   2.12e-11 ***
32  FundValue6     -7.623e-02   1.330e-02    -5.730   1.34e-08 ***
33  FundValue7     -7.379e-02   1.406e-02    -5.247   1.89e-07 ***
34  FundValue8     -1.632e-01   1.557e-02   -10.480   < 2e-16  ***
35  FundValue9     -6.131e-02   1.566e-02    -3.916   9.64e-05 ***
36  FundValue10    -1.320e-01   1.544e-02    -8.554   < 2e-16  ***
37  ---
38  Signif. codes:  0 '***' 0.001 '**' 0.01 '*' 0.05 '.' 0.1
        ' ' 1
39
40  Residual standard error: 16990 on 976 degrees of freedom
41  Multiple R-squared:  0.6945,     Adjusted R-squared:
        0.6873
42  F-statistic: 96.49 on 23 and 976 DF,  p-value: < 2.2e-16
```

Since the variable recordID contains the identifying keys, it does not help predict the fair market values. As a result, we excluded this variable in the regression formula.

In the above model summary, we notice that the variable gender is displayed as genderM and the variable prodType is split into four variables. In fact, the two variables gender and prodType are categorical variables, which are converted to binary **dummy variables** automatically by R. See the previous section on the role of binary variables.

From the regression coefficients shown in the model summary, we see that the variables issueDate, matDate, age, gmdbAmt, gmwbAmt, and gmmbAmt have positive impact on the fair market values. This sounds reasonable as the higher the value of each of these variables, the higher the fair market values.

Once we have the regression model, we can use it to predict the fair market values of the guarantees embedded in the variable annuity contracts. For example, we use the regression model to predict the fair market values of the guarantees in the training dataset and the test dataset as follows:

```
1 > yhat <- predict(fit1, dat10kTrain)
2 > dMin <- min(dat10kTrain$fmv)
3 > dMax <- max(dat10kTrain$fmv)
4 > dev.new(width=4, height=4)
5 > par(mar=c(4,4,1,1))
6 > plot(dat10kTrain$fmv, yhat, xlab="Calculated FMV", ylab
    ="Predicted FMV")
7 > lines(c(dMin, dMax), c(dMin, dMax))
8 >
9 > yhat <- predict(fit1, dat10kTest)
0 > dMin <- min(dat10kTest$fmv)
1 > dMax <- max(dat10kTest$fmv)
2 > dev.new(width=4, height=4)
3 > par(mar=c(4,4,1,1))
4 > plot(dat10kTest$fmv, yhat, xlab="Calculated FMV", ylab=
    "Predicted FMV")
5 > lines(c(dMin, dMax), c(dMin, dMax))
```

In the above R code, we first used the function `predict` to estimate the fair market values. Then we created scatter plots of the fair market values predicted by the model and those calculated by the Monte Carlo simulation model. The resulting scatter plots are shown in Figure 5.2. From the figures, we see that most of the predicted fair market values approximately match the calculated fair market values. For some contracts, however, the predicted fair market values are close to zero but the calculated fair market values are very large. This indicates that we can further improve this linear regression model, but this is out of scope of this case study.

Our goal is to estimate the aggregate fair market value at the portfolio level. We can calculate the predicted fair market value of the portfolio and the percentage difference between the predicted fair market value and the calculated fair market value at the portfolio level as follows:

```
1 > yhat <- predict(fit1, dat10k)
2 > fmvdiff <- sum(yhat) - sum(dat10k$fmv)
3 > fmvdiff / sum(dat10k$fmv)
4 [1] 0.0165042
```

From the above output, we see that the percentage difference is around 1.65%. In other words, the linear regression model is able to produce a very accurate

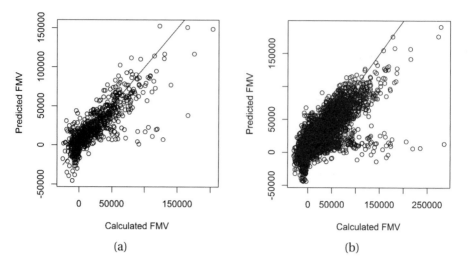

Figure 5.2: *Scatter plots of the predicted fair market values and the calculated fair market values. (a) Fair market values from the training dataset. (b) Fair market values from the test dataset.*

estimate of the fair market value of the portfolio. In addition, building the linear regression model and using the model to estimate the fair market values takes much less time than the Monte Carlo simulation model. See the exercise below.

Exercise 5.2. Suppose that it took the Monte Carlo simulation model 3 hours to calculate the fair market values of the 10,000 variable annuity contracts in the portfolio. Estimate how much time each of the following components takes:

- Run the Monte Carlo simulation model to calculate the fair market values of 1,000 selected variable annuity contracts;
- Fit the linear regression model; and
- Use the linear regression model to estimate the fair market value of the whole portfolio of 10,000 contracts.

5.7   Model Evaluation

To measure the performance of the regression model at individual contract level, we use the following six measures: the root mean squared error (**RMSE**), the relative average absolute error (**RAAE**), the R^2, the relative maximum absolute error (**RMAE**), the average percentage error (**APE**), and the average absolute percentage error (**AAPE**).

Let $y_1, y_2, \ldots, y_J$ be the fair market values in the test dataset and let $\hat{y}_1, \hat{y}_2, \ldots, \hat{y}_J$ be the fair market values predicted by the regression model. Then the validation measures are defined as follows:

$$\text{RMSE} = \sqrt{\frac{1}{J}\sum_{l=1}^{J}(\hat{y}_l - y_l)^2}, \tag{5.1a}$$

$$\text{RAAE} = \frac{\sum_{l=1}^{J}|\hat{y}_l - y_l|}{J \times s_y}, \tag{5.1b}$$

$$R^2 = 1 - \frac{\sum_{l=1}^{J}(\hat{y}_l - y_l)^2}{\sum_{l=1}^{J}(\bar{y} - y_l)^2} \tag{5.1c}$$

$$\text{RMAE} = \frac{\max_{1\leq l\leq J}|\hat{y}_l - y_l|}{s_y}, \tag{5.1d}$$

$$\text{APE} = \frac{1}{J}\sum_{l=1}^{J}\frac{\hat{y}_l - y_l}{y_l}, \tag{5.1e}$$

$$\text{AAPE} = \frac{1}{J}\sum_{l=1}^{J}\left|\frac{\hat{y}_l - y_l}{y_l}\right|, \tag{5.1f}$$

where $\bar{y}$ and s_y are the sample mean and sample standard deviation of $y_1, y_2, \ldots, y_J$, respectively.

Exercise 5.3. Write an R function called `calMeasure(y, yhat)` to calculate the validation measures RMSE, RAAE, R^2, RMAE, APE, and AAPE. The function should return the values of these measures in a list with names `rmse`, `raae`, `rsquared`, `rmae`, `ape`, `aape`, respectively.

Let `calMeasure` be the function defined in Exercise 5.3. Then we can calculate the validation measures as follows:

```
 1 > yhat <- predict(fit1, dat10kTest)
 2 > calMeasure(dat10kTest$fmv, yhat)
 3 $rmse
 4 [1]  17958.8
 5
 6 $raae
 7 [1]  0.3698167
 8
 9 $rsquared
10 [1]  0.6564983
11
12 $rmae
13 [1]  8.883246
14
15 $ape
16 [1]  -0.06891369
17
18 $aape
19 [1]  3.870861
```

The measure RMSE is in dollar units and it is hard to interpret the measure by just looking at its value. All other measures are relative measures. The value of RAAE tells us that on average, the absolute difference is about 36.98% of the standard deviation of the calculated fair market values. The value of RMAE tells us that the maximum absolute difference is about 9 times the standard deviation. The values of such validation measures show that the linear regression model does not perform well at the individual contract level, although it produces very accurate estimates at the portfolio level, as we previously mentioned.

5.8   Statistical Inference for Several Coefficients

In this section, we introduce the **general linear hypothesis**, which involves a set of regression coefficients.

As we can see from the model summary in Section 5.6, the p-value of the dummy variable genderM is about 0.2874, which indicates that this dummy variable is not significant for predicting the fair market value. Let us conduct a hypothesis test at 5% significance level to check whether this dummy variable is significant. To do that, we formulate the following hypothesis:

$$H_0 : \beta_1 = 0, \quad H_a : \beta_1 \neq 0.$$

The corresponding general linear hypothesis in matrix form is given by

$$H_0 : \mathbf{C\beta} = \mathbf{d}, \quad H_a : \mathbf{C\beta} \neq \mathbf{d},$$

where

$$\mathbf{C} = (0, 1, 0, \ldots, 0), \quad \mathbf{d} = 0.$$

In R, we conduct this general linear hypothesis as follows:

```
1 > fit1 <- lm(fmv ~ . - recordID, data=dat10kTrain)
2 > fit1summary <- summary(fit1)
3 > s <- fit1summary[[6]]  # this is the residual standard
    error
4 > b <- fit1$coefficients
5 > X <- model.matrix(fmv ~ . - recordID, data=dat10kTrain)
6 > k <- ncol(X) - 1
7 > C = matrix(0, nrow=1, ncol=k + 1)
8 > C[1,2] <- 1
9 > p <- 1
10 > d = matrix(0, nrow=1, ncol=1)
11 > fratio <- t( C %*% b - d) %*% solve( C %*% solve(t(X) %
     *% X) %*% t(C) ) %*% ( C %*% b - d) / (p * s^2)
12 > n <- nrow(X)
13 > fvalue <- qf(1-0.05, p, n-(k+1))
14 > fratio
15          [,1]
16 [1,] 1.132899
17 > fvalue
18 [1] 3.851004
```

From the above calculation, we see that the F-ratio is less than the F-value at the 5% significance level. Hence we fail to reject the null hypothesis at the 5% significance level. There is not enough evidence in the training data to show that the variable gender is significant for predicting the fair market value.

———————————————◦———————————————

Exercise 5.4. Write an R program to plot the probability density function of an F-distribution with $df_1 = 1$ and $df_2 = 977$. (Hint: use the R function df to calculate the density of F-distributions.)

Exercise 5.5. Consider the following linear regression model:

```
1 fit1 <- lm(fmv ~ . - recordID, data=dat10kTrain)
```

(a) Formulate a general linear hypothesis in matrix form to test whether the dummy variables of product type jointly affect the fair market value.
(b) Write R code to test the general linear hypothesis at the 1% significance level.

5.9   Summary

In this chapter, we introduced how to build a multiple linear regression model to predict the fair market values of the guarantees embedded in variable annuity contracts. We emphasized that this regression model is more computationally efficient than the underlying Monte Carlo simulation model.

In this case study, we also demonstrated how to evaluate the out-of-sample performance of the regression model. This was accomplished by subdividing the dataset into a training dataset and a test dataset. The training dataset is used to estimate the parameters of the regression model, while the test dataset is used to validate the model.

The fitted regression model was also used to estimate the fair market values of the guarantees embedded in variable annuity contracts. We found that prediction at the portfolio level is much more accurate than that in the individual contract level.

The multiple linear regression model is called a metamodel (Friedman, 2013) of the Monte Carlo simulation model and can be used to replace the Monte Carlo simulation model to value large portfolios of variable annuity contracts. Other metamodels have been proposed to predict the fair market values of the guarantees, see for example, Gan (2013), Gan (2015a), Gan and Lin (2015), Gan and Valdez (2018), and Gan (2018).

Chapter 6

Generalized Linear Models

In previous chapters, we introduced linear regression models and their applications. Linear regression models can be extended in many ways. In this chapter, we introduce generalized linear models, which are widely used extensions.

6.1   Linear Exponential Family of Distributions

The **linear exponential family** of distributions is a wide class of distributions that include many common distributions such as the normal distribution. A distribution is said to belong to the linear exponential family if it can be expressed in the following form:

$$f(y; \theta, \phi) = \exp\left(\frac{y\theta - b(\theta)}{\phi} + S(y, \phi)\right), \tag{6.1}$$

where θ and ϕ are parameters, $b(\theta)$ is a function of the parameter θ that does not depend on y or ϕ, and $S(y, \phi)$ is a function of y and the parameter ϕ that does not depend on θ.

Based on the probability distribution function given in Equation (6.1), we can calculate the mean and the variance of a linear exponential family distribution as follows (see Exercise 6.2):

$$E[Y] = b'(\theta), \tag{6.2}$$

$$\mathrm{Var}(Y) = \phi b''(\theta). \tag{6.3}$$

Table 6.1 gives some distributions that belong to the linear exponential family. Table 6.2 presents the corresponding parameterizations of these distributions in the linear exponential family form given in Equation (6.1).

Distribution	Density	Support
Normal	$\dfrac{1}{\sigma\sqrt{2\pi}}\exp\left(-\dfrac{(y-\mu)^2}{2\sigma^2}\right)$	$(-\infty,\infty)$
Bernoulli	$p^y(1-p)^{1-y}$	$\{0,1\}$
Poisson	$\dfrac{\lambda^y e^{-\lambda}}{y!}$	$\{0,1,2,\dots\}$
Gamma	$\dfrac{1}{\lambda^\alpha \Gamma(\alpha)}y^{\alpha-1}e^{-\lambda y}$	$(0,\infty)$

Table 6.1: *Some examples of distributions in the linear exponential family and their probability distribution functions.*

Distribution	θ	ϕ	$b(\theta)$	$S(y,\phi)$
Normal	μ	σ^2	$\dfrac{\theta^2}{2}$	$-\dfrac{y^2}{2\phi}-\dfrac{1}{2}\ln(2\pi\phi)$
Bernoulli	$\ln\dfrac{p}{1-p}$	1	$\ln(1+e^\theta)$	0
Poisson	$\ln\lambda$	1	e^θ	$-\ln y!$
Gamma	$-\dfrac{1}{\alpha\beta}$	$\dfrac{1}{\alpha}$	$\ln(-\theta)$	$-\dfrac{1}{\phi}\ln\phi-\ln\Gamma(\dfrac{1}{\phi})+(\dfrac{1}{\phi}-1)\ln y$

Table 6.2: *General forms of some distributions in the linear exponential family.*

Exercise 6.1. The **inverse Gaussian distribution** is a member of the linear exponential family and has the following probability distribution function:

$$f(y;\mu,\lambda)=\left(\frac{\lambda}{2\pi y^3}\right)^{\frac{1}{2}}\exp\left[\frac{-\lambda(y-\mu)^2}{2\mu^2 y}\right].$$

Write the distribution in the form given in Equation (6.1) by finding θ, ϕ, $b(\theta)$ and $S(y,\phi)$.

Exercise 6.2. Let Y be a random variable following an exponential family distribution defined in Equation (6.1).

(a) Show that the **moment generating function** of Y is given by

$$E\left[\exp(tY)\right] = \exp\left(\frac{b(\theta + \phi t) - b(\theta)}{\phi}\right).$$

(Hint: When t is sufficiently small, we can assume that $f(y; \theta + \phi t, \phi)$ is a distribution function.)

(b) Show that
$$E[Y] = b'(\theta)$$

and
$$\text{Var}(Y) = \phi b''(\theta),$$

where $b'(\theta)$ and $b''(\theta)$ denote the first and the second derivatives of $b(\theta)$, respectively.

6.2 GLM Models

The **generalized linear model** (GLM) is a widely used family of regression models that includes linear regression models introduced in previous chapters. The GLM provides a unifying framework to handle dependent variables that are discrete, continuous, or a mixture.

In the GLM context, we assume that the mean of the response (i.e., the dependent variable) can be expressed as a function of linear combinations of the explanatory variables, i.e.,

$$\mu_i = E[y_i], \tag{6.4a}$$

$$\eta_i = \mathbf{x}_i'\boldsymbol{\beta} = g(\mu_i). \tag{6.4b}$$

Here $\mathbf{x}_i = (1, x_{i1}, x_{i2}, \ldots, x_{ik})'$ is a vector of regressor values, μ_i is the mean response for the ith case, and η_i is a systematic component of the GLM. The function $g(\cdot)$ is known and is referred to as the **link function**. The inverse of the link function is called the **mean function** of the model, i.e.,

$$\mu_i = g^{-1}(\mathbf{x}_i'\boldsymbol{\beta}).$$

In the GLM defined in Equation (6.4), we allow the mean response to vary by observations and keep the parameters in $\boldsymbol{\beta}$ to be the same among different observations.

Distribution	Mean Function	Variance Function	Canonical Link Function
Normal	θ	1	μ
Bernoulli	$\dfrac{e^\theta}{1+e^\theta}$	$\mu(1-\mu)$	$\ln\dfrac{\mu}{1-\mu}$
Poisson	e^θ	μ	$\ln\mu$
Gamma	$-\dfrac{1}{\theta}$	μ^2	$-\dfrac{1}{\mu}$

Table 6.3: *Mean functions, variance functions, and canonical link functions for some common distributions.*

There are different choices of link functions for a particular distribution. The link function that is the inverse of the mean function $b'(\theta)$ is called the **canonical link function**. Table 6.3 gives the canonical link functions for some common distributions.

In GLMs, we make the following assumptions:

(a) $x_{i1}, x_{i2}, \ldots, x_{in}$ are nonstochastic variables.
(b) $y_1, y_2, \ldots, y_n$ are independent.

In particular, we assume that the dependent variable follows a distribution from the linear exponential family. We do not assume that the dependent variable has constant variance. Instead, we assume that the variance is a function of the mean, i.e.,

$$\text{Var}(y_i) = \phi v(\mu_i). \tag{6.5}$$

The variance functions of some distributions are given in Table 6.3.

In a GLM, we allow the parameters θ and ϕ to vary by observation. The parameter θ is linked to the systematic component $\mathbf{x}_i'\boldsymbol{\beta}$ through the mean function $b'(\theta)$ and the link function g:

$$\theta_i = (b')^{-1}(\mu_i) = (b')^{-1}(g^{-1}(\mathbf{x}_i'\boldsymbol{\beta})) = (g \circ b')^{-1}(\mathbf{x}_i'\boldsymbol{\beta}), \tag{6.6}$$

where $\boldsymbol{\beta}$ is a vector of parameters to be estimated from the data. Unlike the parameter θ, the parameter ϕ varies by observation through the following form:

$$\phi_i = \frac{\phi}{w_i}, \tag{6.7}$$

where $w_1, w_2, \ldots, w_n$ are known prior weights.

From Table 6.2, we see that the parameter ϕ is known for some distributions and unknown for other distributions. Once the parameters $\boldsymbol{\beta}$ are estimated from the data, we can use the GLM to make a prediction at a new point $\mathbf{x}_*$ as follows:

$$y_* = \mu_* = g^{-1}(\mathbf{x}_*' \hat{\boldsymbol{\beta}}), \tag{6.8}$$

where $\hat{\boldsymbol{\beta}}$ denotes the estimated parameters.

6.3   Maximum Likelihood Estimation

The method of **maximum likelihood** is commonly used to estimate the parameters of a GLM from a dataset. In the method of maximum likelihood, the parameters are estimated from the data by maximizing the following **log-likelihood function**:

$$
\begin{aligned}
L(\boldsymbol{\beta}, \phi) &= \sum_{i=1}^{n} \left(\frac{y_i \theta_i - b(\theta_i)}{\phi_i} + S(y_i, \phi_i) \right) \\
&= \sum_{i=1}^{n} \left(w_i \frac{y_i (g \circ b')^{-1}(\mathbf{x}_i' \boldsymbol{\beta}) - g^{-1}(\mathbf{x}_i' \boldsymbol{\beta})}{\phi} + S(y_i, \frac{\phi}{w_i}) \right).
\end{aligned}
\tag{6.9}
$$

If ϕ is known, we do not need to estimate ϕ. If the link function is canonical, then $g = (b')^{-1}$ and

$$\theta_i = (b')^{-1}(\mu_i) = g(\mu_i) = \mathbf{x}_i' \boldsymbol{\beta}.$$

In such cases, the log-likelihood function given above can be simplified to be

$$L(\boldsymbol{\beta}, \phi) = \sum_{i=1}^{n} \left(w_i \frac{y_i \mathbf{x}_i' \boldsymbol{\beta} - b(\mathbf{x}_i' \boldsymbol{\beta})}{\phi} + S(y_i, \frac{\phi}{w_i}) \right). \tag{6.10}$$

Taking derivatives of the log-likelihood function with respect to $\boldsymbol{\beta}$ gives the **score function**:

$$
\begin{pmatrix}
\dfrac{\partial L(\boldsymbol{\beta}, \phi)}{\partial \beta_0} \\[2mm]
\dfrac{\partial L(\boldsymbol{\beta}, \phi)}{\partial \beta_1} \\[2mm]
\vdots \\[2mm]
\dfrac{\partial L(\boldsymbol{\beta}, \phi)}{\partial \beta_k}
\end{pmatrix}
=
\begin{pmatrix}
\dfrac{1}{\phi} \sum_{i=1}^{n} w_i (y_i - b'(\mathbf{x}_i' \boldsymbol{\beta})) \\[2mm]
\dfrac{1}{\phi} \sum_{i=1}^{n} w_i x_{i1} (y_i - b'(\mathbf{x}_i' \boldsymbol{\beta})) \\[2mm]
\vdots \\[2mm]
\dfrac{1}{\phi} \sum_{i=1}^{n} w_i x_{ik} (y_i - b'(\mathbf{x}_i' \boldsymbol{\beta}))
\end{pmatrix},
\tag{6.11}
$$

which can be written compactly as follows:

$$\frac{\partial L(\boldsymbol{\beta}, \phi)}{\partial \boldsymbol{\beta}} = \frac{1}{\phi} \sum_{i=1}^{n} w_i(y_i - b'(\mathbf{x}_i'\boldsymbol{\beta}))\mathbf{x}_i = \frac{1}{\phi}\mathbf{X}' \begin{pmatrix} w_1(y_1 - b'(\mathbf{x}_1'\boldsymbol{\beta})) \\ w_2(y_2 - b'(\mathbf{x}_2'\boldsymbol{\beta})) \\ \vdots \\ w_n(y_n - b'(\mathbf{x}_n'\boldsymbol{\beta})) \end{pmatrix}. \tag{6.12}$$

Equating the score function to zero gives the **normal equations**:

$$\mathbf{X}' \begin{pmatrix} w_1(y_1 - b'(\mathbf{x}_1'\boldsymbol{\beta})) \\ w_2(y_2 - b'(\mathbf{x}_2'\boldsymbol{\beta})) \\ \vdots \\ w_n(y_n - b'(\mathbf{x}_n'\boldsymbol{\beta})) \end{pmatrix} = \mathbf{0}, \tag{6.13}$$

where $\mathbf{X}$ is the design matrix (see Equation (3.4)). We can get the **maximum likelihood estimators** of $\boldsymbol{\beta}$ by solving the above normal equations.

Under broad conditions, the score function has a large sample normal distribution with mean $\mathbf{0}$ and variance $I(\boldsymbol{\beta})$, where $I(\boldsymbol{\beta})$ is the **information matrix** defined by

$$I(\boldsymbol{\beta}) = -E\left[\frac{\partial^2 L(\boldsymbol{\beta}, \phi)}{\partial \boldsymbol{\beta}\partial \boldsymbol{\beta}'}\right]. \tag{6.14}$$

The log-likelihood function has two basic properties. The first basic property is that the expected value of the score function is equal to zero, i.e.,

$$E\left[\frac{\partial L(\boldsymbol{\beta}, \phi)}{\partial \boldsymbol{\beta}}\right] = \mathbf{0}. \tag{6.15}$$

The second basic property is that the log-likelihood function satisfies the following equation:

$$E\left[\frac{\partial^2 L(\boldsymbol{\beta}, \phi)}{\partial \boldsymbol{\beta}\partial \boldsymbol{\beta}'}\right] + E\left[\frac{\partial L(\boldsymbol{\beta}, \phi)}{\partial \boldsymbol{\beta}} \cdot \frac{\partial L(\boldsymbol{\beta}, \phi)}{\partial \boldsymbol{\beta}'}\right] = \mathbf{0}, \tag{6.16}$$

where

$$\frac{\partial^2 L(\boldsymbol{\beta}, \phi)}{\partial \boldsymbol{\beta}\partial \boldsymbol{\beta}'} = \begin{pmatrix} \dfrac{\partial^2 L(\boldsymbol{\beta}, \phi)}{\partial \beta_0 \partial \beta_0} & \dfrac{\partial^2 L(\boldsymbol{\beta}, \phi)}{\partial \beta_0 \partial \beta_1} & \cdots & \dfrac{\partial^2 L(\boldsymbol{\beta}, \phi)}{\partial \beta_0 \partial \beta_k} \\ \dfrac{\partial^2 L(\boldsymbol{\beta}, \phi)}{\partial \beta_1 \partial \beta_0} & \dfrac{\partial^2 L(\boldsymbol{\beta}, \phi)}{\partial \beta_1 \partial \beta_1} & \cdots & \dfrac{\partial^2 L(\boldsymbol{\beta}, \phi)}{\partial \beta_1 \partial \beta_k} \\ \vdots & \vdots & \ddots & \vdots \\ \dfrac{\partial^2 L(\boldsymbol{\beta}, \phi)}{\partial \beta_k \partial \beta_0} & \dfrac{\partial^2 L(\boldsymbol{\beta}, \phi)}{\partial \beta_k \partial \beta_1} & \cdots & \dfrac{\partial^2 L(\boldsymbol{\beta}, \phi)}{\partial \beta_k \partial \beta_k} \end{pmatrix},$$

and
$$\frac{\partial L(\boldsymbol{\beta},\phi)}{\partial \boldsymbol{\beta}'} = \left(\frac{\partial L(\boldsymbol{\beta},\phi)}{\partial \boldsymbol{\beta}}\right)' = \left(\frac{\partial L(\boldsymbol{\beta},\phi)}{\partial \beta_0} \quad \frac{\partial L(\boldsymbol{\beta},\phi)}{\partial \beta_1} \quad \cdots \quad \frac{\partial L(\boldsymbol{\beta},\phi)}{\partial \beta_k}\right).$$

From Equation (6.16), the information matrix can also be written as

$$I(\boldsymbol{\beta}) = E\left[\frac{\partial L(\boldsymbol{\beta},\phi)}{\partial \boldsymbol{\beta}} \cdot \frac{\partial L(\boldsymbol{\beta},\phi)}{\partial \boldsymbol{\beta}'}\right]. \tag{6.17}$$

Under broad conditions, the maximum likelihood estimator $\hat{\boldsymbol{\beta}}$ has a large sample normal distribution with mean $\boldsymbol{\beta}$ and variance $I(\boldsymbol{\beta})^{-1}$, where $I(\boldsymbol{\beta})$ is the information matrix defined in Equation (6.14). This result is helpful for calculating the standard errors of the parameter estimates.

Exercise 6.3. Let y_i and $\mathbf{x}_i = (1, x_{i1}, \ldots, x_{ik})'$ be the observed values of the dependent variable and the regressors for the ith case, respectively. Suppose that $y_1, y_2, \ldots, y_n$ are independently and normally distributed and that the weights $w_1 = w_2 = \ldots = w_n = 1$. Consider a GLM with the normal distribution for the dependent variable and the canonical link function.

(a) Write out the log-likelihood function for the GLM.

(b) Calculate the maximum likelihood estimator $\hat{\boldsymbol{\beta}}$.

(c) Calculate the information matrix $I(\boldsymbol{\beta})$.

(d) Calculate the variance-covariance matrix $\text{Var}(\hat{\boldsymbol{\beta}})$.

6.4 Residuals

Residuals are important for regression modeling for the following reasons: first, diagnosing the fit of a regression model usually involves examining the residuals; second, residuals are the building blocks for many goodness-of-fit measures. In linear regression models, the residuals are defined as the differences between the given values and the fitted values of the dependent variable, i.e., $y_i - \hat{\mu}_i$. These residuals are referred to as **raw residuals** in the GLM context.

For linear regression models where the dependent variable is normally distributed, analyzing the raw residuals helps to

- discover nonlinear patterns in the independent variables;

- identify influential points; and

- reveal other patterns in the data such as heteroscedasticity.

However, analyzing the raw residuals in a GLM context can be meaningless. In this section, we introduce some general forms of generalized residuals that are more useful than the raw residual in a GLM context.

The first form of generalized residual is the **Pearson residual** defined by

$$R_p(y_i; \mathbf{x}_i, \boldsymbol{\beta}, \phi) = \frac{y_i - \hat{\mu}_i}{\sqrt{\text{Var}(y_i)}}, \tag{6.18}$$

which is the raw residual scaled by the standard deviation of y_i. As pointed out in (McCullagh and Nelder, 1989, p38), one disadvantage of the Pearson residual is that its distribution is often skewed when the dependent variable follows non-normal distributions.

The second form of generalized residual is the **Anscombe residual** defined by

$$R_a(y_i; \mathbf{x}_i, \boldsymbol{\beta}, \phi) = \frac{h(y_i) - E[h(y_i)]}{\sqrt{\text{Var}(h(y_i))}}, \tag{6.19}$$

where $h(\cdot)$ is a known function that is selected so that $h(y_i)$ is approximately normally distributed. The function $h(\cdot)$ is complicated and is different when the dependent variable follows different distributions. See (Frees, 2009) for some examples of the function $h(\cdot)$.

The third form of generalized residual is the **deviance residual** defined by

$$R_d(y_i; \mathbf{x}_i, \boldsymbol{\beta}, \phi) = \text{sgn}(y_i - \hat{\mu}_i)\sqrt{2\left(\ln f(y_i; \theta_{i, Sat}, \phi) - \ln f(y_i; \hat{\theta}_i, \phi)\right)}, \tag{6.20}$$

where $\theta_{i, Sat}$ is the parameter from the saturated model and $\hat{\theta}_i$ is the parameter estimated by the method of maximum likelihood.

6.5 Model Evaluation

For a GLM, we usually have the following relationship:

$$\sum_{i=1}^{n}(y_i - \bar{y})^2 \neq \sum_{i=1}^{n}(y_i - \hat{y}_i)^2 + \sum_{i=1}^{n}(\hat{y}_i - \bar{y})^2.$$

As a result, we do not get the same statistic as in the linear regression models when defining R^2. However, there are some alternative R^2 measures for GLMs

(Frees, 2009, Chapter 11). In this section, we introduce some goodness-of-fit statistics and information criteria to evaluate GLMs. It is a good practice to use several goodness-of-fit statistics for model evaluation in order to increase validity of models.

One widely used goodness-of-fit statistic for evaluating GLMs is the **Pearson chi-square statistic**. The Pearson chi-square statistic is defined as

$$\chi^2 = \sum_{i=1}^{n} \frac{(y_i - \hat{\mu}_i)^2}{\text{Var}(y_i)} = \sum_{i=1}^{n} \frac{(y_i - \hat{\mu}_i)^2}{\phi v(\hat{\mu}_i)}, \tag{6.21}$$

where $\hat{\mu}_i$ is an estimator of μ_i.

Another goodness-of-fit statistic for evaluating GLMs is the **deviance statistic**, which is defined by

$$D = 2\phi(L_{max} - L(\hat{\boldsymbol{\beta}}, \phi)), \tag{6.22}$$

where $\hat{\boldsymbol{\beta}}$ is the vector of parameters estimated by the method of maximum likelihood and L_{max} is the largest possible value of the log-likelihood function. The largest possible value of the log-likelihood function is calculated by

$$L_{max} = \sum_{i=1}^{n} f(y_i; \theta_{i,Sat}, \phi),$$

where $\theta_{i,Sat}$ is the solution to the following equation

$$\frac{\partial}{\partial \theta_i} f(y_i; \theta_i, \phi) = \frac{y_i - b'(\theta_i)}{\phi} = 0.$$

The value L_{max} is the value of the log-likelihood function for the **saturated model**, which provides the best possible fit by allowing as many parameters as observations.

Information criteria can also be used to compare different GLMs. Two commonly used information criteria are the **AIC** (Akaike's Information Criterion) and the **BIC** (Bayesian Information Criterion). The AIC is defined as

$$AIC = -2L(\hat{\boldsymbol{\beta}}, \phi) + 2K, \tag{6.23}$$

where K is the number of parameters. For example, if there are $k+1$ regressors and ϕ is known, then $K = k+1$. If there are $k+1$ regressors and ϕ is unknown, then $K = k+2$. Given two GLMs, we prefer the GLM with lower AIC.

The BIC is defined as

$$BIC = -2L(\hat{\boldsymbol{\beta}}, \phi) + K \ln n, \tag{6.24}$$

where K is the number of parameters and n is the number of observations. If n is large, the BIC penalizes the complexity of the model more than does the AIC. Given two GLMs, we prefer the GLM with lower BIC.

Exercise 6.4. For $i = 1, 2, \ldots, n$, let y_i and $\hat{\mu}_i$ denote the observed values of the dependent variable and the estimator of μ_i under a GLM with the canonical link function for a distribution, respectively. Calculate the deviance statistics for the following distributions:

(a) Normal.

(b) Bernoulli.

(c) Poisson.

6.6 Summary

In this chapter, we introduced generalized linear models (GLM), which provide a unifying framework to handle dependent variables that are discrete, continuous, or a mixture. A GLM consists of several components: a distribution for the dependent variable (the random component), a linear combination of independent variables (the systematic component), and a link function. We also introduced the method of maximum likelihood for estimating parameters for GLMs and some goodness-of-fit measures. For more information about GLMs, readers are referred to McCullagh and Nelder (1989), Dobson and Barnett (2008a), and Frees (2009).

6.7 End-of-Chapter Exercises

Exercise 6.5. The claims department of an insurance company is evaluating the effect of implementing different strategies to increase efficiency in processing claims. The data used consists of the reduction in days of completion (Y) as the response variable with the type of strategy implemented (X1) and the age of the policyholders (X2). The strategies are labeled as A, B and C. The R output for the regression model, call this Model I, using only X1 as independent variable is given below:

```
1 Coefficients:
2           Estimate Std. Error t value Pr(>|t|)
3 (Intercept)    5.000       1.000   5.000 0.000739 ***
4 X1B            8.000       1.414   5.657 0.000311 ***
5 X1C            4.000       1.414   2.828 0.019773 *
6 ---
7 Signif. codes:  0 '***' 0.001 '**' 0.01 '*' 0.05 '.' 0.1
       ' ' 1
8
9 Residual standard error: 2 on 9 degrees of freedom
10 Multiple R-squared:  0.7805,  Adjusted R-squared:  0.7317
11 F-statistic:     16 on 2 and 9 DF,  p-value: 0.001088
```

The R output for the regression model, call this Model II, using both X1 and X2 as independent variables is given below:

```
1 Coefficients:
2           Estimate Std. Error t value Pr(>|t|)
3 (Intercept) 2.21089     1.29634   1.705 0.126497
4 X1B         7.20311     1.12969   6.376 0.000215 ***
5 X1C         3.96680     1.08979   3.640 0.006589 **
6 X2          0.06641     0.02482   2.675 0.028123 *
7 ---
8 Signif. codes:  0 '***' 0.001 '**' 0.01 '*' 0.05 '.' 0.1
       ' ' 1
9
10 Residual standard error: 1.541 on 8 degrees of freedom
11 Multiple R-squared:  0.8841,  Adjusted R-squared:  0.8407
12 F-statistic: 20.35 on 3 and 8 DF,  p-value: 0.0004223
```

(a) For Model I, express the linear regression model used with the error component.

(b) For Model I, interpret the estimated coefficients of the variables X1B and X1C.

(c) Re-write the linear regression model in Part (a) as a one-way analysis of variance (ANOVA) model in the form:

$$Y_{ij} = \alpha + \tau_j + \epsilon_{ij},$$

for $i = 1, 2, \ldots, 12$ and for strategy $j =$ A, B, C.

(d) For Model II, interpret the estimated coefficient of X2.

(e) Which of the two models are considered better in describing the data? Give
     an explanation.

Exercise 6.6. In understanding what affects the monthly rent of apartments in a
certain district, the following regression model

$$Y_i = \alpha + \beta_1 X1_i + \beta_2 X2_i + \epsilon_i,$$

for $i = 1, 2, \ldots, n$ is fitted to the data with the response variable Y (monthly rent
per square foot) and predictor variables X1 (distance from the city center in
miles) and X2 (indicator 1 if two bedroom, 0 if one bedroom). The fitted model is
summarized below:

```
1  Coefficients:
2              Estimate  Std. Error  t value  Pr(>|t|)
3  (Intercept)  0.96856    0.03033   31.930   < 2e-16  ***
4  X1          -0.10992    0.01946   -5.649   2.72e-06 ***
5  X2          -0.10422    0.03609   -2.888   0.0068   **
6  ---
7  Signif. codes:  0 '***' 0.001 '**' 0.01 '*' 0.05 '.' 0.1
8      ' ' 1
9  Residual standard error: 0.1065 on 33 degrees of freedom
10 Multiple R-squared:  0.5889,  Adjusted R-squared:  0.564
11 F-statistic: 23.63 on 2 and 33 DF,  p-value: 4.272e-07
```

An interaction term (X1*X2) equal to the product of X1 and X2 was introduced to
the model

$$Y_i = \alpha + \beta_1 X1_i + \beta_2 X2_i + \beta_3 X1_i * X2_i + \epsilon_i,$$

for $i = 1, 2, \ldots, n$ and the fitted model is summarized below:

```
1  Coefficients:
2              Estimate  Std. Error  t value  Pr(>|t|)
3  (Intercept)  0.972781   0.036406  26.720   < 2e-16  ***
4  X1          -0.115085   0.030905  -3.724   0.000756 ***
5  X2          -0.112500   0.052833  -2.129   0.041016 *
6  X1:X2        0.008731   0.040174   0.217   0.829326
7  ---
8  Signif. codes:  0 '***' 0.001 '**' 0.01 '*' 0.05 '.' 0.1
       ' ' 1
9
10 Residual standard error: 0.1081 on 32 degrees of freedom
11 Multiple R-squared:  0.5895,  Adjusted R-squared:  0.551
12 F-statistic: 15.32 on 3 and 32 DF,  p-value: 2.354e-06
```

(a) For the model without interaction, interpret the estimated coefficients of X1 and X2.

(b) For the model with interaction, how do you interpret the estimated coefficient of the interaction term X1*X2? Justify your answer.

Exercise 6.7. You are given the following estimated regression model:

$$\hat{y} = -0.2 + 2.5x_1 + -1.5x_2 + 0.5x_1 * x_2.$$

You are to evaluate the quality of the goodness of fit of this model using the test data given below:

y	-8	-45	3	-5	-15
x_1	1	0	1	1	0
x_2	0	6	3	5	3

(a) Calculate the average percentage error (APE).

(b) Calculate the average absolute percentage error (AAPE).

(c) What can you conclude when these two values are compared?

Exercise 6.8. Consider a special case of the Inverse Gaussian where $\lambda = \mu^2$. The density function has the expression:

$$f(y; \mu) = \frac{\mu}{\sqrt{2\pi} y^{3/2}} \exp\left[-\frac{1}{2}\frac{(y-\mu)^2}{y}\right]$$

(a) Find expressions for θ, ϕ, $b(\theta)$ and $S(y, \phi)$.

(b) Demonstrate that the variance function has the expression $V(\mu) = \frac{1}{2}\mu^3$.

(c) Find the canonical link function $g(\mu)$.

(d) Show that the deviance statistic can be written as

$$D = 2\sum_{i=1}^{n}\frac{(y_i - \hat{\mu}_i)^2}{\hat{\mu}_i^2 y_i}.$$

Exercise 6.9. A Poisson regression model is to be fitted to the data of the form (y_i, x_i) where y_i refers to the frequency of claims, x_i is a regressor variable referring to gender with $x_i = 1$ for male and $x_i = 0$ for female. The index i refers to the observation. The link function can be expressed as

$$\log(\mu_i) = \beta_0 + \beta_1 x_i.$$

Now, suppose the observations are ordered in the sense that the first n_1 observations are males and the subsequent n_2 observations are females. In effect, the link function can be written as

$$\log(\mu_i) = \begin{cases} \beta_0 + \beta_1, & \text{for } i = 1, 2, \ldots, n_1 \\ \beta_0, & \text{for } i = n_1 + 1, n_1 + 2, \ldots, n_1 + n_2 \end{cases}$$

(a) Show that the log-likelihood can be expressed as

$$(\beta_0 + \beta_1) \sum_{i=1}^{n_1} y_i - n_1 \exp(\beta_0 + \beta_1) + \beta_0 \sum_{i=n_1+1}^{n_1+n_2} y_i - n_2 \exp(\beta_0) + \text{constant}$$

where the 'constant' is independent of β_0 and β_1.

(b) Derive the maximum likelihood estimates of β_0 and β_1. Interpret these estimates.

(c) Define

$$\bar{y}_M = \frac{1}{n_1} \sum_{i=1}^{n_1} y_i \quad \text{and} \quad \bar{y}_F = \frac{1}{n_2} \sum_{i=n_1+1}^{n_1+n_2} y_i$$

to be the average number of claims for males and females, respectively. Show that the deviance statistic for this model can be written as

$$D = 2 \sum_{i=1}^{n_1} \left[y_i \log(y_i / \bar{y}_M) - (y_i - \bar{y}_M) \right] + 2 \sum_{i=n_1+1}^{n_1+n_2} \left[y_i \log(y_i / \bar{y}_F) - (y_i - \bar{y}_F) \right].$$

(d) Derive the maximum likelihood estimate of β_0 and the deviance statistic in the case where $\beta_1 = 0$.

Chapter 7

Case Study: Predicting Demand for Term Life Insurance

In this case study, we introduce logistic and probit regression models for binary dependent variables. After working through this case study, readers should be able to

- Fit logistic and probit regression models

- Understand and use the method of maximum likelihood

- Understand and calculate the Rand Accuracy measure

7.1 Problem Description

Term life insurance is a type of life insurance that covers only a part of your lifetime (Hungelmann, 2009). It provides coverage at a fixed rate of payments for a limited period of time and only pays a death benefit if the policyholder dies within the designated term.

Life insurance companies are interested in knowing who buys term life insurance, or the demand side of the market for term life insurance. In this case study, we would like to analyze the characteristics of customers and build regression models to predict whether a customer buys term life insurance.

The dependent variable is binary: the value of the dependent variable is 1 if the customer bought term life insurance; the value is 0 if the customer did not buy term life insurance. As a result, the linear regression models we introduced in previous case studies do not work well here. We will use nonlinear regression techniques to model such binary dependent variables.

7.2 Data Description

To build models for predicting who buys term life insurance, we obtain a random sample of 500 households with positive incomes from the 2004 Survey of Consumer Finances (SCF), which is a nationally representative sample that contains extensive information on assets, liabilities, and demographic characteristics of sampled persons. Among the 500 households, 275 families purchased term life insurance.

The dataset is saved in a CSV file named `termlifepos.csv` and contains seven variables, which are described in Table 7.1. The dependent variable is `facepos`, which is a binary variable with value 1 if the customer bought term life insurance and value 0 if the customer did not buy term life insurance. The other six variables are independent variables.

Variable	Description
facepos	Indicator of term life insurance purchase
gender	Gender of the respondent
age	Age of the customer
marstat	Marital status of the respondent
edu	Number of years of education of the respondent
numhh	Number of household members
lnincome	Log income of the respondent

Table 7.1: *A list of variables of the term life insurance data.*

The variable `gender` is a binary variable with values 0 and 1 indicating female and male, respectively. The variable `marstat` is a categorical variable with values 0, 1, and 2 indicating other, married, and living together, respectively. The rest of the variables are all continuous variables. Since the income of the respondent has a wide range, the log income is used here in order to reduce the variability of the variable.

7.3 Loading Data into R

Suppose that the current working directory contains the file `termlifepos.csv`. Then we can load the data into R and display the summary as follows:

```
1 > term <- read.csv("termlifepos.csv")
2 > summary(term)
3    facepos            gender              age
```

```
 4    Min.    :0.00      Min.     :0.000     Min.     :20.00
 5    1st Qu.:0.00      1st Qu.:1.000     1st Qu.:37.00
 6    Median :1.00      Median :1.000     Median :47.00
 7    Mean    :0.55      Mean     :0.826     Mean     :47.16
 8    3rd Qu.:1.00      3rd Qu.:1.000     3rd Qu.:58.00
 9    Max.    :1.00      Max.     :1.000     Max.     :85.00
10        marstat            edu               numhh
11    Min.    :0.00      Min.     : 2.00     Min.     :1.00
12    1st Qu.:0.00      1st Qu.:12.00     1st Qu.:2.00
13    Median :1.00      Median :14.00     Median :2.00
14    Mean    :0.79      Mean     :14.06     Mean     :2.87
15    3rd Qu.:1.00      3rd Qu.:16.00     3rd Qu.:4.00
16    Max.    :2.00      Max.     :17.00     Max.     :9.00
17        lnincome
18    Min.    :2.415
19    1st Qu.:4.447
20    Median :4.732
21    Mean    :4.744
22    3rd Qu.:5.025
23    Max.    :7.875
```

From the summary we see that the categorical variables gender and marstat are treated as numerical variables. We can convert them to factors as follows:

```
 1  > term$gender <- factor(term$gender)
 2  > term$marstat <- factor(term$marstat)
 3  > summary(term)
 4      facepos        gender         age            marstat
 5    Min.    :0.00    0: 87   Min.     :20.00     0:136
 6    1st Qu.:0.00    1:413   1st Qu.:37.00     1:333
 7    Median :1.00            Median :47.00     2: 31
 8    Mean    :0.55            Mean     :47.16
 9    3rd Qu.:1.00            3rd Qu.:58.00
10    Max.    :1.00            Max.     :85.00
11        edu               numhh            lnincome
12    Min.    : 2.00    Min.     :1.00     Min.     :2.415
13    1st Qu.:12.00    1st Qu.:2.00     1st Qu.:4.447
14    Median :14.00    Median :2.00     Median :4.732
15    Mean     :14.06    Mean     :2.87     Mean     :4.744
16    3rd Qu.:16.00    3rd Qu.:4.00     3rd Qu.:5.025
17    Max.     :17.00    Max.     :9.00     Max.     :7.875
```

Once we have converted the variables gender and marstat, we see the frequencies of the categories in the summary of the data. For example, we can see that

333 of the 500 respondents are married and 413 of them are male. We can also deduce from the summary statistics that more than half have college education and more than half are at least 47 years old.

Exercise 7.1. Consider the term life insurance data `term` and use the function `table` to find out how many married respondents are male and how many male respondents purchased term life insurance.

7.4   Binary Dependent Variables

In Chapter 5, we introduced binary independent variables, which are used to represent categorical explanatory variables. A **binary dependent variable** can be used to build a model to predict whether an event has occurred or a subject has a particular characteristic of interest.

A binary dependent variable is a binary random variable that has a **Bernoulli distribution**. Let $\pi_i = P(y_i = 1)$, i.e., π_i is the probability that $y_i = 1$. Then $P(y_i = 0) = 1 - \pi_i$,

$$E[y_i] = 0 \times P(y_i = 0) + 1 \times P(y_i = 1) = \pi_i,$$

and

$$\mathrm{Var}(y_i) = \pi_i(1 - \pi_i).$$

We can treat the binary variable `facepos` as a continuous variable and fit a linear model as follows:

$$y_i = \beta_0 + \beta_1 x_{i1} + \cdots + \beta_k x_{ik} + \epsilon_i. \tag{7.1}$$

The linear model given in Equation (7.1) is known as the **linear probability model**. We fit a linear probability model for the data as follows:

```
> fit1 <- lm(facepos ~ ., data=term)
> summary(fit1)

Call:
lm(formula = facepos ~ ., data = term)

Residuals:
```

```
 8      Min       1Q    Median        3Q       Max
 9  -0.7696  -0.4882    0.2931    0.4086    0.7469
10
11  Coefficients:
12                 Estimate  Std. Error  t value  Pr(>|t|)
13  (Intercept)  -0.1347102   0.2047611   -0.658    0.5109
14  gender1      -0.0083410   0.0812460   -0.103    0.9183
15  age           0.0001227   0.0017319    0.071    0.9436
16  marstat1      0.1574873   0.0776315    2.029    0.0430 *
17  marstat2     -0.0607523   0.1105810   -0.549    0.5830
18  edu           0.0198001   0.0081623    2.426    0.0156 *
19  numhh         0.0081397   0.0171758    0.474    0.6358
20  lnincome      0.0596283   0.0414731    1.438    0.1511
21  ---
22  Signif. codes:
23  0 '***' 0.001 '**' 0.01 '*' 0.05 '.' 0.1 ' ' 1
24
25  Residual standard error: 0.4838 on 492 degrees of freedom
26  Multiple R-squared:  0.0694,   Adjusted R-squared:
        0.05616
27  F-statistic: 5.242 on 7 and 492 DF,  p-value: 8.754e-06
```

We then plot the fitted values and the residuals of the linear probability model as follows:

```
1  > par(mar=c(4,4,1,1), mfrow=c(1,2))
2  > plot(fit1$fitted.values, ylab="Predicted Values")
3  > plot(fit1$residuals, ylab="Residuals")
```

The resulting plots are shown in Figure 7.2. From the figure, we see that the predicted probabilities are between 0 and 1. Since the given probabilities are either 0 or 1, the residuals of the linear probability model are scattered in two clusters.

Although linear probability models allow us to interpret the parameters conveniently, they suffer from the following drawbacks:

- Fitted values can be negative or larger than 1.
- The variance of the response is not constant.
- Residual analysis is not meaningful.

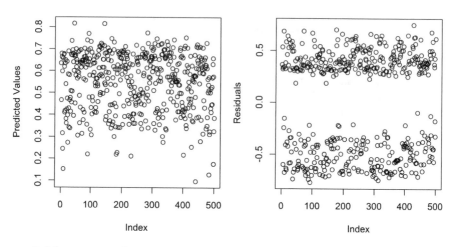

Table 7.2: *Fitted values and residuals of the linear probability model.*

7.5 Logistic and Probit Regression Models

Using nonlinear functions of explanatory variables allows us to circumvent the drawbacks of linear probability models. We can express the conditional expectation of the response given the explanatory variables as a function of explanatory variables as follows:

$$\pi_i = P(y_i = 1|\mathbf{x}_i) = \pi(\mathbf{x}_i'\boldsymbol{\beta}). \tag{7.2}$$

The **logistic function** and the cumulative distribution function of the normal distribution are two special cases of the function $\pi(\cdot)$. The logistic function is defined as

$$\pi(z) = \frac{e^z}{1 + e^z}. \tag{7.3}$$

If the logistic function is used, the regression model is referred to as the **logistic regression model**. The cumulative distribution function of the normal distribution is defined as

$$\pi(z) = \Phi(z), \tag{7.4}$$

where $\Phi(\cdot)$ is the standard normal distribution function given by

$$\Phi(z) = \int_{-\infty}^{z} \frac{1}{\sqrt{2\pi}} e^{-\frac{1}{x^2}} \mathrm{d}x.$$

If the cumulative distribution function of the normal distribution is used, the resulting regression model is called the **probit regression** model.

The inverse function, π^{-1}, of the function π is referred to as the **link function**. The link function of the logistic regression has the following explicit form:

$$\text{logit}(p) = \ln \frac{p}{1-p}.$$

The link function of the probit regression does not admit a closed-form expression.

Exercise 7.2. Compare the logistic function and the cumulative distribution function of the normal distribution by plotting the two functions in one plot with different colors. (Hint: Use the R function pnorm to calculate the cumulative distribution function of the normal distribution)

The logistic and probit regression models are nonlinear regression models and cannot be interpreted straightforwardly. However, they can be interpreted by the threshold method. Suppose that there exists an underlying linear model:

$$y_i^* = \mathbf{x}_i' \boldsymbol{\beta} + \epsilon_i^*,$$

where the response y_i^* is not observable. However, we observe when the response crosses a threshold d:

$$y_i = \begin{cases} 0, & \text{if } y_i^* \le d, \\ 1, & \text{if } y_i^* > d. \end{cases}$$

Suppose that the disturbance ϵ_i^* follows a logistic distribution with mean $-d$ and standard deviation 1, that is,

$$P(\epsilon_i^* \le a) = \frac{1}{1 + e^{-a-d}}.$$

Then we have

$$
\begin{aligned}
\pi_i &= P(y_i = 1 | \mathbf{x}_i) = P(y_i^* > d) = P(\epsilon_i^* > d - \mathbf{x}_i' \boldsymbol{\beta}) \\
&= P(\epsilon_i^* < \mathbf{x}_i' \boldsymbol{\beta} - d) \\
&= \frac{1}{1 + \exp(-\mathbf{x}_i' \boldsymbol{\beta})} \\
&= \pi(\mathbf{x}_i' \boldsymbol{\beta}).
\end{aligned}
\tag{7.5}
$$

The probit regression can be interpreted similarly by assuming the disturbance ϵ_i^* follows a normal distribution.

7.6   The Method of Maximum Likelihood

Since the logistic and probit regression models are nonlinear, the customary method of estimation for such models is the **method of maximum likelihood**. In this section, we introduce the method of maximum likelihood and how to fit the logistic and probit regression models in R using this method.

The **likelihood** refers to the observed value of the probability function. For the ith observation, the likelihood is given by

$$\begin{cases} 1 - \pi_i, & \text{if } y_i = 0; \\ \pi_i, & \text{if } y_i = 1, \end{cases} \tag{7.6}$$

which can be expressed compactly as

$$(1 - \pi_i)^{(1 - y_i)} \pi_i^{y_i}. \tag{7.7}$$

Suppose that the observations are independent. Then the likelihood of the dataset is the product of the likelihoods of all observations, i.e.,

$$\prod_{i=1}^{n} (1 - \pi_i)^{(1 - y_i)} \pi_i^{y_i}.$$

Taking logarithms and using Equation (7.5), the log-likelihood of the dataset is the sum of the log-likelihoods of the observations:

$$L(\boldsymbol{\beta}) = \sum_{i=1}^{n} \left[y_i \ln \pi(\mathbf{x}_i' \boldsymbol{\beta}) + (1 - y_i) \ln(1 - \pi(\mathbf{x}_i' \boldsymbol{\beta})) \right]. \tag{7.8}$$

The method of maximum likelihood tries to find the values of $\boldsymbol{\beta}$ that maximize the log-likelihood of the dataset. An optimization procedure is usually required to find the values of $\boldsymbol{\beta}$ that maximize the log-likelihood. Such procedures are beyond the scope of this book.

In R, we fit a logistic regression model to the dataset using the function glm as follows:

```
1 > fit1 <- glm(facepos ~ ., family=binomial(link = 'logit')
    , data=term)
2 > summary(fit1)
3
4 Call:
5 glm(formula = facepos ~ ., family = binomial(link = "
      logit"),
6     data = term)
7
```

```
Deviance Residuals:
    Min       1Q   Median       3Q      Max
 -1.690   -1.160    0.834    1.022    1.654

Coefficients:
                Estimate Std. Error z value Pr(>|z|)
(Intercept) -2.7427365  0.9029121  -3.038  0.00238 **
gender1     -0.0331925  0.3458716  -0.096  0.92355
age          0.0004917  0.0074693   0.066  0.94751
marstat1     0.6431316  0.3304364   1.946  0.05162 .
marstat2    -0.2824027  0.4868637  -0.580  0.56188
edu          0.0855904  0.0357964   2.391  0.01680 *
numhh        0.0366896  0.0743323   0.494  0.62160
lnincome     0.2602722  0.1817494   1.432  0.15213
---
Signif. codes:
0 '***' 0.001 '**' 0.01 '*' 0.05 '.' 0.1 ' ' 1

(Dispersion parameter for binomial family taken to be 1)

    Null deviance: 688.14  on 499  degrees of freedom
Residual deviance: 652.68  on 492  degrees of freedom
AIC: 668.68

Number of Fisher Scoring iterations: 4
```

The name GLM refers to generalized linear models and represents a large class of distribution models that can accommodate both discrete and continuous dependent variables. Although a linear regression model is a special case of a GLM, the syntax of the glm function is a little bit different from that of the lm function. We need to specify a link function for the glm function. In the above example, we specified the logit function as the link function to fit a logistic regression model.

The model summary shows that only the variables marstat1 and edu are significant for predicting the purchase of term life insurance as the two variables have relatively small p-values.

In the model summary, we also see the **AIC** value. Here AIC refers to Akaike's information criterion and is defined as

$$AIC = 2(k+1) - 2L(\boldsymbol{\beta}), \qquad (7.9)$$

where $k+1$ represents the number of parameters. The AIC can be used to select the best from several models. If we have several models for a dataset, we prefer the model that has the lowest AIC. As indicated in Equation (7.9), the AIC includes a penalty for introducing too many independent variables.

Using the definition given in Equation (7.9), we can calculate the AIC for the logistic regression model as follows:

```
1 > logistic <- function(x) {
2 +    return(1 / (1 + exp(-x)) )
3 + }
4 > X <- model.matrix(facepos ~ ., data=term)
5 > xbeta <- X %*% as.matrix(fit1$coefficients, ncol=1)
6 > y <- term$facepos
7 > Lbeta <- sum( y * log( logistic(xbeta) ) + (1-y) * log(
     1 - logistic(xbeta) ) )
8 > k <- ncol(X) - 1
9 > 2 * (k+1) - 2 * Lbeta
10 [1]  668.68
```

The AIC calculated above matches the AIC shown in the model summary.

Exercise 7.3. Write R code to do the following:

(a) Fit a probit regression model to the term life insurance dataset with `marstat` and `edu` as explanatory variables. (Hint: use `link = 'probit'` in the `glm` function.)

(b) Calculate the AIC of the fitted model.

(c) Between the full logistic regression model and this probit model, which one do you prefer?

7.7 Model Evaluation

Since the logistic and probit regression models are nonlinear regression models, it does not make sense to evaluate these models with R^2. As mentioned in the previous section, for these types of models, we can use the AIC to compare different models on the same dataset. In this section, we introduce an out-of-sample validation measure.

We use the **Rand Accuracy** (Powers, 2011) to evaluate the out-of-sample performance of the logistic and probit regression models. To calculate the Rand

Accuracy measure, we first convert the predicted values from the logistic or probit regression model into zeros and ones. For example, if the predicted value of the model is less than 0.5, we convert the predicted value to 0. If the predicted value is greater than or equal to 0.5, we convert it to 1. Then we can create a 2×2 confusion matrix from the four outcomes as shown in Table 7.3.

		Predicted Response	
		Positive	Negative
Observed	Positive	True Positive	False Negative (Type II error)
Response	Negative	False Positive (Type I error)	True Negative

Table 7.3: *The confusion matrix of outcomes from a binary classification model.*

The Rand Accuracy is defined as

$$ACC = \frac{TP + TN}{n}, \tag{7.10}$$

where TP denotes the number of true positive outcomes, TN denotes the number of true negative outcomes, and n is the total number of observations.

The Rand Accuracy measure ranges from 0 to 1. A higher value of the Rand Accuracy measure indicates better agreement between the predicted responses and the observed responses. In other word, we prefer a model that has a higher Rand Accuracy measure.

Exercise 7.4. Write an R function named calACC(p1, p2) to calculate the Rand Accuracy measure based on Equation (7.10), where the two arguments p1 and p2 denote the vector of observed responses and the vector of predicted responses, respectively. You can assume that p1 and p2 contain only zeros and ones.

To measure the out-of-sample performance of the logistic regression model, we split the dataset into two subsets, use one subset to fit a logistic regression model, and use the other subset for testing purpose. We can do these steps as follows:

```
> set.seed(1)
> ind <- sample(1:nrow(term), 400)
```

```
3 > termTrain <- term[ind,]
4 > termTest <- term[-ind,]
5 > fit3 <- glm(facepos ~ marstat + edu,family=binomial(
    link = 'logit'), data=termTrain)
6 > yhat <- predict(fit3, termTest)
7 > pyhat <- 1 / ( 1 + exp(-yhat) )
8 > pyhat01 <- round(pyhat)
9 > calACC(pyhat01, termTest$facepos)
10 [1] 0.63
```

In the above code, we converted the predicted responses to probabilities, which were again converted to zeros and ones. Then we calculated the Rand Accuracy measure using the R function from Exercise 7.4. The Rand Accuracy measure of this model is about 0.63, which indicates that about 63% of the testing data are predicted correctly by the model.

Exercise 7.5. Let $Y_1, Y_2, \ldots, Y_n$ be n random variables that represent the claim counts of n automobile policies. Show that for $j = 0, 1, \ldots$, the expected number of policies with j claims is given by

$$N_j = \sum_{i=1}^{n} P(Y_i = j).$$

Exercise 7.6. Let `termTrain` and `termTest` be two subsets created by the following R code:

```
1 set.seed(1)
2 ind <- sample(1:nrow(term), 300)
3 termTrain <- term[ind,]
4 termTest <- term[-ind,]
```

Write R code to fit a full probit regression model (i.e., a probit regression model that uses all the explanatory variables) to the dataset `termTrain` and calculate the Rand Accuracy measure of this model based on the dataset `termTest`.

7.8 Summary

In this chapter, we introduced linear probability models, logistic regression models, and probit regression models for binary dependent variables. Linear probability models suffer from the drawbacks that the fitted values can be negative or larger than 1. Logistic and probit regression models circumvent these drawbacks by using a nonlinear function to transform the fitted values to probabilities. Both models focus on binary dependent variables. We also introduced how to fit logistic and probit regression models in R. To assess the performance of various models, we introduced the AIC as a measure to compare several models and the Rand Accuracy to measure the out-of-sample performance of nonlinear regression models. For more information about regression models for binary data, readers are referred to (Faraway, 2005) and (Frees, 2009).

7.9 End-of-Chapter Exercises

Exercise 7.7. Consider an underlying linear model $y_i^* = \mathbf{x}_i'\boldsymbol{\beta} + \epsilon_i^*$, where the response y_i^* is unobservable, but instead we observe the response y_i when y_i^* crosses a threshold d as follows:

$$
y_i = \begin{cases} 0, & \text{if } y_i^* \le d; \\ 1, & \text{if } y_i^* > d; \end{cases}
$$

Assume the disturbance ϵ_i^* follows a normal distribution with mean $-d$ and variance 1. Show that

$$
\pi_i = P(y_i = 1 | \mathbf{x}_i) = \Phi(\mathbf{x}_i'\boldsymbol{\beta}),
$$

where $\Phi(\cdot)$ is the cumulative distribution function of a standard normal random variable.

Exercise 7.8. Consider the logistic regression model expressed as:

$$
\ln\left(\frac{\pi}{1-\pi}\right) = \beta_0 + \beta_1 x_1 + \beta_2 x_2,
$$

where x_1 is a binary variable and x_2 is a continuous variable. Suppose π is the probability that a disease develops. The ratio $\frac{\pi}{1-\pi}$ refers to the odds that a disease develops.

(a) Show that the odds ratio of going from $x_1 = 0$ to $x_1 = 1$ is

$$
e^{\beta_1} = \frac{\text{odds when } x_1 = 1}{\text{odds when } x_1 = 0}.
$$

Interpret this odds ratio.

(b) Show that the odds ratio of going from $x_2 = c$ to $x_2 = c+1$, where c is a fixed constant, is

$$
e^{\beta_2} = \frac{\text{odds when } x_2 = c+1}{\text{odds when } x_2 = c}.
$$

Interpret this odds ratio.

(c) Consider the estimated logistic regression model

$$\ln\left(\frac{\hat{\pi}}{1-\hat{\pi}}\right) = 3.54 + 2.75\,\text{gender} - 1.15\,\text{dosage},$$

where the variable gender is male when equal to 1 and female when equal to 0, and the variable dosage is measured in milliliters. Give an interpretation of the coefficients of gender and dosage.

Exercise 7.9. Consider the dataset dfA created by the following piece of R code:

```
1  set.seed(1)
2  vE <- rlogis(1000, location=3)
3  vX <- runif(1000, min=-2, max=2)
4  ystar <- 2 + 3 * vX + vE
5  y <- as.numeric(ystar > 3)
6  dfA <- data.frame(Y=y, X=vX)
```

In the dataset, X and Y denote the independent and the dependent variables, respectively.

(a) Describe how the dataset was generated.

(b) Fit a probit regression model and a logistic regression model to the dataset. Which model provides a better fit in terms of AIC?

Exercise 7.10. Consider the dataset dfB created by the following piece of R code:

```
1  set.seed(1)
2  vE <- rnorm(2000, mean=3)
3  vX <- runif(2000, min=-1, max=1)
4  ystar <- 2 + 3 * vX + vE
5  y <- as.numeric(ystar > 3)
6  dfB <- data.frame(Y=y, X=vX)
```

In the dataset, X and Y denote the independent and the dependent variables, respectively.

(a) Describe how the dataset was generated.

(b) Fit a probit regression model and a logistic regression model to the dataset. Which model provides a better fit in terms of AIC?

Chapter 8

Case Study: Modeling the Number of Auto Claims

In this case study, we introduce Poisson regression and negative binomial regression models for count-dependent variables. After working through this case study, readers should be able to

- Fit Poisson regression models and negative binomial regression models to count dependent variables

- Understand and use the method of maximum likelihood

- Understand and calculate the Pearson goodness-of-fit measure

8.1   Problem Description

Ratemaking refers to the determination of insurance prices in the property & casualty (P&C) insurance industry (Werner and Modlin, 2010). A simple model to set the price of a product is

$$Price = Cost + Profit.$$

This simple model reflects the cost associated with the product and an acceptable margin for profit. For many non-insurance products, the production cost is known before the product is sold. Unlike these non-insurance products, insurance is a promise to do something in the future if certain events happen during a specified time period. As a result, applying the above model to price an insurance product is not straightforward because the production cost of the insurance product is unknown before the product is sold.

To address the aforementioned problem, we can build models based on historical data to estimate the cost. To estimate the cost of car insurance, for example, we can build models to estimate the number of automobile claims (frequency) and the claim amounts (severity) based on historical data. In this case study, we introduce models to estimate the number of automobile claims.

8.2   Data Description

To illustrate how to model the frequency of automobile claims, we obtain a subset of the Singapore automobile insurance data that was studied by Frees and Valdez (2008). This dataset is also available in the R package insuranceData (See Exercise A.48). In the R package, the name of the dataset is SingaporeAuto.

Suppose that the R package insuranceData is installed. Then we can load the dataset into the R workspace as follows:

```
 1 > library(insuranceData)
 2 > data(SingaporeAuto)
 3 > head(SingaporeAuto)
 4   SexInsured  Female  VehicleType  PC  Clm_Count
 5 1           U       0            T   0          0
 6 2           U       0            T   0          0
 7 3           U       0            T   0          0
 8 4           U       0            T   0          0
 9 5           U       0            T   0          0
10 6           U       0            T   0          0
11   Exp_weights       LNWEIGHT  NCD  AgeCat  AutoAge0  AutoAge1
12 1   0.6680356  -0.40341383   30       0         0         0
13 2   0.5667351  -0.56786326   30       0         0         0
14 3   0.5037645  -0.68564629   30       0         0         0
15 4   0.9144422  -0.08944106   20       0         0         0
16 5   0.5366188  -0.62246739   20       0         0         0
17 6   0.7529090  -0.28381095   20       0         0         0
18   AutoAge2  AutoAge  VAgeCat  VAgecat1
19 1        0        0        0         2
20 2        0        0        0         2
21 3        0        0        0         2
22 4        0        0        0         2
23 5        0        0        0         2
24 6        0        0        0         2
```

In the above code, we first loaded the package using the function library. Then we loaded the dataset using the function data by specifying the name of the dataset.

From the first few rows of the dataset, we see that this dataset contains 15 variables. Since some variables contain duplicated information, we focus on the following variables: `Female`, `PC`, `Clm_Count`, `Exp_weights`, `NCD`, `AgeCat`, and `VAgecat1`. These variables are described in Table 8.1.

Variable	Description
Female	Binary (equal to 1 if the insured is female)
PC	Binary (equal to 1 if the car is an automobile)
Clm_Count	Integer (the number of claims)
Exp_weights	Exposure (the fraction of the year that a policyholder had insurance coverage)
NCD	Categorical (No claims discount)
AgeCat	Categorical (Age category of a policyholder. Categories 0, 2, 3, 4, 5, 6, 7 represent age groups 0-21, 22-25, 26-35, 36-45, 46-55, 56-65, 66 and over, respectively)
VAgecat1	Categorical (Vehicle age category. Categories 2, 3, 4, 5, 6 represent vehicle age groups 0-2, 3-5, 6-10, 11-15, 16 and older, respectively.)

Table 8.1: *Description of the Singapore automobile data.*

We can create a new dataset with relevant variables as follows:

```
> datAuto <- SingaporeAuto[, c("Clm_Count", "Female", "PC
  ", "Exp_weights", "NCD", "AgeCat", "VAgecat1")]
> datAuto$NCD <- factor(datAuto$NCD, levels=c(50, 0, 10,
  20, 30, 40))
> datAuto$AgeCat <- factor(datAuto$AgeCat, levels=c(7, 0,
  2, 3, 4, 5, 6))
> datAuto$VAgecat1 <- factor(datAuto$VAgecat1, levels=c
  (6, 2, 3, 4, 5))
> summary(datAuto)
 Clm_Count            Female               PC
 Min.   :0.00000   Min.   :0.00000   Min.   :0.0000
 1st Qu.:0.00000   1st Qu.:0.00000   1st Qu.:0.0000
 Median :0.00000   Median :0.00000   Median :1.0000
 Mean   :0.06989   Mean   :0.09355   Mean   :0.5134
 3rd Qu.:0.00000   3rd Qu.:0.00000   3rd Qu.:1.0000
 Max.   :3.00000   Max.   :1.00000   Max.   :1.0000

 Exp_weights          NCD        AgeCat   VAgecat1
 Min.   :0.005476   50:1419    7:  17    6: 218
```

```
16 1st Qu.:0.279261      0 :2010      0:3640      2:4406
17 Median :0.503764      10:1458      2: 141      3: 771
18 Mean    :0.519859      20:1836      3:1476      4: 924
19 3rd Qu.:0.752909      30: 411      4:1516      5:1164
20 Max.    :1.000000      40: 349      5: 536
21                                      6: 157
```

We saved the new dataset to an R data frame named datAuto. We also converted
the categorical variables to factors. We reordered the levels of the factors so the
reference level will be the first level we specified. For example, the reference level
of NCD will be 50. The NCD variable refers to the discount of the premium based
on the policyholder's past claim. Since the variables Female and PC are binary
variables with values of 0 and 1, we do not need to convert them to factors.

Exercise 8.1. Write R code to calculate the distribution of claim counts by gender,
claim counts by age category, and claim counts by vehicle age category. (Hint:
Use the table function.)

8.3   Poisson Regression Models

The **Poisson distribution** is a fundamental distribution used for counts. The
probability density function of the Poisson distribution is given by

$$P(y = j) = \frac{\mu^j}{j!} e^{-\mu}, \quad j = 0, 1, 2, \ldots,$$

where μ is the mean of the distribution.

   Let $x_1, x_2, \ldots, x_n$ be the observations of the explanatory variables and let y_1,
$y_2, \ldots, y_n$ be the corresponding responses. Under the Poisson regression model,
the response y_i is assumed to follow a Poisson distribution with mean μ_i, which
is assumed to be an exponential function of $x_i' \beta$. In other words, we have

$$E[y_i] = \mu_i = E_i \exp\left(x_i' \beta\right),$$

where $\beta = (\beta_0, \beta_1, \ldots, \beta_k)'$ is a vector of parameters and E_i is the exposure. For
the automobile claim data, the exposure is the fraction of the year that a policy-
holder had insurance coverage. The exposure E_i is a known number and is not a
parameter.

We use the method of maximum likelihood to estimate the parameters $\boldsymbol{\beta}$. The likelihood of the ith observation is given by

$$P(y = y_i) = \frac{\mu_i^{y_i}}{y_i!} e^{-\mu_i}.$$

The likelihood of the dataset is calculated as

$$\prod_{i=1}^{n} P(y = y_i),$$

from which we get the log-likelihood of the dataset:

$$
\begin{aligned}
L(\boldsymbol{\beta}) &= \sum_{i=1}^{n} (-\mu_i + y_i \ln \mu_i - \ln y_i!) \\
&= \sum_{i=1}^{n} (-E_i \exp(\mathbf{x}_i'\boldsymbol{\beta}) + y_i (\ln E_i + \mathbf{x}_i'\boldsymbol{\beta}) - \ln y_i!).
\end{aligned}
\tag{8.1}
$$

The term $\ln E_i$ in the above equation is called an **offset**.

Since the log-likelihood is a nonlinear function of the parameters, we rely on a numerical procedure to find the values of the parameters that maximize the log-likelihood. In R, we fit a Poisson regression model to the dataset as follows:

```
 1 > fit1 <- glm(Clm_Count ~ Female + PC + NCD + AgeCat +
     VAgecat1, offset=log(Exp_weights), family=poisson(
     link='log'), data=datAuto)
 2 > summary(fit1)
 3
 4 Call:
 5 glm(formula = Clm_Count ~ Female + PC + NCD + AgeCat +
     VAgecat1,
 6 family = poisson(link = "log"), data = datAuto, offset =
     log(Exp_weights))
 7
 8 Deviance Residuals:
 9 Min       1Q    Median       3Q       Max
10 -0.8204  -0.4331  -0.3163  -0.2069    3.7803
11
12 Coefficients:
13 Estimate Std. Error z value Pr(>|z|)
14 (Intercept) -13.94760   284.66051   -0.049  0.96092
15 Female       -0.17420     0.15511   -1.123  0.26139
16 PC           10.75870   284.65919    0.038  0.96985
17 NCD0          0.70934     0.14324    4.952 7.34e-07 ***
```

```
18 NCD10               0.41010      0.16421    2.497   0.01251 *
19 NCD20               0.27481      0.16875    1.628   0.10343
20 NCD30               0.31825      0.21029    1.513   0.13019
21 NCD40              -0.03578      0.25625   -0.140   0.88895
22 AgeCat0            10.17915    284.66009    0.036   0.97147
23 AgeCat2            -0.69884      0.77560   -0.901   0.36757
24 AgeCat3            -0.53937      0.71729   -0.752   0.45208
25 AgeCat4            -0.59228      0.71567   -0.828   0.40791
26 AgeCat5            -0.77587      0.73042   -1.062   0.28813
27 AgeCat6            -0.22631      0.74957   -0.302   0.76271
28 VAgecat12           1.61740      0.51115    3.164   0.00155 **
29 VAgecat13           1.55057      0.51570    3.007   0.00264 **
30 VAgecat14           1.12749      0.51888    2.173   0.02979 *
31 VAgecat15           0.36382      0.53116    0.685   0.49337
32 ---
33 Signif. codes:
34 0 '***' 0.001 '**' 0.01 '*' 0.05 '.' 0.1 ' ' 1
35
36 (Dispersion parameter for poisson family taken to be 1)
37
38 Null deviance: 2716.9  on 7482   degrees of freedom
39 Residual deviance: 2605.7  on 7465   degrees of freedom
40 AIC: 3636.8
41
42 Number of Fisher Scoring iterations: 10
```

In fitting the Poisson model with `glm`, we usually specify "log" as the link function and incorporate the exposure using offset. From the above model summary, we see that variables `NCD` and `VAgecat1` are significant for predicting the claim frequency.

Exercise 8.2. Let `fit1` be a Poisson regression model created by the following R code:

```
1 fit1 <- glm(Clm_Count ~ Female + PC + NCD + AgeCat +
     VAgecat1, offset=log(Exp_weights), family=poisson(
     link='log'), data=datAuto)
```

Write R code to

(a) Calculate the log-likelihood function $L(\boldsymbol{\beta})$ for this model. (Hint: use the R function `lfactorial` to calculate $\ln y_i!$.)

(b) Calculate the AIC of this model, where AIC is defined as

$$AIC = 2(k+1) - 2L(\boldsymbol{\beta}),$$

where $k+1$ represents the number of parameters. Does the AIC calculated above match the AIC given in the model summary?

For $i = 1, 2, \ldots, n$, the ith fitted value of the Poisson regression model is $E[y_i] = \mu_i = \exp(\mathbf{x}'_i \boldsymbol{\beta})$. Given the mean μ_i, we can calculate the probabilities when $y_i = j$ for $j = 0, 1, 2, \ldots$. By summing the probabilities $P(y_i = j)$ for all $i = 1, 2, \ldots, n$, we get the estimated number of policies with j claims. For example, we can estimate the number of policies with 0 claims, 1 claim, 2 claims, 3 claims, and 4 claims as follows:

```
 1 > vj <- c(0:4)
 2 > njhat <- matrix(0, nrow=1, ncol=length(vj))
 3 > colnames(njhat) <- vj
 4 > for(j in vj) {
 5 +     njhat[j+1] <- sum(dpois(j, fit1$fitted.values))
 6 + }
 7 > njhat
 8            0         1        2        3          4
 9 [1,] 6987.298 469.6269 24.90036 1.128134 0.04492483
10 > with(datAuto, table(Clm_Count))
11 Clm_Count
12    0    1    2    3
13 6996  455   28    4
```

From the above output, we see that the estimated number of policies with 0 claims is 6987.298. The actual number of policies with 0 claims is 6996. The estimated number of policies with 3 claims is 1.128134. The actual number of policies with 3 claims is 4. It seems that the Poisson regression model provides a good fit for the dataset. In Section 8.5, we will introduce a statistic to better quantify the goodness of fit.

8.4 Negative Binomial Regression Models

The Poisson regression model introduced in the previous section is simple but too restrictive. The Poisson regression model assumes **equidispersion**, that is, the mean is equal to the variance. Many datasets do not satisfy this condition. In this section, we introduce negative binomial regression models to address this drawback.

The **negative binomial distribution** has the following probability density function

$$P(y = j) = \binom{j + r - 1}{r - 1} p^r (1 - p)^j, \tag{8.2}$$

where $r > 0$ and $p \in (0, 1)$ are parameters. The parameter r represents the number of failures until the experiment is stopped and the parameter p represents the success probability in each experiment.

The mean and the variance of a variable y that follows a negative binomial distribution are given by

$$E[y] = \frac{r(1 - p)}{p}, \quad \mathrm{Var}(y) = \frac{r(1 - p)}{p^2}.$$

Since the mean and the variance of a negative binomial distribution are not equal, we do not have the equidisperson problem when fitting a negative binomial model to a dataset.

To fit a negative binomial regression model to a count dependent variable, we let the parameter p to vary by observation i. In particular, we incorporate the independent variables into the model as follows:

$$\mu_i = \frac{r(1 - p_i)}{p_i} = E_i \exp\left(\mathbf{x}_i' \boldsymbol{\beta}\right), \tag{8.3}$$

where r and $\boldsymbol{\beta}$ are parameters to be estimated, and E_i is the exposure. The log-likelihood function of the negative binomial regression model is given by

$$
\begin{aligned}
L(\boldsymbol{\beta}) \\
= \ & \sum_{i=1}^{n} \ln P(y = y_i) \\
= \ & \sum_{i=1}^{n} \left(\ln \binom{y_i + r - 1}{r - 1} + r \ln p_i + y_i \ln(1 - p_i) \right) \\
= \ & \sum_{i=1}^{n} \left(\ln \binom{y_i + r - 1}{r - 1} + r \ln \frac{r}{r + \mu_i} + y_i \ln \frac{\mu_i}{r + \mu_i} \right) \\
= \ & \sum_{i=1}^{n} \left(\ln(y_i + r - 1)! - \ln(r - 1)! - \ln y_i! + r \ln \frac{r}{r + \mu_i} + y_i \ln \frac{\mu_i}{r + \mu_i} \right). \tag{8.4}
\end{aligned}
$$

The method of maximum likelihood is also used to estimate the parameters.

To fit a negative binomial regression model in R, we use the function `glm.nb` from the R package `MASS`, which must be downloaded and installed in R. The following R code shows how to fit a negative binomial regression model to the claim count variable:

```
> library(MASS)
> fit2<-glm.nb(Clm_Count ~ Female + PC + NCD + AgeCat +
    VAgecat1 + offset(log(Exp_weights)), link=log, data
    =datAuto)
> summary(fit2)

Call:
glm.nb(formula = Clm_Count ~ Female + PC + NCD + AgeCat +
    VAgecat1 +
    offset(log(Exp_weights)), data = datAuto, link = log,
        init.theta = 2.465841279)

Deviance Residuals:
    Min       1Q    Median       3Q       Max
-0.8020  -0.4291  -0.3144  -0.2068    3.4440

Coefficients:
                Estimate Std. Error z value Pr(>|z|)
(Intercept)   -2.195e+01  1.554e+04  -0.001  0.99887
Female        -1.777e-01  1.584e-01  -1.122  0.26179
PC             1.876e+01  1.554e+04   0.001  0.99904
NCD0           7.114e-01  1.461e-01   4.868 1.13e-06 ***
NCD10          4.112e-01  1.674e-01   2.456  0.01403 *
NCD20          2.780e-01  1.718e-01   1.619  0.10549
NCD30          3.268e-01  2.140e-01   1.527  0.12670
NCD40         -2.904e-02  2.595e-01  -0.112  0.91090
AgeCat0        1.817e+01  1.554e+04   0.001  0.99907
AgeCat2       -6.949e-01  7.981e-01  -0.871  0.38389
AgeCat3       -5.435e-01  7.395e-01  -0.735  0.46235
AgeCat4       -5.948e-01  7.378e-01  -0.806  0.42014
AgeCat5       -7.791e-01  7.526e-01  -1.035  0.30055
AgeCat6       -2.098e-01  7.721e-01  -0.272  0.78582
VAgecat12      1.615e+00  5.142e-01   3.141  0.00168 **
VAgecat13      1.549e+00  5.189e-01   2.986  0.00283 **
VAgecat14      1.128e+00  5.219e-01   2.162  0.03065 *
VAgecat15      3.641e-01  5.340e-01   0.682  0.49540
---
Signif. codes:  0 '***' 0.001 '**' 0.01 '*' 0.05 '.' 0.1
    ' ' 1

(Dispersion parameter for Negative Binomial(2.4658)
    family taken to be 1)
```

```
37
38     Null deviance: 2524.8   on 7482   degrees of freedom
39 Residual deviance: 2417.1   on 7465   degrees of freedom
40 AIC: 3634.8
41
42 Number of Fisher Scoring iterations: 1
43
44
45               Theta:   2.47
46           Std. Err.:   1.40
47
48  2 x log-likelihood:   -3596.75
```

In the above code, we first loaded the R package MASS using the function library. Then we called the function glm.nb to fit the model. The parameter theta in the model summary corresponds to the parameter r in Equation (8.3).

Exercise 8.3. Write R code to calculate the log-likelihood $L(\boldsymbol{\beta})$ of the following negative binomial regression model:

```
1 fit2<-glm.nb(Clm_Count ~ Female + PC + NCD + AgeCat +
      VAgecat1 +  offset(log(Exp_weights)),link=log, data=
      datAuto)
```

Does $2L(\boldsymbol{\beta})$ match the "2 x log-likelihood" given in the model summary?

We can also compare the frequencies of the claims estimated by the model and those from the actual data as follows:

```
1 > vj <- c(0:4)
2 > njhat <- matrix(0, nrow=1, ncol=length(vj))
3 > colnames(njhat) <- vj
4 > for(j in vj) {
5 +     njhat[j+1] <- sum(dnbinom(j, size=fit2$theta, mu=
      fit2$fitted.values))
6 + }
7 > njhat
8               0         1          2         3          4
9 [1,] 6996.94 451.8095 31.63446 2.403226 0.1944642
10 > with(datAuto, table(Clm_Count))
11 Clm_Count
```

```
12│    0      1      2      3
13│ 6996    455     28      4
```

In the above code, we used the R function `dnbinom` to calculate the probability from a negative binomial distribution. In our code, we called this function with three parameters: `x`, `size`, and `mu`. The parameter `x` specifies the count; the parameter `size` corresponds to the parameter r; the parameter `mu` corresponds to the mean μ_i.

The estimated number of policies with 0 claims is 6996.94, which is very close to the actual number of policies with 0 claims. The estimated number of policies with 3 claims is also close to the actual number of policies with 3 claims. It seems that the negative binomial regression model is also a good candidate model for the dataset.

8.5 Model Evaluation

To examine regression models for count dependent variables, it is common to use the **Pearson's chi-square statistic**, which is defined as:

$$\chi^2 = \sum_{j=0}^{m} \frac{(O_j - E_j)^2}{E_j}, \tag{8.5}$$

where O_j is the actual number of policies that have j claims, E_j is the estimated number of policies that have j claims, m is the maximum number of claims considered over all policies.

For example, we can calculate the Pearson's chi-square statistics for the Poisson model and the negative binomial model as follows:

```
 1 > # calculate actual count frequency
 2 > y <- datAuto$Clm_Count
 3 > m <- 4
 4 > 0 <- matrix(0, nrow=1, ncol=m+1)
 5 > colnames(0) <- 0:m
 6 > for(j in 0:m) {
 7 +        0[j+1] <- sum(y==j)
 8 + }
 9 > # calculate count frequency from fit1
10 > fit1 <- glm(Clm_Count ~ Female + PC + NCD + AgeCat +
     VAgecat1, offset=log(Exp_weights), family=poisson(
     link='log'), data=datAuto)
11 > fit1E <- matrix(0, nrow=1, ncol=m+1)
12 > colnames(fit1E) <- 0:m
```

```
13 > for(j in 0:m) {
14 +       fit1E[j+1] <-  sum(dpois(j, fit1$fitted.values))
15 + }
16 > # calculate count frequency from fit2
17 > library(MASS)
18 > fit2<-glm.nb(Clm_Count ~ Female + PC + NCD + AgeCat +
      VAgecat1 + offset(log(Exp_weights)),link=log, data=
      datAuto)
19 > fit2E <- matrix(0, nrow=1, ncol=m+1)
20 > colnames(fit2E) <- 0:m
21 > for(j in 0:m) {
22 +       fit2E[j+1] <-  sum(dnbinom(j, size=fit2$theta, mu=
      fit2$fitted.values))
23 + }
24 > 0
25              0    1    2 3 4
26 [1,] 6996 455 28 4 0
27 > fit1E
28              0             1             2             3             4
29 [1,] 6987.298 469.6269 24.90036 1.128134 0.04492483
30 > fit2E
31              0             1             2             3             4
32 [1,] 6996.94 451.8095 31.63446 2.403226 0.1944642
33 > sum( (0-fit1E)^2 / fit1E )
34 [1] 8.208022
35 > sum( (0-fit2E)^2 / fit2E )
36 [1] 1.695625
```

The above output shows that the Pearson's chi-square statistics for the Poisson model and the negative binomial model are about 8.2 and 1.7, respectively. The results show that the negative binomial model is better than the Poisson model because the former has a lower statistic.

———————————————————⌒———————————————————

Exercise 8.4. Calculate the Pearson's chi-square statistics for the following four models:

```
1 m1 <- glm(Clm_Count ~ 1, family=poisson(link='log'), data
     =datAuto)
2 m2 <- glm(Clm_Count ~ 1, offset=log(Exp_weights), family=
     poisson(link='log'), data=datAuto)
3 m3 <- glm(Clm_Count ~ Female + PC + NCD + AgeCat +
     VAgecat1, offset=log(Exp_weights), family=poisson(
     link='log'), data=datAuto)
```

```
4 m4 <- glm.nb(Clm_Count ~ Female + PC + NCD + AgeCat +
    VAgecat1 + offset(log(Exp_weights)), link=log, data=
    datAuto)
```

Which model is the best?

8.6 Summary

In this chapter, we introduced the Poisson regression model and the negative binomial regression model for datasets with count-dependent variables. The Poisson regression model assumes equidispersion, which means that the mean and the variance of the underlying count dependent variable are equal. Insurance claim data usually exhibits overdispersion, which means that the variance of the count dependent variable is larger than the mean. With an additional parameter, the negative binomial regression model is more flexible than the Poisson regression model and can be used to model overdispersion. We also introduced the Pearson's chi-square statistic to measure the goodness-of-fit of models for count-dependent variables. For more information about models for count data, readers are referred to (Faraway, 2005), (de Jong and Heller, 2008), and (Frees, 2009).

8.7 End-of-Chapter Exercises

Exercise 8.5. One application of the Poisson regression model is for the prediction of incurred but not reported (IBNR) claims reserves. For a certain portfolio of general insurance policies, denote by y_{ij} the claims that occur in accident year i, but are paid in development year j, where $i, j = 1, 2, ..., t$ with observable claims only for $i + j \leq t + 1$. For this portfolio for a 3-year development period, the observed incremental claims are usually represented in a claims triangle run-off as shown below:

Accident	Development Year		
Year	1	2	3
1	2,541	1,029	217
2	2,824	790	
3	1,981		

The objective is to estimate the unobserved claims at the bottom-half of this triangle. Assume that y_{ij} is modeled as a Poisson distribution with mean $\alpha_i \beta_j$.

(a) Derive explicit forms for the maximum likelihood estimators for the parameters α_i and β_j.

(b) Using the result in (a), calculate the maximum likelihood estimates for α_i and β_j for $i, j = 1, 2, 3$.

(c) Using the result in (b), give estimates of the bottom half of the triangle.

Chapter 9

Case Study: Modeling the Loss Severity of Auto Claims

In this case study, we consider the use of generalized linear models to examine the loss severity of insurance claims. For empirical investigation, we use a dataset containing one-year vehicle insurance policies. After working through this case study, readers will be able to

- Fit gamma regression models to insurance claim amounts

- Understand and use the method of maximum likelihood to estimate the model parameters

- Make predictions based on the fitted models

- Evaluate the models based on deviance

9.1 Problem Description

Two-part models (Frees, 2009; Antonio and Valdez, 2012) are popular models for modeling insurance claims. In a two-part model, an insurance claim is decomposed into two components: the **frequency** component and the **severity** component. In other words, the claim of a subject is modeled as

$$\text{Claim Recorded} = r \times y, \tag{9.1}$$

where r is a binary variable indicating whether the subject has an insurance claim and y is a continuous variable denoting the amount of the claim.

The two-part model given in Equation (9.1) has several advantages. First, it allows us to model the frequency and the severity separately. For example, we can use a binary regression model (e.g., the probit and logistic regression models described in Chapter 7) to model r and a linear regression model to model y. Second, it allows us to use different sets of explanatory variables for the frequency and the severity components.

In many situations, the frequency of claims may exceed one. For automobile insurance, for example, a policyholder may have more than one claim in a year. The two-part model given in Equation (9.1) can be extended to model the frequency that may exceed one. For $i = 1, 2, \ldots, n$, we observe the following data for the ith subject:

- the number of claims N_i.

- the amounts of these N_i claims: $y_{i1}, y_{i2}, \ldots, y_{iN_i}$.

Sometimes we are only interested in the **aggregate loss** for the ith subject:

$$S_i = y_{i1} + y_{i2} + \cdots + y_{iN_i}.$$

In this case, we decompose the joint distribution of the dependent variables as

$$f(N, S) = f_1(N) \times f_2(S|N), \tag{9.2}$$

where $f(N, S)$ denotes the joint distribution of N and S, $f_1(N)$ denotes the probability of having N claims, and $f_2(S|N)$ denotes the conditional density of the aggregate loss S given N.

A count regression model is used to model the frequency component of the two-part model given in Equation (9.2). For example, the Poisson and negative binomial models can be used to model the frequency. We already introduced the Poisson and negative binomial models in Chapter 8.

A regression model for continuous data is used to model the severity component conditional on $N > 0$. Since the severity component is usually nonnegative and skewed to the right, options for modeling the severity component include (de Jong and Heller, 2008):

- use a transformation (e.g., log transformation) to transform the responses and use a normal linear regression model on the transformed responses.

- use a generalized linear model with a response distribution that is concentrated on the non-negative axis and can handle skewness. Typical distributions include the gamma and inverse Gaussian distributions.

For the purpose of this case study, we emphasize the gamma regression model to model the severity component. For a more in-depth statistical analysis of modeling insurance claims, see Antonio and Valdez (2012).

9.2 Data Description

In this case study, we consider a vehicle insurance dataset obtained from de Jong and Heller (2008). This dataset contains 67,856 one-year vehicle insurance policies taken out in 2004 or 2005. Among these policies, 4,624 policies had at least one claim. This dataset is also available in the R package `insuranceData` (See Exercise A.48). The name of the dataset in the R package is `dataCar`.

Variable	Description
veh_value	Vehicle value in $10,000s
exposure	Exposure of the policy
clm	Occurrence of claim (0=No, 1=Yes)
numclaims	Number of claims
claimcst0	Claim amount (0 if no claim)
veh_body	Vehicle body type
veh_age	Vehicle age (1=New, 2,3,4)
gender	Gender of the policyholder
area	Area of residence
agecat	Age band of the policyholder (1=Youngest,2,3,4,5,6)
X_OBSTAT_	A factor with only one level

Table 9.1: *Variables of the vehicle insurance dataset* `dataCar`.

The dataset `dataCar` contains observations on 11 variables, which are described in Table 9.1. To load the dataset into the R workspace and show the summary of the dataset, we proceed as follows:

```
> library(insuranceData)
> data(dataCar)
> summary(dataCar)
   veh_value            exposure              clm
 Min.   : 0.000    Min.   :0.002738    Min.   :0.00000
 1st Qu.: 1.010    1st Qu.:0.219028    1st Qu.:0.00000
 Median : 1.500    Median :0.446270    Median :0.00000
 Mean   : 1.777    Mean   :0.468651    Mean   :0.06814
 3rd Qu.: 2.150    3rd Qu.:0.709103    3rd Qu.:0.00000
 Max.   :34.560    Max.   :0.999316    Max.   :1.00000

   numclaims             claimcst0            veh_body
 Min.   :0.00000    Min.   :    0.0      SEDAN  :22233
 1st Qu.:0.00000    1st Qu.:    0.0      HBACK  :18915
 Median :0.00000    Median :    0.0      STNWG  :16261
```

```
16  Mean    :0.07276    Mean    :  137.3    UTE     : 4586
17  3rd Qu.:0.00000    3rd Qu.:    0.0    TRUCK   : 1750
18  Max.    :4.00000    Max.    :55922.1    HDTOP   : 1579
19                                          (Other): 2532
20       veh_age          gender      area           agecat
21  Min.    :1.000    F:38603    A:16312    Min.    :1.000
22  1st Qu.:2.000    M:29253    B:13341    1st Qu.:2.000
23  Median :3.000                C:20540    Median :3.000
24  Mean    :2.674                D: 8173    Mean    :3.485
25  3rd Qu.:4.000                E: 5912    3rd Qu.:5.000
26  Max.    :4.000                F: 3578    Max.    :6.000
27
28                    X_OBSTAT_
29  01101      0      0      0:67856
```

From the output, we see that the variable X_OBSTAT_ is a factor with only one
level. The variables clm and numclaims are treated as numerical variables. To
show the counts of the two variables, we use the table function as follows:

```
1  > table(dataCar[,"clm"])
2
3      0      1
4  63232   4624
5  > table(dataCar[,"numclaims"])
6
7      0      1      2      3      4
8  63232   4333    271     18      2
```

From the output, we see that 4,624 observations had at least one claim. Among
these 4,624 observations, 271 had two claims, 18 had three claims, and 2 had four
claims.

Since we want to build models for loss severity, we are only interested in the
observations with at least one claim. We can extract the relevant data in R as
follows:

```
1  > vnames <- c("claimcst0", "veh_value", "numclaims", "veh
     _body", "veh_age", "gender", "area", "agecat")
2  > dataCar2 <- dataCar[dataCar[,"clm"]==1, vnames]
3  > dim(dataCar2)
4  [1] 4624       8
5  > summary(dataCar2)
6     claimcst0              veh_value            numclaims
7   Min.    :  200.0    Min.    : 0.000    Min.    :1.000
8   1st Qu.:  353.8    1st Qu.: 1.100    1st Qu.:1.000
```

```
 9  Median :    761.6    Median :  1.570    Median :1.000
10  Mean   :  2014.4    Mean   :  1.859    Mean   :1.068
11  3rd Qu.:  2091.4    3rd Qu.:  2.310    3rd Qu.:1.000
12  Max.   :55922.1    Max.   : 13.900    Max.   :4.000
13
14      veh_body            veh_age          gender      area
15  SEDAN  :1476    Min.    :1.000    F:2648    A:1085
16  HBACK  :1264    1st Qu.:2.000    M:1976    B: 965
17  STNWG  :1173    Median :3.000              C:1412
18  UTE    : 260    Mean   :2.626              D: 496
19  HDTOP  : 130    3rd Qu.:4.000              E: 386
20  TRUCK  : 120    Max.   :4.000              F: 280
21  (Other): 201
22      agecat
23  Min.   :1.000
24  1st Qu.:2.000
25  Median :3.000
26  Mean   :3.325
27  3rd Qu.:4.000
28  Max.   :6.000
```

The new data frame dataCar2 contains 4,624 observations on eight variables, which include the dependent variable claimcst0. We did not include clm, exposure, or X_OBSTAT_. The reason is that the information contained in clm is captured by numclaims; the variable exposure is used to model the frequency rather than the severity; the variable X_OBSTAT_ contains identical values. In our remaining analysis, we will work with the data frame dataCar2.

Exercise 9.1. Plot the claim amount from dataCar2 in a histogram and comment on the distribution of the claim amount.

Exercise 9.2. Write R code to do the following:

- Calculate the mean of the claim amount for each vehicle body type.

- Sort the means in increasing order.

- Plot the means and label each point using the vehicle body type name.

(Hint: use the aggregate function.)

9.3   The Gamma Regression Model

The **gamma distribution** is a two-parameter family of probability distributions for continuous data. There are several parameterizations for the gamma distribution. Here, a parameterization refers to a way of defining the parameters necessary for a specification of a model. One common parameterization is to use a shape parameter k and a scale parameter θ. In this parameterization, the probability density function of the gamma distribution is given by

$$f(x;k,\theta) = \frac{x^{k-1}\exp\left(-\dfrac{x}{\theta}\right)}{\theta^k\Gamma(k)}, \quad x > 0, \tag{9.3}$$

where $k > 0$, $\theta > 0$, and $\Gamma(k)$ is the **gamma function** defined as

$$\Gamma(k) = \int_0^\infty x^{k-1}e^{-x}\mathrm{d}x.$$

If a random variable S follows a gamma distribution with parameters k and θ, we write

$$S \sim \mathrm{Gamma}(k,\theta).$$

The expectation and variance of S are given by

$$E[S] = k\theta \tag{9.4}$$

and

$$\mathrm{Var}(S) = k\theta^2, \tag{9.5}$$

respectively. The **dispersion** parameter of the gamma distribution is

$$\phi = \frac{1}{k}. \tag{9.6}$$

The dispersion parameter is defined for all distributions in the exponential family, which includes the gamma distribution. See de Jong and Heller (2008).

Exercise 9.3. Write an R function named `logdgamma` to calculate the log density of the gamma distribution given by

$$\ln f(x;k,\theta) = k\ln\frac{x}{\theta} - \frac{x}{\theta} - \ln x - \ln\Gamma(k).$$

What is the output of the following R code?

```
1 logdgamma (55922.13, 1, 1)
2 log (dgamma (55922.13, shape=1, scale=1))
```

The gamma regression model is a special **generalized linear model** (**GLM**) that may be described by the following assumptions (Venables and Ripley, 2002):

- The response S_i is observed independently at fixed values of stimulus variables $\mathbf{x}_i = (1, x_{i1}, x_{i2}, \ldots, x_{ip})'$, for $i = 1, 2, \ldots, n$.

- The influence of $\mathbf{x}_i$ on the distribution of S_i can be summarized through a single linear function

$$\eta_i = \mathbf{x}_i'\boldsymbol{\beta} = \beta_0 + \beta_1 x_{i1} + \cdots + \beta_p x_{ip}.$$

The linear function is referred to as the **linear predictor**.

- The distribution of S_i has the probability density function given by $f(S_i; k, \theta_i)$, where f is the gamma density function defined in Equation (9.3), k is the shape parameter, and θ_i is a parameter depending on the linear predictor.

- The mean $\mu_i = k\theta_i$ is a smooth invertible function of the linear predictor, that is,

$$k\theta_i = m(\eta_i)$$

or

$$\eta_i = m^{-1}(k\theta_i) = l(k\theta_i).$$

The inverse function $l(\cdot)$ is referred to as the **link function**.

A common choice of the link function is the log function. In this case, the mean can be written as

$$k\theta_i = \exp(\eta_i) = \exp\left(\mathbf{x}_i'\boldsymbol{\beta}\right). \tag{9.7}$$

The corresponding probability density function can be written as

$$g(S_i; k, \boldsymbol{\beta}) = \frac{\left(\dfrac{kS_i}{\exp(\mathbf{x}_i'\boldsymbol{\beta})}\right)^k \exp\left(-\dfrac{kS_i}{\exp(\mathbf{x}_i'\boldsymbol{\beta})}\right)}{S_i \Gamma(k)}. \tag{9.8}$$

We use the method of maximum likelihood to estimate the parameters k and $\boldsymbol{\beta}$. In particular, we maximize the log-likelihood function, which is expressed as

$$
\begin{aligned}
\ell(k, \boldsymbol{\beta}) &= \sum_{i=1}^{n} \ln g(S_i; k, \boldsymbol{\beta}) \\
&= \sum_{i=1}^{n} k\left[\ln(kS_i) - \mathbf{x}_i'\boldsymbol{\beta}\right] - \sum_{i=1}^{n} \frac{kS_i}{\exp(\mathbf{x}_i'\boldsymbol{\beta})} - \Gamma(k)\sum_{i=1}^{n} \ln S_i. \quad (9.9)
\end{aligned}
$$

The gamma regression model described above does not account for the number of claims. Intuitively, the more claims a policyholder incurs, the higher the claim amount of the policyholder. As a result, it makes sense to incorporate the number of claims in the gamma regression model. To do that, we can just modify the dispersion parameter as follows:

$$
\phi_i = \frac{\phi}{N_i} = \frac{1}{kN_i} = \frac{1}{k_i},
$$

where ϕ_i is the dispersion parameter for the ith observation and k_i is the shape parameter of the ith observation. After the number of claims is incorporated, the probability density function for the ith observation becomes

$$
g(S_i; k, \boldsymbol{\beta}) = \frac{\left(\dfrac{kN_iS_i}{\exp(\mathbf{x}_i'\boldsymbol{\beta})}\right)^{kN_i} \exp\left(-\dfrac{kN_iS_i}{\exp(\mathbf{x}_i'\boldsymbol{\beta})}\right)}{S_i\Gamma(k)}. \quad (9.10)
$$

The corresponding log-likelihood function is given by

$$
\begin{aligned}
\ell(k, \boldsymbol{\beta}) &= \sum_{i=1}^{n} \ln g(S_i; k, \boldsymbol{\beta}) \\
&= \sum_{i=1}^{n} kN_i\left[\ln(kN_iS_i) - \mathbf{x}_i'\boldsymbol{\beta}\right] - \sum_{i=1}^{n} \frac{kN_iS_i}{\exp(\mathbf{x}_i'\boldsymbol{\beta})} - \Gamma(k)\sum_{i=1}^{n} \ln S_i. \quad (9.11)
\end{aligned}
$$

Exercise 9.4. Write an R function named negll(param, X, S, N) to calculate the log-likelihood function defined in Equation (9.11), where param is a vector of parameters $(k, \boldsymbol{\beta})$, X is the design matrix, S is the vector of claim amounts, and N is the vector of claim numbers. What is the output of the following R code?

```
1  N <- dataCar2$numclaims
2  S <- dataCar2$claimcst0
3  X <- model.matrix(claimcst0 ~ 1, data=dataCar2)
4  negll(c(1,log(mean(S))), X=X, S=S, N=N)
```

9.4   Fitting the Gamma Regression Model

In R, we can use the `glm` function to fit a Gamma regression model to the data. To fit an intercept-only Gamma regression model, for example, we proceed as follows:

```
> fit1 <- glm(claimcst0 ~ 1, weights=numclaims,  family=
    Gamma(link=log), data=dataCar2)
> summary(fit1)

Call:
glm(formula = claimcst0 ~ 1, family = Gamma(link = log),
    data = dataCar2,
     weights = numclaims)

Deviance Residuals:
    Min        1Q    Median        3Q       Max
 -1.8354   -1.3732   -0.8837    0.0048    6.7165

Coefficients:
             Estimate Std. Error t value Pr(>|t|)
(Intercept)   7.64160    0.02505     305   <2e-16 ***
---
Signif. codes:
0 '***' 0.001 '**' 0.01 '*' 0.05 '.' 0.1 ' ' 1

(Dispersion parameter for Gamma family taken to be
    3.098419)

    Null deviance: 7705.1  on 4623  degrees of freedom
Residual deviance: 7705.1  on 4623  degrees of freedom
AIC: 85173

Number of Fisher Scoring iterations: 6
```

In the above code, we incorporated the number of claims into the model using the argument `weights`. From the output, we see that the value of the parameter β_0 is 7.64160 and the AIC is 85,173. The dispersion parameter is 3.098419, from which we get the estimate of the shape parameter:

$$k = \frac{1}{\phi} = 0.3227452.$$

However, the above estimate of the shape parameter is not accurate. To get an accurate estimate of the shape parameter, we use the `gamma.shape` function from the R package MASS:

```
1 > library(MASS)
2 > gamma.shape(fit1)
3
4 Alpha:  0.71904865
5 SE:     0.01282174
```

From the output, we see that the value of the shape parameter should be about 0.719.

Instead of using the glm function, we can estimate the parameters by maximizing the log-likelihood function directly. To do that, we can use the optim function to maximize the log-likelihood function as follows:

```
1 > N <- dataCar2$numclaims
2 > S <- dataCar2$claimcst0
3 > X <- model.matrix(claimcst0 ~ 1, data=dataCar2)
4 > initEst <- c(1, log(mean(S)))
5 > res1 <- optim(initEst, negll, NULL,  X=X, S=S, N=N,
     control=list(fnscale=-1, maxit=1000))
6 > res1
7 $par
8 [1]  0.7191074 7.6418826
9
10 $value
11 [1] -39661.53
12
13 $counts
14 function  gradient
15       49        NA
16
17 $convergence
18 [1] 0
19
20 $message
21 NULL
```

In the above R code, the function negll was created in Exercise 9.4. Since the optim function always minimizes a function, we used fnscale=-1 in the control list of the function so that the negative log-likelihood function is minimized. The optimum values of the parameters are given in the vector res1$par. From the output, we see that the optimum values of the parameters match the values from the glm and gamma.shape functions.

Now let us fit a full model to the data using the glm function:

```
 1 > fit2 <- glm(claimcst0 ~ . - numclaims, weights=
     numclaims, family=Gamma(link=log), data=dataCar2)
 2 > summary(fit2)
 3
 4 Call:
 5 glm(formula = claimcst0 ~ . - numclaims, family = Gamma(
     link = log),
 6     data = dataCar2, weights = numclaims)
 7
 8 Deviance Residuals:
 9     Min       1Q    Median       3Q       Max
10  -1.9612   -1.3924   -0.8373    0.0444    6.8190
11
12 Coefficients:
13                Estimate Std. Error t value Pr(>|t|)
14 (Intercept)     7.04358    0.56557  12.454  < 2e-16 ***
15 veh_value       0.01979    0.03354   0.590 0.555211
16 veh_bodyCONVT   0.58887    1.13552   0.519 0.604068
17 veh_bodyCOUPE   0.78254    0.57806   1.354 0.175889
18 veh_bodyHBACK   0.54260    0.54585   0.994 0.320253
19 veh_bodyHDTOP   0.41549    0.56221   0.739 0.459931
20 veh_bodyMCARA  -0.71349    0.70203  -1.016 0.309531
21 veh_bodyMIBUS   0.65829    0.60035   1.097 0.272914
22 veh_bodyPANVN   0.42867    0.58130   0.737 0.460895
23 veh_bodyRDSTR  -0.37414    1.13120  -0.331 0.740851
24 veh_bodySEDAN   0.40046    0.54488   0.735 0.462411
25 veh_bodySTNWG   0.37578    0.54580   0.688 0.491180
26 veh_bodyTRUCK   0.60006    0.56276   1.066 0.286353
27 veh_bodyUTE     0.47147    0.55198   0.854 0.393070
28 veh_age         0.06942    0.03187   2.178 0.029460 *
29 genderM         0.18545    0.05152   3.600 0.000322 ***
30 areaB          -0.05245    0.07333  -0.715 0.474506
31 areaC           0.04496    0.06694   0.672 0.501842
32 areaD          -0.00434    0.09097  -0.048 0.961955
33 areaE           0.14003    0.09954   1.407 0.159583
34 areaF           0.36834    0.11383   3.236 0.001221 **
35 agecat         -0.06120    0.01757  -3.483 0.000500 ***
36 ---
37 Signif. codes:
38 0 '***' 0.001 '**' 0.01 '*' 0.05 '.' 0.1 ' ' 1
39
40 (Dispersion parameter for Gamma family taken to be
     2.931467)
41
```

```
42|      Null deviance:  7705.1   on 4623   degrees of freedom
43| Residual deviance:  7503.9   on 4602   degrees of freedom
44| AIC:  85055
45|
46| Number of Fisher Scoring iterations:  7
```

From the model summary, we see that the vehicle age, gender, residence area, and age band are relatively significant. The vehicle value and vehicle body are not significant. Since the AIC is lower than the intercept-only model, the full model is better than the intercept-only model. As mentioned before, the shape parameter calculated from the dispersion parameter is not accurate. We can get an accurate estimate of the shape parameter as follows:

```
1| > library(MASS)
2| > gamma.shape(fit2)
3|
4| Alpha:  0.73601616
5| SE:     0.01315078
```

Exercise 9.5. Write R code to estimate the parameters of the full gamma regression model directly by using the optim function to maximize the log-likelihood function defined in Equation (9.11). Do the estimates obtained from the optim function closely match those obtained from the glm and gamma.shape functions? Explain.

Exercise 9.6. Use the glm function to fit a reduced gamma regression model to the data with only the variables veh_age, gender, area, and agecat. Between the full model and the reduced model, which one is better in terms of AIC?

9.5 Prediction

Let $\mathbf{x} = (1, x_1, \ldots, x_p)'$ be a vector containing the values of the explanatory variables. Then the predicted claim amount at $\mathbf{x}$ is just the mean of the gamma distribution, that is,

$$\hat{y} = \exp\left(\mathbf{x}\hat{\boldsymbol{\beta}}\right), \tag{9.12}$$

where $\hat{\boldsymbol{\beta}}$ is the vector of estimated regression coefficients.

To calculate the fitted values of the full gamma regression model, for example, we can proceed as follows:

```
1 > betahat <- fit2$coefficients
2 > yhat <- exp(X %*% as.matrix(betahat, ncol=1))
3 > head(yhat)
4          [,1]
5 15 1721.493
6 17 2454.595
7 18 2428.618
8 41 6565.281
9 65 3007.110
10 66 1953.031
```

The fitted values calculated above match the fitted values obtained from the R object fit2:

```
1 > head(fit2$fitted.values)
2        15        17        18        41        65        66
3 1721.493 2454.595 2428.618 3282.640 3007.110 1953.031
```

Exercise 9.7. We can also use the predict function to calculate the predicted values. Write R code to use this function to calculate the fitted values. Then produce a scatter plot of the fitted values against the observed values.

9.6 Model Evaluation

For the normal linear regression model, we define residuals $\hat{\epsilon}_i = y_i - \hat{y}_i$ and their standardized versions to check the appropriateness of the model. The gamma regression model is a generalized linear model, which has assumptions that are different from those of the normal model. These residuals are not normally distributed and do not have constant variance. In this section, we introduce the **deviance residual**, which broadens the definition of residual from the notion of $\hat{\epsilon}_i = y_i - \hat{y}_i$ to a more general quantification of the appropriateness of the model to the data.

For the ith observation, the deviance residual of the gamma regression model is defined as

$$\delta_i = \text{sgn}(y_i - \hat{\mu}_i)\sqrt{2N_i\left(-\ln\frac{y_i}{\hat{\mu}_i} + \frac{y_i - \hat{\mu}_i}{\hat{\mu}_i}\right)},\tag{9.13}$$

where sgn($\cdot$) is the sign function, N_i is the number of claims, and $\hat{\mu}_i$ is the ith predicted value calculated as

$$\hat{\mu}_i = \exp\left(\mathbf{x}_i\hat{\boldsymbol{\beta}}\right).$$

For the definition of the deviance residual in a generalized linear model, see Dobson and Barnett (2008b). Some summary statistics of deviance residuals are shown in the summary of the results produced by the glm function.

The deviance of the gamma regression model is defined as

$$\Delta = \sum_{i=1}^{n}\delta_i^2.\tag{9.14}$$

The deviance is typically used to compare several models. A lower value of the deviance indicates a better fitted model.

In R, we can calculate the deviance residuals of the gamma regression model as follows:

```
1 > plot (dres , resid (fit2))
2 > S <- dataCar2$claimcst0
3 > yhat <- fit2$fitted.values
4 > N <- dataCar2$numclaims
5 > dres <- sign(S-yhat) * sqrt(2 * N * ( -log(S / yhat)
     + (S - yhat) / yhat) )
6 > summary (dres)
7     Min.    1st Qu.    Median     Mean   3rd Qu.      Max.
8 -1.96100  -1.39200  -0.83730  -0.52450   0.04443   6.81900
```

In the above code, we calculated the residual deviance for the full gamma regression model. From the output, we see that the summary statistics of the deviance residuals match those given in the summary of the full model. We can also use the resid function to get the deviance residuals from the fitted model:

```
1 > summary (resid (fit2))
2     Min.    1st Qu.    Median     Mean   3rd Qu.      Max.
3 -1.96100  -1.39200  -0.83730  -0.52450   0.04443   6.81900
```

The deviance of the full gamma regression model is calculated as

```
> sum(dres^2)
[1] 7503.922
> sum(resid(fit2)^2)
[1] 7503.922
> fit2$deviance
[1] 7503.922
```

In the above code, we used three ways to calculate the deviance: using the formula directly, using the `resid` function in R, and using the stored value of the deviance in R.

Exercise 9.8. Let `fitA` and `fitB` be two gamma regression models fitted in the following R code:

```
set.seed(1)
ind <- sample(1:nrow(dataCar2), size=3000)
dataTrain <- dataCar2[ind,]
dataTest <- dataCar2[-ind,]
fitA <- glm(claimcst0 ~ . - numclaims, weights=numclaims,
      family=Gamma(link=log), data=dataTrain)
fitB <- glm(claimcst0 ~ veh_age + gender + area + agecat,
      weights=numclaims, family=Gamma(link=log), data=
      dataTrain)
```

In the above code, the dataset is split into two subsets: one for training and one for testing. The two models are fitted to the training data.

(a) Which model is better in terms of AIC?

(b) Write R code to calculate the out-of-sample deviance using the testing dataset `dataTest`. Which model is better in terms of out-of-sample deviance?

9.7   Summary

In this case study, we introduced the gamma regression model to model the claim amount of vehicle insurance policies. In particular, we introduced how to estimate the parameters using the method of maximum likelihood. We used the `glm` function to fit the model. We also used the `optim` function to fit the model directly by maximizing the log likelihood function. In addition, we described how to use the model to make predictions and how to evaluate the model using deviance residuals.

The gamma regression model is a generalized linear model, which is used to accommodate responses that follow non-normal distributions. For more information about generalized linear models, readers are referred to (de Jong and Heller, 2008), (Dobson and Barnett, 2008b), and (Frees, 2009).

Chapter 10

Decision Trees

In this chapter, we introduce decision trees, which are also referred to as tree-based models. In particular, we introduce regression trees and classification trees. **Decision trees** have the following advantages over traditional regression models:

- Decision trees represent the process of human decision-making more closely than do the regression models described in previous chapters.
- Decision trees can be visualized graphically. As a result, trees can be interpreted and understood easily by people.
- Decision trees can handle categorical and ordinal independent variables straightforwardly without the need to create dummy variables.

10.1   Tree-Based Models

Tree-based models involve dividing the predictor space (i.e., the space formed by independent variables) into a number of simple regions. Tree-based models can be applied to regression problems where the dependent variable is quantitative and classification problems where the dependent variable is qualitative. Using a tree to make a prediction for a new observation is straightforward. To do that, we first find the region to which the new observation belongs and then use the mean or the mode of the region as the prediction.

10.1.1   Regression Trees

To build a regression tree, we divide the predictor space into non-overlapping regions. For the sake of simplicity and easy interpretation of the resulting model, we divide the predictor space into high-dimensional boxes or rectangles. In

particular, we divide the predictor space into J boxes such that the following
objective function

$$f(R_1, R_2, \ldots, R_J) = \sum_{j=1}^{J} \sum_{i=1}^{n} I_{R_j}(\mathbf{x}_i)(y_i - \mu_j)^2 \tag{10.1}$$

is minimized, where I is an indicator function, R_j denotes the set of indices of
the observations that belong to the jth box, μ_j is the mean response of the observations in the jth box, $\mathbf{x}_i$ is the vector of predictor values for the ith observation,
and y_i is the response value for the ith observation. Here $I_{R_j}(\mathbf{x}_i)$ is defined as
follows:

$$I_{R_j}(\mathbf{x}_i) = \begin{cases} 1, & \text{if } \mathbf{x}_i \in R_j, \\ 0, & \text{otherwise.} \end{cases}$$

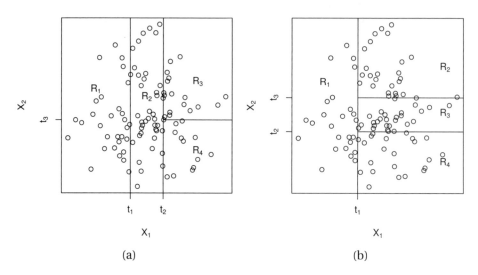

Figure 10.1: *Examples of dividing a two-dimensional predictor space into four
boxes.*

A natural way to divide the predictor space into J boxes proceeds as follows.
First, we split the predictor space into two boxes. Then we split one box into
another two boxes. We continue the process until we get J boxes. Figure 10.1
shows two examples of how a two-dimensional predictor space is divided into
four boxes. In Figure 10.1(a), for example, we have

$$R_1 = \{\mathbf{x} : x_1 < t_1\}, \quad R_2 = \{\mathbf{x} : t_1 < x_1 < t_2\}$$

$$R_3 = \{\mathbf{x} : x_1 > t_2, x_2 > t_3\}, \quad R_4 = \{\mathbf{x} : x_1 > t_2, x_2 < t_3\}.$$

The tree corresponding to the split shown in Figure 10.1(a) is shown in Figure 10.2.

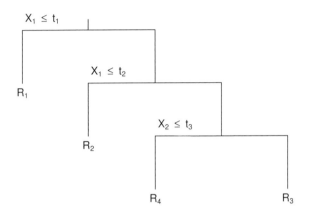

Figure 10.2: *A decision tree corresponding to the split given in Figure 10.1(a).*

Suppose that there are k predictor variables and the jth predictor has n distinct values, where n is the sample size. Then there are $k(n-1)$ ways to divide the predictor space into two boxes. Similarly, there are $k(n-2)$ ways to divide the two boxes into three boxes. Hence there are

$$\prod_{j=1}^{J-1}(k(n-j)) = k^{J-1}\prod_{j=1}^{n}(n-j)$$

ways to divide the predictor space into J boxes. It is not computationally feasible to enumerate all the divisions to find the best division that minimizes the objective function given in Equation (10.1).

The **recursive binary splitting** method can be used to find the approximately optimal division. This method is a top-down, greedy method in that it starts with the whole predictor space and repeats using a greedy strategy to select a box and divide it into two until J boxes have been created. In particular, this method first splits the whole predictor space into two boxes by finding j and t to minimize the following objective function

$$\sum_{i=1}^{n}\left[I_{R_1(j,t)}(\mathbf{x}_i)(y_i - \mu_1(j,t))^2 + I_{R_2(j,t)}(\mathbf{x}_i)(y_i - \mu_2(j,t))^2\right],$$

where

$$R_1(j,t) = \{\mathbf{x}: x_j < t\}, \quad R_2(j,t) = \{\mathbf{x}: x_j > t\},$$

$$\mu_1(j, t) = \frac{1}{|R_1(j, t)|} \sum_{i=1}^{n} I_{R_1(j,t)}(\mathbf{x}_i) y_i,$$

and

$$\mu_2(j, t) = \frac{1}{|R_2(j, t)|} \sum_{i=1}^{n} I_{R_2(j,t)}(\mathbf{x}_i) y_i.$$

The predictor j ranges from 1 to k and the cutpoint t can take at most $n - 1$ distinct values. Hence there are at most $k(n - 1)$ combinations. The greedy strategy finds the best combination by calculating the objective function values on all the $k(n - 1)$ combinations.

Then the recursive binary splitting method repeats the above process for each of the existing boxes until there are J boxes. The number of objective function evaluations is

$$\sum_{j=1}^{J-1} (k(n - j)) = \frac{(2n - J)(J - 1)k}{2},$$

which is not a big number when both n and k are not large.

Selecting the number of boxes, J, is also important in building a regression tree. If J is too small, we get a small tree, which might lead to biased predictions. If J is too large, we get a large and complex tree, which might lead to overfitting of the data. In general, there are two approaches to determine the number of boxes. The first approach is to use the aforementioned process to build the tree only so long as the decrease in the objective function exceeds some threshold. If the threshold is set to be high enough, then this approach can lead to small trees. However, one disadvantage of this approach is that the tree building process might be terminated early and a late good split will be missed.

Another approach is to use a **tree pruning** technique, which determines the number of boxes by first building a large tree T_0 and then pruning it back to obtain a subtree. It is computationally infeasible to consider all subtrees to select the best subtree that has the lowest test error rate. **Cost complexity pruning**, also known as **weakest link pruning**, is a pruning technique that considers a small number of subtrees (James et al., 2013).

The cost complexity pruning method requires a nonnegative tuning parameter α, which is also called the **complexity parameter**. Given α, the cost complexity pruning method finds a subtree T of the large tree T_0 such that the following objective function

$$f_\alpha(T) = \sum_{j=1}^{|T|} \sum_{i=1}^{n} I_{R_j}(\mathbf{x}_i)(y_i - \mu_j)^2 + \alpha|T| \tag{10.2}$$

is minimized, where $|T|$ denotes the number of terminal nodes in T and R_j represents the jth terminal node of T. When $\alpha = 0$, the subtree T that minimizes the objective function given in Equation (10.2) is simply T_0. When α increases, subtrees with many terminal nodes will be penalized by the term $\alpha|T|$. As a result, larger values of α will lead to smaller trees. When we increase the value of α from zero, we get a nested sequence of subtrees of T_0. In fact, it has been shown that (Breiman et al., 1984):

- If T_1 and T_2 are subtrees of T_0 with $f_\alpha(T_1) = f_\alpha(T_2)$, then either T_1 is a subtree of T_2 or T_2 is a subtree of T_1.

- If $\alpha_1 < \alpha_2$, then either $T_{\alpha_1} = T_{\alpha_2}$ or T_{α_2} is a strict subtree of T_{α_1}, where T_α denotes the subtree of T_0 that minimizes the objective function given in Equation (10.2).

Algorithm 10.1: Building a regression tree with cross-validation.

Input: A dataset X, K, N_{min}
Output: Optimal regression tree

1 Fit a large regression tree T_0 to the dataset X by using the recursive binary splitting method. Stop only when each terminal node has fewer than N_{min} observations;

2 Compute intervals $I_1 = [0, \alpha_1]$, $I_2 = (\alpha_1, \alpha_2]$, ..., $I_m = (\alpha_{m-1}, \infty]$ such that all $\alpha \in I_j$ share the same minimizing subtrees of T_0;
    /* β_j is a typical value in the interval I_j.   */

3 Set $\beta_0 = 0$, $\beta_1 = \sqrt{\alpha_1 \alpha_2}$, ..., $\beta_{m-1} = \sqrt{\alpha_{m-1}\alpha_m}$, $\beta_m = \infty$;
    /* Use K-fold cross-validation to select α */

4 Divide the dataset X into K groups $G_1, G_2, ..., G_K$, each of which contains about n/K observations;

5   Fit a regression tree on the dataset except the kth group G_k and determine subtrees T_{β_1}, T_{β_2}, ..., T_{β_m} for this reduced data set;

6   Compute the predicted response for each observation in the kth group G_k and the mean squared prediction error, under each of the models T_{β_1}, T_{β_2}, ..., T_{β_m};

7   Average the mean squared prediction error for each of models, and use the 1-SE rule to select the complexity parameter β_*;

8 Return the subtree of T_0 that corresponds to β_*;

The task of building an optimal regression tree is related to choosing the optimal complexity parameter α. This can be accomplished by cross-validation. The detailed steps are given in Algorithm 10.1. Instead of selecting the subtree that minimizes the mean squared prediction error, we use the **1-SE rule** to select the subtree to avoid overfitting the data. Under the 1-SE rule, we select the smallest subtree whose mean squared prediction error is within $e_b + se(e_b)$, where e_b is the lowest error estimate and $se(e_b)$ is the standard error of the estimate.

Exercise 10.1. Draw a decision tree corresponding to the split given in Figure 10.1(b).

Exercise 10.2. Describe the recursive binary splitting method for building regression trees.

Exercise 10.3. Describe two approaches for selecting the number of boxes. Why is one approach preferable to the other?

10.1.2 Classification Trees

The process of building a classification tree is similar to that of building a regression tree. Since classification trees are used to predict a qualitative response, however, we cannot use the sum of squared errors to define objective functions or use the mean response of a region to predict the response for a new observation. With a classification tree, we use the mode (i.e., the most frequently occurring value) of a region to predict the response of an observation that belongs to the region.

There are several criteria for choosing classification trees. The first one is **classification error rate** defined by

$$E(R_1, R_2, \ldots, R_J) = \sum_{j=1}^{J} \left(1 - \max_{1 \leq k \leq K} p_{jk} \right), \tag{10.3}$$

where p_{jk} denotes the proportion of observations in R_j that are from the kth class. If the response in each region is dominated by a single class, then the value of E will be close to zero. Given two classification trees with the same number of regions, we prefer the one with lower classification error rate. A disadvantage of the classification error rate is that it is not sensitive for growing trees and does poorly for imbalanced data.

The second criterion is the **Gini index** defined as

$$G(R_1, R_2, \ldots, R_J) = \sum_{j=1}^{J} \sum_{k=1}^{K} p_{jk}(1 - p_{jk}). \tag{10.4}$$

The Gini index measures the total variation across the K classes. If the response in each region is dominated by a single class, then all of the p_{jk}'s are close to zero or one. In such cases, the value of G will close to zero. Given two classification trees with the same number of regions, we prefer the one with lower Gini index.

The third criterion is the **cross-entropy** defined by

$$D(R_1, R_2, \ldots, R_J) = -\sum_{j=1}^{J} \sum_{k=1}^{K} p_{jk} \ln p_{jk}. \tag{10.5}$$

Since

$$\lim_{x \to 0} x \ln x = 0 \text{ and } \lim_{x \to 1} x \ln x = 0,$$

the cross-entropy is close to zero if all of the p_{jk}'s are close to zero or one. The cross-entropy is similar to the Gini index. Given two classification trees with the same number of regions, we prefer the one with lower cross-entropy.

The Gini index and the cross-entropy are more sensitive to tree growing than is the classification error rate. As a result, both the Gini index and the cross-entropy are typically used to measure the quality of a particular split in the classification tree building process. However, all three measures can be used in tree pruning. If the goal is to get a pruned tree that has the lowest classification error rate, then the classification error rate is preferable in the pruning process.

Exercise 10.4. Describe the difference of regression trees and classification trees and compare the process of building a regression tree with that of building a classification tree.

10.2 Prediction Models

In terms of predictive accuracy, tree-based models generally do not perform to the level of other regression and classification approaches. However, aggregating many decision trees has the potential to improve the predictive accuracy significantly. In this section, we introduce some prediction models that aggregate trees. In particular, we introduce bagging, boosting, and random forests, which can be used to improve statistical learning methods in terms of predictive accuracy.

10.2.1   Bagging

Bagging is a general-purpose method for reducing the variance of a statistical learning model. To apply this method to regression trees, we first generate M different bootstrapped training datasets, each of which is a random sample. Then we build a regression tree for each of the M bootstrapped training datasets. These regression trees are grown deep without pruning. Finally, we average all the predictions from the M regression trees:

$$f_{bag}(\mathbf{x}) = \frac{1}{M} \sum_{l=1}^{M} f_l(\mathbf{x}), \tag{10.6}$$

where $f_l(\mathbf{x})$ is the predicted value from the lth regression tree.

To apply bagging to classification trees, the process is similar. However, we cannot just average the predictions because the predictions are qualitative. One possible approach to average all the predictions is to use the mode of the predictions, i.e., the most frequently predicted class.

Bagging can reduce the variance of a tree-based model. However, it is not as straightforward to interpret the resulting model as in the case of a single tree because many trees are combined. One way to mitigate the side effect of the bagging method is to calculate some variable importance measure that gives a summary of the importance of each predictor in splitting the trees.

10.2.2   Boosting

Boosting is another general-purpose method for improving the accuracy of a statistical learning model. Like bagging, boosting also involves creating many trees. In boosting, however, trees are created sequentially. The idea of boosting is to fit a small tree each time to the residuals from the previous tree. A shrunken version of the new tree is added to the previous tree and the residuals are also updated. The process is repeated many times to arrive at a final boosted model.

Algorithm 10.2 shows the pseudo-code of the boosting method for regression trees. From the pseudo-code, we see that the trees are created sequentially and each tree is created based on a previous tree. The final boosted model is

$$f(\mathbf{x}) = \sum_{l=1}^{M} \lambda f_l(\mathbf{x}),$$

where f_l is the lth tree created in the boosting process.

Algorithm 10.2: Pseudo-code of the boosting method for regression trees.

Input: A training dataset $\{(\mathbf{x}_i, y_i) : i = 1, 2, \ldots, n\}$, J, M, λ
Output: The boosted model

1 Set $f(\mathbf{x}_i) = 0$ and $e_i = y_i$ for all $i = 1, 2, \ldots, n$;
2 **for** $l = 1$ *to* M **do**
3   Fit a regression tree f_l with J regions to the dataset
        $\{(\mathbf{x}_i, e_i) : i = 1, 2, \ldots, n\}$;
        `/* Update f by adding a shrunken version of the new`
           `tree.`   `*/`
4     $f \leftarrow f + \lambda f_l$;
        `/* Update the residuals.`   `*/`
5     $e_i \leftarrow e_i - \lambda f_l(\mathbf{x}_i)$;
6 **end**
7 Return the boosted model f;

The boosting method requires several tuning parameters: J, M, and λ. The parameter J specifies the size of the new trees created in each step. Usually J is set to be a small number, e.g., $J = 2$. The parameter M specifies how many trees to be created. Usually M is set to a much larger value than J. However, a large value of M can overfit the data. Cross-validation can be used to find an appropriate value for M. The parameter λ is referred to as the shrinkage parameter and is set to a small positive number, e.g., $\lambda = 0.01$. The parameter λ controls the learning speed of the boosting method. A smaller value of λ requires a large value of M to get satisfactory prediction accuracy.

10.2.3 Random Forests

The **random forest method** is similar to the bagging method in that both methods create many trees and average these trees to create a final model. The difference between the random forest method and the bagging method is in how the trees are created. In the bagging method, each tree is fitted to a bootstrapped training sample by using all the predictors. In the random forest method, however, only a small subset of the predictors is used to fit a tree to a bootstrapped training sample.

In bagging, the trees are highly correlated because all predictors are considered to decide each split. In the random forest method, the trees are not highly correlated because only a subset of the predictors is considered to decide each split. Since the trees created in the random forest method are less correlated, the average of these trees has less variance and is more reliable.

The number of predictors used for each split is a tuning parameter of the random forest method. Suppose that the dataset has k predictors. Typically, the random forest method uses about $\sqrt{k}$ predictors for each split to create a tree. If all the predictors are used, then the random forest method is the same as the bagging method.

10.3   Comparison with Linear Models

The tree-based models introduced in this chapter are quite different from the linear models introduced in previous chapters. Tree-based models have the following form:

$$y = \sum_{j=1}^{J} I_{R_j}(\mathbf{x}) \mu_j.$$

In contrast, linear models have the following form:

$$y = f(\beta_0 + \beta_1 x_1 + \ldots + \beta_k x_k).$$

To determine which model to use for a particular problem, we can follow the following rule of thumb. If the response and the predictors are thought to have an approximately linear relationship, then linear models are likely to outperform tree-based models, which do not exploit the linear structure. If the relationship between the response and the predictors is nonlinear or interactions exist between variables, then tree-based models may outperform linear models. The relative performance of linear models and tree-based models can be assessed by out-of-sample validation techniques, which can be used to measure the accuracy of any predictive models.

Exercise 10.5. Describe and compare the three prediction models: bagging, boosting, and random forests.

10.4   Summary

In this chapter, we introduced tree-based models, which are useful alternatives to the linear models introduced in previous chapters. An advantage of tree-based models is that they are easy to understand and interpret. When a single tree is used, however, tree-based models do not perform as well as linear models in terms of predictive accuracy. To improve the predictive accuracy, we introduced some prediction models such as bagging, boosting, and random forests, which are general-purpose methods for improving the accuracy of statistical learning models. For more information about tree-based models, readers are referred to (Breiman et al., 1984) and (James et al., 2013, Chapter 8).

10.5 End-of-Chapter Exercises

Exercise 10.6. Consider the following dataset

i	x_{i1}	x_{i2}	y_i
1	1	2	8
2	2	1	6
3	2	3	14
4	3	1	8
5	3	2	13

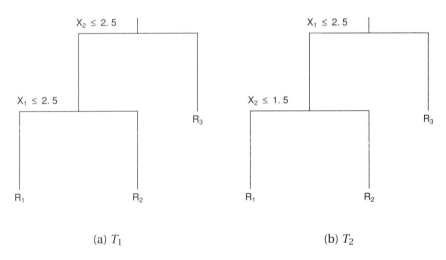

(a) T_1 (b) T_2

Figure 10.3: *Two decision trees For Exercise 10.6.*

Figure 10.3 shows two decision trees for the dataset.

(a) For each decision tree, calculate the mean responses μ_1, μ_2, and μ_3 of the regions R_1, R_2, and R_3, respectively.

(b) For each decision tree, calculate the value of the objective function defined in Equation (10.1). In terms of the objective function values, which decision tree is better?

(c) Use each decision tree to predict the response at $(2,2)$.

Exercise 10.7. Use the recursive binary splitting method to build a regression tree with three boxes for the dataset given in Exercise 10.6.

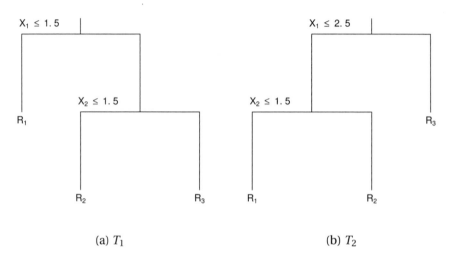

(a) T_1 (b) T_2

Figure 10.4: *Two decision trees for Exercise 10.8.*

Exercise 10.8. Consider the following dataset

i	x_{i1}	x_{i2}	y_i
1	1	1	C
2	1	2	C
3	1	3	B
4	2	1	C
5	2	3	A
6	3	1	B
7	3	2	A
8	3	3	A

Figure 10.4 shows two decision trees for the above dataset. Calculate the classification error, the Gini index, and the cross-entropy for each of the two decision trees.

Chapter 11

Case Study: Decision Trees

In this chapter, we illustrate how to apply tree-based models to solve a real-world problem in insurance. In particular, we introduce how to estimate the fair market values of the guarantees embedded in variable annuities using regression trees. After working through this case study, readers will be able to

- Fit regression trees to data
- Calculate and understand various validation measures
- Evaluate the out-of-sample performance of models
- Use prediction models such as bagging, boosting, and random forests to improve regression trees

11.1   Preparing Data

In this case study, we use the same dataset used in Chapter 5. For a description of the problem and the dataset, readers can read Chapter 5.

To fit regression trees to this dataset, we first load the dataset into R as follows:

```
1  inforce <- read.csv("inforce10k.csv")
2  fmv <- read.csv("fmv_seriatim.csv")
```

Then we merge the inforce data and the fair market values by the following R code:

```
1  inforce2 <- merge(inforce, fmv, by.x = "recordID", by.y =
       "RecordID")
```

Finally, we select the variables and split the dataset into a training set and a test set as follows:

```
1  vNames <- c("recordID", "gender", "prodType", "issueDate"
     , "matDate", "age", "gmdbAmt", "gmwbAmt", "
     gmwbBalance", "gmmbAmt", "withdrawal", paste("
     FundValue", 1:10, sep=""), "fmv")
2  dat10k <- inforce2[,vNames]
3
4  set.seed(1)
5  vInd <- sample(1:nrow(dat10k), size=1000)
6  dat10kTrain <- dat10k[vInd,]
7  dat10kTest <- dat10k[-vInd,]
```

As mentioned in Section 5.4, we select these variables to build a predictive model because these variables are used to calculate the fair market values and are not constants.

11.2 Fitting Regression Trees

Instead of implementing the recursive binary splitting algorithm, we use existing R packages to fit regression trees to the data. There are two commonly used R packages for tree-based models: `tree` and `rpart`. In this case study, we use the `rpart` package to fit regression trees.

To use the `rpart` package, we first load the package with the following code:

```
1  library(rpart)
```

Then we can fit a regression tree to the training dataset by using the `rpart` function:

```
1  tree1 <- rpart(fmv ~ . - recordID, data=dat10kTrain,
     method = "anova")
```

The `rpart` requires three arguments: the formula, the data, and the method. The formula is similar to the formula used in regression modeling function such as `lm` and `glm`. Since our dependent variable is continuous, we use the anova method for the `rpart` function.

Once we have fitted the regression tree, we can see the tree as follows:

```
1  > tree1
2  n= 1000
3
4  node), split, n, deviance, yval
5        * denotes terminal node
```

```
 1) root 1000 922451000000   18647.160
   2) prodType=DBRP,DBRU,WB 598 243614000000    4360.767
     4) age< 56.45753 444   87410390000     1054.518
       8) gmwbAmt< 16396.94 376   40774990000    -1418.781 *
       9) gmwbAmt>=16396.94 68   31617300000   14730.410 *
     5) age>=56.45753 154 137357000000   13893.070
      10) gmdbAmt< 460547.1 133   31138410000     6364.449 *
      11) gmdbAmt>=460547.1 21   50936600000   61574.320
        22) matDate< 47369.5 10    2696859000   20865.790 *
        23) matDate>=47369.5 11   16602590000   98582.070 *
   3) prodType=MB,WBSU 402 375224100000   39899.050
     6) gmwbBalance< 327097.5 313 133380800000   29104.500
      12) FundValue2< 46231.89 209   52947850000
          22917.500 *
      13) FundValue2>=46231.89 104   56355120000
          41538.000
        26) gmmbAmt< 348539.3 66   23384740000   33695.020
            *
        27) gmmbAmt>=348539.3 38   21859330000   55160.010
            *
     7) gmwbBalance>=327097.5 89   77106940000   77861.900
      14) gmwbBalance< 506272.7 62   20783470000
          67418.250 *
      15) gmwbBalance>=506272.7 27   34032820000
          101843.600 *
```

The above output shows how the splits of the regression tree are done. In particular, we see the rules for splitting the node, the number of observations, and the mean response. For example, the root node contains all the observations and is split into two nodes by the variable prodType. Observations with a prodType value of DBRP, DBRU, and WB belong to the left child; observations with a prodType value of MB and WBSU belong to the right child.

To visualize the regression tree, we can plot the tree by using the following code:

```
par(mar=c(1,1,1,1))
plot(tree1, uniform=T, margin=0.05)
text(tree1, use.n = TRUE)
```

In the above code, we first plot the regression tree using the plot function. Then we add labels to the tree by using the text function. The resulting regression tree is shown in Figure 11.1.

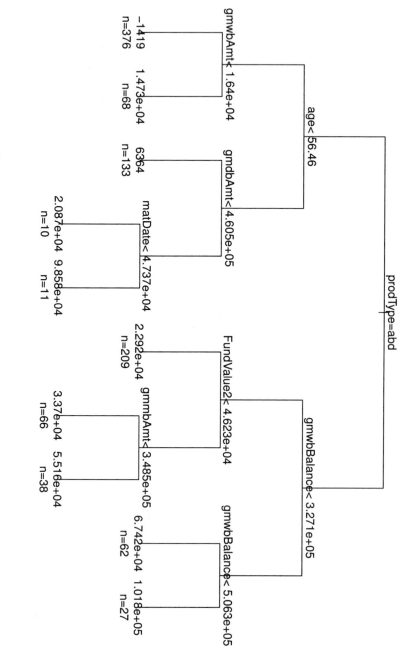

Figure 11.1: A regression tree fitted to the training dataset.

The regression tree shown in Figure 11.1 shows how each node is split. If a categorical variable is used to split a node, the rule is specified by letters. For example, the rule prodType=abd in the root node means that observations in the first, second, and fourth categories of the prodType variable belong to the left child. You can see the order of the categories by using the levels function as follows:

```
> levels(dat10kTrain$prodType)
[1] "DBRP"  "DBRU"  "MB"    "WB"    "WBSU"
```

In the terminal nodes of the tree, we also see the number of observations and the mean response.

The measures of variable importance can be obtained from the summary of the tree object as follows:

```
> vImp <- tree1summary$variable.importance
> vImp
     prodType   gmwbBalance       gmwbAmt       gmdbAmt
 303612846550  263078933815  230820036350  219885957953
     gmmbAmt    FundValue2       matDate    FundValue8
 171616339078   63028624946   31637150837   27584439384
   withdrawal    FundValue1     issueDate    FundValue7
  25356189686   23390915917   22146005586   19083126852
          age   FundValue10    FundValue6    FundValue9
  18846660005   16456012052   11272072258    7403880331
   FundValue4    FundValue3    FundValue5
   4385944289    2631566573    2631566573
```

The measure of variable importance for a variable is the sum of the goodness-of-split measures for each split that the variable is used as the primary or surrogate variable[1]. We can scale these measures and plot them in a bar plot as follows:

```
vImp <- vImp * 100 / max(vImp)
ind <- order(vImp)
par(las=2) # make label text perpendicular to axis
par(mar=c(3,8,1,1)) # increase y-axis margin.
barplot(vImp[ind], main="", horiz=TRUE, names.arg=names(
    vImp[ind]))
```

The resulting bar plot is shown in Figure 11.2, from which we see that the most important variable is prodType.

---

[1]A surrogate variable is used to split an observation if the primary variable has missing values in the observation.

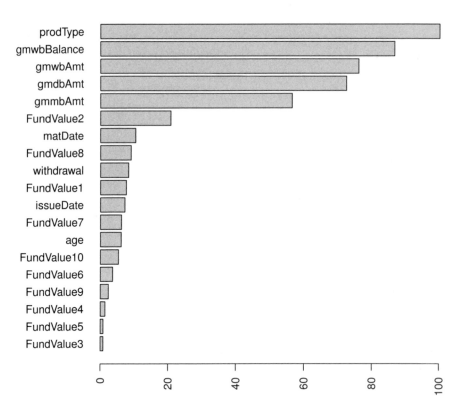

Figure 11.2: *Variables ordered by the scaled importance measures.*

Exercise 11.1. Consider the regression tree fitted by the following code:

```
tree1 <- rpart(fmv ~ . - recordID, data=dat10kTrain,
    method = "anova")
```

(a) Find out the observations in the training dataset that belong to Node 10. (The rules can be found in the output if you type tree1 in the R Console.)

(b) Calculate the mean response of Node 10.

11.3   Pruning Trees

To prune the regression tree, we first need to select an optimal value for the complexity parameter α. We use the 1-SE rule to select the complexity parameter. To do that, we print the complexity parameter table as follows:

```
> printcp(tree1)

Regression tree:
rpart(formula = fmv ~ . - recordID, data = dat10kTrain,
    method = "anova")

Variables actually used in tree construction:
[1] age            FundValue2  gmdbAmt     gmmbAmt
[5] gmwbAmt        gmwbBalance matDate     prodType

Root node error: 9.2245e+11/1000 = 922450994

n= 1000

          CP nsplit rel error   xerror       xstd
1 0.329137       0   1.00000  1.00342  0.076924
2 0.178585       1   0.67086  0.68783  0.065632
3 0.040180       2   0.49228  0.51395  0.054901
4 0.034297       4   0.41192  0.48167  0.050366
5 0.026102       5   0.37762  0.45962  0.042111
6 0.024165       6   0.35152  0.44755  0.041011
7 0.016281       7   0.32735  0.43594  0.037977
8 0.012045       8   0.31107  0.41936  0.037239
9 0.010000       9   0.29903  0.41436  0.037158
```

The table shows the complexity parameter values (the CP column), the corresponding cross-validation errors (the xerror column), and the standard errors of the error estimates (the xstd column). The number of splits is also shown in the table. Using the 1-SE rule, we select the complexity parameter value of the smallest subtree whose xerror is lower than the lowest xerror plus its xstd. In this case, the lowest xerror plus its xstd is $0.41436 + 0.037158 = 0.451518$. The smallest subtree whose error estimate is less than 0.451518 has 6 splits or 7 terminal nodes. The corresponding complexity parameter is 0.024165.

We can also plot the error estimates as a function of the complexity parameter α as follows:

```
1 > par(mar=c(4,4,3,1))
2 > plotcp(tree1)
```

The resulting plot is shown in Figure 11.3 The dotted horizontal line corresponds to the lowest error estimate plus its standard error. From the figure, we see that the subtree with 7 splits is the best subtree according to the 1-SE rule.

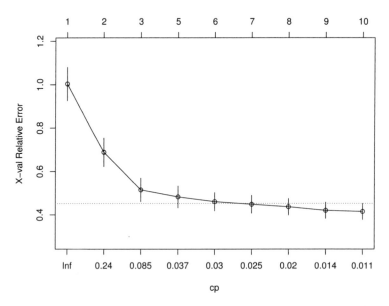

Figure 11.3: *Cross-validation errors for different complexity parameter values.*

Now we have selected an optimal value of the complexity parameter. We can prune the regression tree and plot the tree as follows:

```
1 tree2 <- prune(tree1, cp=0.02)
2 dev.new(width=10,height=6)
```

```
3 par(mar = c(1,1,1,1))
4 plot(tree2, uniform=T, margin=0.05)
5 text(tree2, use.n = TRUE)
```

We used a complexity parameter of 0.02. In fact, we can use any values in the interval (0.016281, 0.024165] because the complexity parameters in this interval share the same subtree. The pruned regression tree is shown in Figure 11.4.

11.4 Prediction with a Single Tree

We have fitted a regression tree to the training dataset. We can use the fitted regression tree to predict the response for the test dataset. To do that, we use the predict function as follows:

```
1 > yhat_tree1 <- predict(tree1, dat10kTest)
2 > head(yhat_tree1)
3          1         2         3         4         5
4  -1418.781 -1418.781 -1418.781 33695.021 -1418.781
5          6
6  98582.067
```

We can produce a scatter plot between the fair market values calculated by Monte Carlo and those predicted by the regression tree:

```
1 dev.new(width=4, height=4)
2 par(mar=c(4,4,1,1))
3
4 plot(dat10kTest$fmv, yhat_tree1, xlab="Monte Carlo", ylab
     ="Tree model")
```

The resulting scatter plot is shown in Figure 11.5. Since the regression tree model uses the mean response in each terminal node to predict the response of an observation that belongs to the terminal node, the predictions of many observations are the same.

We can calculate the percentage error of the regression tree at the portfolio level by using the following code:

```
1 > totalFMV_mc <- sum(dat10kTest$fmv)
2 > totalFMV_tree1 <- sum(yhat_tree1)
3 > (totalFMV_tree1 - totalFMV_mc) / totalFMV_mc
4 [1] 0.009703155
```

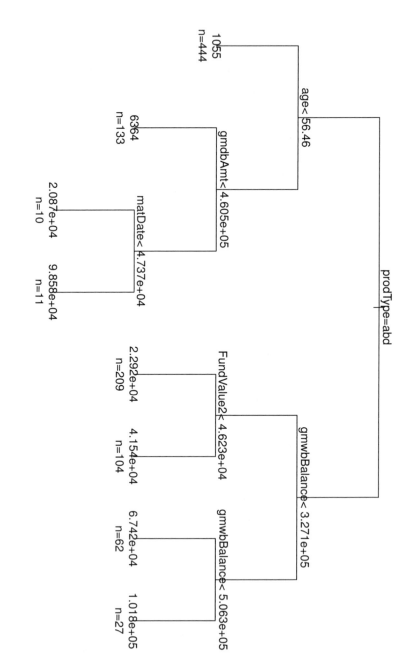

Figure 11.4: A pruned regression tree for the training dataset.

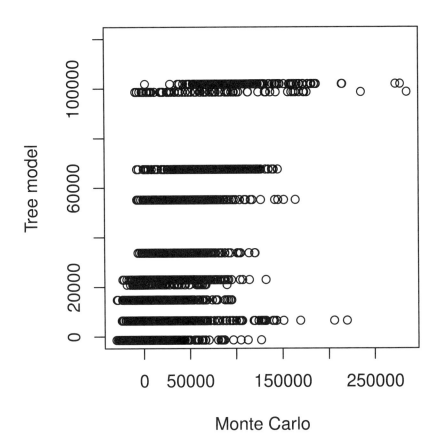

Figure 11.5: *A scatter plot between the fair market values calculated by Monte Carlo and those predicted by the regression tree.*

From the output, we see that the percentage error is about 0.97%, meaning that the total fair market value of the portfolio predicted by the regression tree model is quite close to that calculated by Monte Carlo. We can also calculate the percentage error of the linear regression model:

```
1 > lm1 <- lm(fmv ~ . - recordID, data=dat10kTrain)
2 > yhat_lm1 <- predict(lm1, dat10kTest)
3 > totalFMV_lm1 <- sum(yhat_lm1)
4 > (totalFMV_lm1 - totalFMV_mc) / totalFMV_mc
5 [1] 0.01838693
```

The output shows that the percentage error of the linear regression model is higher that that of the regression tree model. In terms of percentage error at the portfolio level, the regression tree model outperforms the linear regression model.

Exercise 11.2. The R^2 for a general predictive model is defined as

$$R^2 = 1 - \frac{\sum_{i=1}^{n}(y_i - \hat{y}_i)^2}{\sum_{i=1}^{n}(y_i - \bar{y})^2},$$

where y_i denotes the response of the ith observation given in the dataset, $\hat{y}_i$ denotes the response of the ith observation predicted by the predictive model, and $\bar{y}$ is the mean response given in the dataset. Consider the regression tree and the linear regression model fitted by the following code:

```
1  tree1 <- rpart(fmv ~ . - recordID, data=dat10kTrain,
      method = "anova")
2  lm1 <- lm(fmv ~ . - recordID, data=dat10kTrain)
```

Calculate the R^2 for the two models based on the test dataset dat10kTest. Based on the R^2, which model provides a better fit?

Exercise 11.3. Consider the regression trees fitted by the following code:

```
1  tree1 <- rpart(fmv ~ . - recordID, data=dat10kTrain,
      method = "anova")
2  tree2 <- prune(tree1, cp=0.02)
```

The second regression tree is a pruned tree. Calculate the R^2 of the two trees for the test dataset dat10kTest. Based on the R^2, which tree provides a better fit to the test dataset?

11.5 Prediction with Many Trees

In this section, we apply the prediction models such as bagging, boosting, and random forests to predict the response. For bagging and random forests, we use the R package randomForest. Bagging is a special case of random forests when all predictors are used to split a node.

We perform bagging as follows:

```
1 > set.seed(1)
2 > bag1 <- randomForest(formula=fmv ~ . - recordID, data=
    dat10kTrain, mtry=20, importance=TRUE)
3 > bag1
4
5 Call:
6  randomForest(formula = fmv ~ . - recordID, data =
       dat10kTrain,        mtry = 20, importance = TRUE)
7                  Type of random forest: regression
8                        Number of trees: 500
9 No. of variables tried at each split: 20
10
11           Mean of squared residuals: 220022345
12                     % Var explained: 76.15
```

We set mtry to 20, which is the number of predictors of the dataset. To see how the bagged model performs, we can use it to predict the response of the test dataset:

```
1 > yhat_bag1 <- predict(bag1, dat10kTest)
2 > dev.new(width=4, height=4)
3 > par(mar=c(4,4,1,1))
4 > plot(dat10kTest$fmv, yhat_bag1, xlab="Monte Carlo",
    ylab="Bagged Tree model")
5 > abline(0,1)
```

The scatter plot between the fair market values calculated by Monte Carlo and those predicted by the bagged model is shown in Figure 11.6. Comparing Figure 11.6 with Figure 11.5, we see that the scatter plot produced by the bagged model is much better.

Creating a random forest is the same as bagging except that we use a smaller value for the argument mtry:

```
1 > set.seed(1)
2 > bag2 <- randomForest(formula=fmv ~ . - recordID, data=
    dat10kTrain, mtry=4, importance=TRUE)
3 > bag2
4
5 Call:
6  randomForest(formula = fmv ~ . - recordID, data =
       dat10kTrain,        mtry = 4, importance = TRUE)
7                  Type of random forest: regression
8                        Number of trees: 500
9 No. of variables tried at each split: 4
```

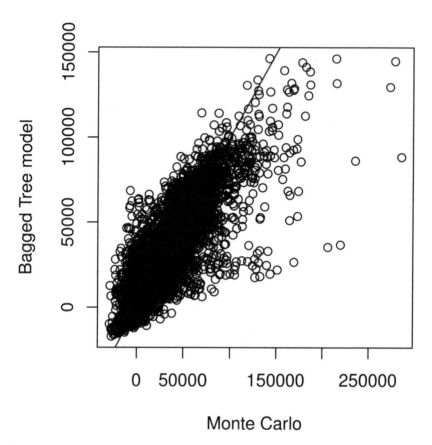

Figure 11.6: *A scatter plot between the fair market values calculated by Monte Carlo and those predicted by the bagged model.*

```
10
11          Mean of squared residuals: 258321147
12                   % Var explained: 72
```

To see the performance of the random forest of the regression trees, we proceed as follows:

```
1 > yhat_bag2 <- predict(bag2, dat10kTest)
2 > dev.new(width=4, height=4)
3 > par(mar=c(4,4,1,1))
4 > plot(dat10kTest$fmv, yhat_bag2, xlab="Monte Carlo",
      ylab="Bagged Tree model")
5 > abline(0,1)
```

The scatter plot produced by the above code is shown in Figure 11.7. If we compare Figures 11.6 and 11.7, we see that the random forest performs similarly to the bagged model.

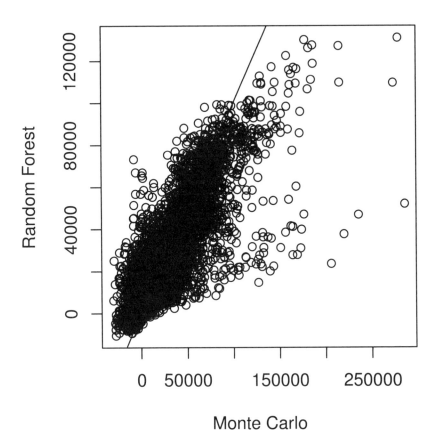

Figure 11.7: *A scatter plot between the fair market values calculated by Monte Carlo and those predicted by the random forest.*

To fit boosted regression trees, we use the gbm function from the gbm package as follows:

```
> set.seed(1)
> boost1 <- gbm(formula=fmv ~ . - recordID , data=
    dat10kTrain , distribution="gaussian", n.trees=5000,
    interaction.depth=3)
> summary(boost1)
                  var         rel.inf
gmwbBalance gmwbBalance  29.669398764
```

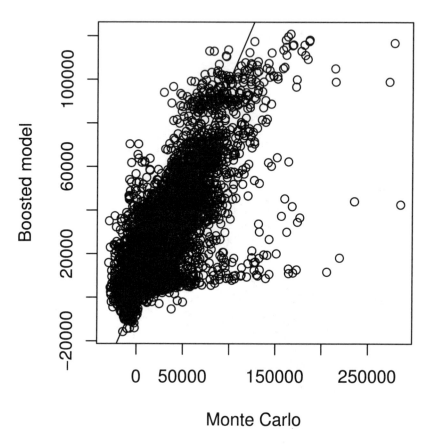

Figure 11.8: *A scatter plot between the fair market values calculated by Monte Carlo and those predicted by the boosted model.*

```
 6 prodType      prodType  25.014841257
 7 gmwbAmt       gmwbAmt   10.492172473
 8 age                age   6.976059405
 9 gmmbAmt       gmmbAmt    6.655199472
10 gmdbAmt       gmdbAmt    4.406193262
11 FundValue2    FundValue2 4.380892866
12 matDate        matDate   2.197005041
13 issueDate    issueDate   1.935611055
14 FundValue8    FundValue8 1.881573088
15 FundValue4    FundValue4 1.708283092
16 FundValue7    FundValue7 1.654809913
17 FundValue9    FundValue9 0.897291196
18 FundValue10  FundValue10 0.697465456
```

19	FundValue3	FundValue3	0.470416527
20	withdrawal	withdrawal	0.315998536
21	FundValue1	FundValue1	0.306106116
22	FundValue5	FundValue5	0.234908884
23	FundValue6	FundValue6	0.100482383
24	gender	gender	0.005291214

In the above function gbm, we set the number of trees to 5000 and limit the depth of each tree to 3. Since the response is continuous, we set the distribution to gaussian. The summary of the boosted model shows the relative influence of the predictors. From the output, we see that gmwbBalance, prodtype, and gmwbAmt are the most important variables.

To see the out-of-sample performance of the boosted model, we proceed as follows:

```
1 > yhat_boost1 <- predict(boost1, newdata=dat10kTest, n.
     trees=5000)
2 > dev.new(width=4, height=4)
3 > par(mar=c(4,4,1,1))
4 > plot(dat10kTest$fmv, yhat_boost1, xlab="Monte Carlo",
     ylab="Boosted model")
5 > abline(0,1)
```

The scatter plot produced by the above code is shown in Figure 11.8. If we compare Figures 11.8, 11.6, and 11.7, we see that the boosted model performs similarly to the bagged model.

Exercise 11.4. Using the test dataset dat10kTest, calculate the R^2 for the following three models:

```
1 set.seed(1)
2 bag1 <- randomForest(formula=fmv ~ . - recordID, data=
     dat10kTrain, mtry=20, importance=TRUE)
3 set.seed(1)
4 bag2 <- randomForest(formula=fmv ~ . - recordID, data=
     dat10kTrain, mtry=4, importance=TRUE)
5 set.seed(1)
6 boost1 <- gbm(formula=fmv ~ . - recordID, data=
     dat10kTrain, distribution="gaussian", n.trees=5000,
     interaction.depth=3)
```

In terms of the R^2, which model performs the best?

11.6 Summary

In this chapter, we demonstrated how to build tree-based models by using the variable annuity dataset from a previous chapter. In particular, we introduced how to fit regression trees and use the fitted trees to predict the responses of new observations. In addition, we introduced how to create bagged models, boosted models, and random forests for improved predictions. For more examples of tree-based models, readers are referred to (James et al., 2013).

11.7 End-of-Chapter Exercises

Exercise 11.5. Consider the demand for term life insurance dataset used in Chapter 7 (i.e., `termlifepos.csv`). The dataset is split into training and testing subsets as follows:

```
1 term <- read.csv("termlifepos.csv")
2 term$gender <- factor(term$gender)
3 term$marstat <- factor(term$marstat)
4 set.seed(1)
5 ind <- sample(1:nrow(term), 300)
6 termTrain <- term[ind,]
7 termTest <- term[-ind,]
```

(a) Use the `rpart` package to fit a classification tree using the training subset `termTrain`.

(b) Plot and interpret the classification tree.

(c) Create a bar plot of the variable importance and interpret.

(d) Use the classification tree to predict the response variable for the testing subset `termTest` and produce the confusion matrix.

(e) Repeat (d) using bagging, boosting, and random forests. Which model is the best in terms of prediction accuracy?

Part II

Unsupervised Learning

Chapter 12

Data Clustering

In this chapter, we introduce data clustering, which refers to a process of finding homogeneous groups or clusters in a dataset. Unlike the linear models and tree-based models introduced in previous chapters, data clustering is a form of unsupervised learning and works with unlabeled data, that is, the dependent variable is not required.

12.1   The Basics of Data Clustering

Data clustering, also known as **cluster analysis**, refers to a process of dividing a set of objects into groups or clusters such that objects in the same clusters are similar and objects in different clusters are quite distinct. An object is also referred to as a record, an individual, an item, a data point, or an observation. In data clustering, we typically work with the cases-by-variables data structure, or tabular data structure as shown in Equation (12.1), where each row represents an observation and each column represents a variable, an attribute, or a feature.

$$X = \begin{pmatrix} \mathbf{x}_1' \\ \mathbf{x}_2' \\ \vdots \\ \mathbf{x}_n' \end{pmatrix} = \begin{pmatrix} x_{11} & x_{12} & \cdots & x_{1d} \\ x_{21} & x_{22} & \cdots & x_{2d} \\ \vdots & \vdots & \ddots & \vdots \\ x_{n1} & x_{n2} & \cdots & x_{nd} \end{pmatrix} \tag{12.1}$$

A variable can be broadly classified as discrete or continuous. A **discrete variable** usually takes on a limited number of values; while a **continuous variable** can take on a value between any two values. In terms of measurement scales, a variable can be classified as nominal, ordinal, interval, and ratio. **Nominal variables** (also called categorical variables) take discrete values that do not have a natural ordering. Ordinal variables take discrete values that have a natural

191

order. Interval variables take continuous values that have a specific order and equal measurement units. Ratio variables are interval variables where the values have a clearly defined zero. For example, a temperature is considered an interval variable but not a ratio variable because a zero temperature does not indicate "no heat." An account value is an example of ratio variables because $1,000 is twice as much as $500.

Depending on the types of the variables, a dataset can be generally classified as discrete, continuous, or mixed-type. In a discrete dataset, all variables are discrete. In a continuous dataset, all variables are continuous. If a dataset has both discrete and continuous variables, then it is a mixed-type dataset. Clustering algorithms are usually different for different types of datasets.

It is difficult to formally define clusters (Everitt et al., 2011). However, there are some operational definitions of clusters. For example, Bock (1989) suggested the following criteria for data points in a cluster:

(a) Share the same or closely related properties;

(b) Have small mutual distances;

(c) Have "contacts" or "relations" with at least one other data point in the cluster; and

(d) Can be clearly distinguishable from the data points that are not in the cluster.

Figure 12.1 shows two datasets with different types of clusters. The first dataset contains three compact clusters; while the second dataset contains two chained clusters.

Dissimilarity measures (also referred to as **distance measures**) are usually required in data clustering because almost all clustering algorithms rely on some distance measures to define clustering criteria. A distance measure D is a binary function that has the following properties:

(a) $D(\mathbf{x}, \mathbf{x}) \geq 0$ (Nonnegativity);

(b) $D(\mathbf{x}, \mathbf{y}) = D(\mathbf{y}, \mathbf{x})$ (Symmetry);

(c) $D(\mathbf{x}, \mathbf{y}) = 0$ if and only if $\mathbf{x} = \mathbf{y}$ (Reflexivity);

(d) $D(\mathbf{x}, \mathbf{z}) \leq D(\mathbf{x}, \mathbf{y}) + D(\mathbf{y}, \mathbf{z})$ (Triangle inequality),

where $\mathbf{x}, \mathbf{y}$, and $\mathbf{z}$ are arbitrary data points. The smaller the distance between two data points, the more similar the two points.

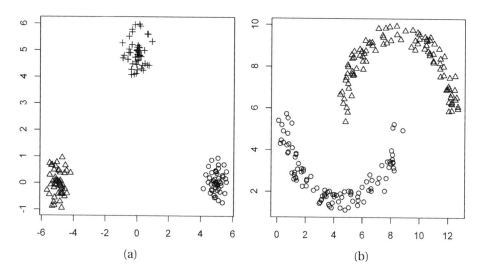

Figure 12.1: *Two datasets with different types of clusters.*

A widely used distance measure for continuous data is the **Minkowski distance** defined by

$$D_{min}(\mathbf{x}, \mathbf{y}) = \left(\sum_{j=1}^{d} |x_j - y_j|^p \right)^{\frac{1}{p}}, \tag{12.2}$$

where d is the dimensionality of the dataset and $p \geq 1$. The well-known **Euclidean distance** is a special case of the Minkowski distance when $p = 2$.

A commonly used distance measure for discrete data (e.g., categorical data) is the simple matching distance defined by

$$D_{sim}(\mathbf{x}, \mathbf{y}) = \sum_{j=1}^{d} \delta(x_j, y_j), \tag{12.3}$$

where $\delta(\cdot, \cdot)$ is defined as

$$\delta(x_j, y_j) = \begin{cases} 0, & \text{if } x_j = y_j, \\ 1, & \text{if } x_j \neq y_j. \end{cases} \tag{12.4}$$

Clustering algorithms can be broadly divided into two categories: partitional clustering algorithms and hierarchical clustering algorithms. A partitional clustering algorithm divides a dataset into a single partition; while a hierarchical clustering algorithm divides a dataset into a sequence of nested partitions. Figure 12.2 shows a diagram of different categories of clustering algorithms.

There are two types of partitional clustering algorithms: hard clustering algorithms (also called crisp clustering algorithms) and soft clustering algorithms (also referred to as fuzzy clustering algorithms). In hard clustering, each data point belongs to exactly one cluster. In soft clustering, a data point can belong to multiple clusters with some weights that specify the degrees of membership.

There are also two types of hierarchical clustering algorithms: agglomerative algorithms and divisive algorithms. An agglomerative hierarchical clustering algorithm uses a bottom-up approach by starting with every data point as a cluster and repeatedly merging the closest pair of clusters based on some criterion until only one cluster is left. In contrast, a divisive hierarchical clustering algorithm uses a top-down approach by starting with the whole dataset as a single cluster and repeatedly splitting large clusters into small ones until every cluster contains only one data point.

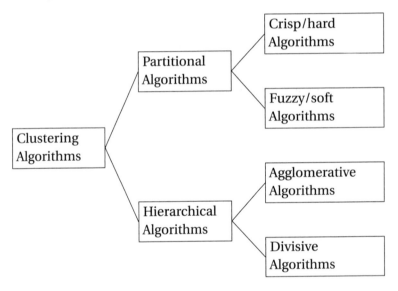

Figure 12.2: *Taxonomy of clustering algorithms.*

Exercise 12.1. For a d-dimensional dataset, the Euclidean distance between two points is defined as

$$D(\mathbf{x}, \mathbf{y}) = \sqrt{\sum_{j=1}^{d} (x_j - y_j)^2}.$$

Show that

(a) For arbitrary real numbers, a_j and b_j, for $j = 1, 2, \ldots, d$, the following inequality holds:

$$\sum_{j=1}^{d} a_j b_j \leq \sqrt{\sum_{j=1}^{d} a_j^2 \sum_{j=1}^{d} b_j^2}.$$

(b) The Euclidean distance $D(\cdot, \cdot)$ satisfies the triangle inequality, i.e.,

$$D(\mathbf{x}, \mathbf{z}) \leq D(\mathbf{x}, \mathbf{y}) + D(\mathbf{y}, \mathbf{z}).$$

Exercise 12.2. Consider the following 2-dimensional dataset [1]:

Point	$V1$	$V2$
$\mathbf{x}_1$	1	2
$\mathbf{x}_2$	1	2.5
$\mathbf{x}_3$	3	1
$\mathbf{x}_4$	4	0.5
$\mathbf{x}_5$	4	2

Calculate the pairwise Euclidean distances for the above dataset.

12.2 Hierarchical Algorithms

As mentioned before, there are two types of hierarchical algorithms: agglomerative algorithms and divisive algorithms. Divisive algorithms are usually more time-consuming than agglomerative algorithms because there are many nontrivial ways to divide a cluster. In this section, we introduce some agglomerative algorithms.

The pseudo-code of a typical agglomerative hierarchical algorithm is shown in Algorithm 12.1. From the pseudo-code, we see that agglomerative hierarchical clustering algorithms require calculating the distances between clusters in order to decide which two clusters to merge at each step. There are different ways

---

[1] This dataset was obtained from (Gan et al., 2007, p119).

to calculate the distances between two clusters. Different ways of calculating distances leads to different agglomerative algorithms.

Algorithm 12.1: Pseudo-code of an agglomerative hierarchical algorithm.

Input: A dataset $\{x_1, x_2, \ldots, x_n\}$
Output: Nested partitions
1 Let C_i be the cluster containing only x_i for $i = 1, 2, \ldots, n$;
2 Calculate the distance between C_i and C_j for all $1 \le i \le n$ and $1 \le j \le k$;
3 **repeat**
4   Merge two clusters that have the minimum distance to form a new cluster;
5   Calculate the distances between the new cluster and the remaining clusters
6 **until** *Only one cluster is left*;
7 Return the nested partitions;

The Lance-Williams formula (Lance and Williams, 1967) is a recurrence formula that calculates the distance between a cluster and another cluster formed by the fusion of two clusters. Let C_i, C_j and C_k be three clusters and let $C_i \cup C_j$ be the cluster formed by the fusion of clusters C_i and C_j. Then, the Lance-Williams formula calculates the distance between C_k and $C_i \cup C_j$ as follows:

$$
\begin{aligned}
& D(C_k, C_i \cup C_j) \\
= \ & \alpha_i D(C_k, C_i) + \alpha_j D(C_k, C_j) + \\
& \beta D(C_i, C_j) + \gamma |D(C_k, C_i) - D(C_k, C_j)|,
\end{aligned} \tag{12.5}
$$

where α_i, α_j, β, and γ are parameters. The subscripts i and j in α_i and α_j indicate that α_i and α_j may depend on the clusters C_i and C_j, respectively. Some commonly used values for these parameters are shown in Table 12.1. Depending on the values of the parameters, agglomerative hierarchical clustering algorithms can be called single-linkage, complete-linkage, group average, weighted group average, Ward's, centroid, and median methods.

In the single-linkage algorithm, the distance between two clusters is the minimum possible distance between a data point in the first cluster and a data point in the second cluster (See Exercise 12.3). In the complete-linkage algorithm, the distance between two clusters is the maximum possible distance between a data point in the first cluster and a data point in the second cluster (See Exercise 12.4).

In the group average algorithm, the distance between two clusters is the average of the distances between the points in two clusters. To see this, we

Table 12.1: *Commonly used values for the parameters of the Lance-Williams formula given in Equation (12.5), where n_i, n_j, and n_k denote the number of data points in clusters C_i, C_j, and C_k, respectively.*

Algorithm	α_i	α_j	β	γ
Single-linkage	$\dfrac{1}{2}$	$\dfrac{1}{2}$	0	$-\dfrac{1}{2}$
Complete-linkage	$\dfrac{1}{2}$	$\dfrac{1}{2}$	0	$\dfrac{1}{2}$
Group average	$\dfrac{n_i}{n_i + n_j}$	$\dfrac{n_j}{n_i + n_j}$	0	0
Weighted group average	$\dfrac{1}{2}$	$\dfrac{1}{2}$	0	0
Centroid	$\dfrac{n_i}{n_i + n_j}$	$\dfrac{n_j}{n_i + n_j}$	$-\dfrac{n_i n_j}{(n_i + n_j)^2}$	0
Median	$\dfrac{1}{2}$	$\dfrac{1}{2}$	$-\dfrac{1}{4}$	0
Ward's	$\dfrac{n_i + n_k}{n_i + n_j + n_k}$	$\dfrac{n_j + n_k}{n_i + n_j + n_k}$	$-\dfrac{n_k}{n_i + n_j + n_k}$	0

assume that

$$D(C, C') = \frac{1}{|C| \cdot |C'|} \sum_{\mathbf{x} \in C, \mathbf{y} \in C'} D(\mathbf{x}, \mathbf{y}),$$

where C and C' are two nonempty, mutually exclusive clusters, $|C|$ denotes the number of points in C, and $D(\mathbf{x}, \mathbf{y})$ denotes the distance between two points. Then from the Lance-Williams formula, we have

$$
\begin{aligned}
&D(C_k, C_i \cup C_j) \\
=\ &\frac{|C_i|}{|C_i| + |C_j|} \frac{\sum_{\mathbf{x} \in C_k, \mathbf{y} \in C_i} D(\mathbf{x}, \mathbf{y})}{|C_k| \cdot |C_i|} + \frac{|C_j|}{|C_i| + |C_j|} \frac{\sum_{\mathbf{x} \in C_k, \mathbf{y} \in C_j} D(\mathbf{x}, \mathbf{y})}{|C_k| \cdot |C_j|} \\
=\ &\frac{1}{(|C_i| + |C_j|)|C_k|} \sum_{\mathbf{x} \in C_k, \mathbf{y} \in C_i \cup C_j} D(\mathbf{x}, \mathbf{y}). \tag{12.6}
\end{aligned}
$$

Hierarchical clustering results can be visualized by **dendrograms**. Figure 12.3 shows two examples of dendrograms produced by the single-linkage and the complete-linkage algorithms for the dataset given in Exercise 12.2. The vertical axis shows the distances when two clusters are merged.

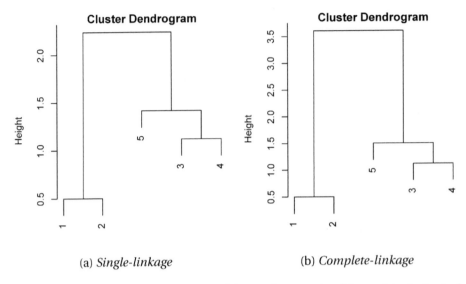

(a) *Single-linkage*   (b) *Complete-linkage*

Figure 12.3: *Dendrograms produced by agglomerative hierarchical clustering algorithms..*

Exercise 12.3. Let C_i, C_j, and C_k be three mutually exclusive and nonempty clusters. Show that under the single-linkage algorithm, the distance between C_k and $C_i \cup C_j$ can be calculated as

$$D(C_k, C_i \cup C_j) = \min\{D(C_k, C_i), D(C_k, C_j)\}.$$

Exercise 12.4. Let C_i, C_j, and C_k be three mutually exclusive and nonempty clusters. Show that under the complete-linkage algorithm, the distance between C_k and $C_i \cup C_j$ can be calculated as

$$D(C_k, C_i \cup C_j) = \max\{D(C_k, C_i), D(C_k, C_j)\}.$$

Exercise 12.5. Consider the dataset given in Exercise 12.2. Let the pairwise Manhattan distances between the data points be given below:

Point 1	Point 2	Distance
1	2	0.5
1	3	3
1	4	4.5
1	5	3
2	3	3.5
2	4	5
2	5	3.5
3	4	1.5
3	5	2
4	5	1.5

Use the Manhattan distance to measure the dissimilarity between individual data points and answer the following questions.

(a) Under the group average algorithm, which two points will be merged first?

(b) Let C_1 be the first cluster formed by merging two points. Calculate the distances between C_1 and the three remaining points under the group average algorithm.

12.3 Partitional Algorithms

The k-**means** algorithm is perhaps the most widely used partitional clustering algorithm due to its simplicity and efficiency. The k-means algorithm was independently developed by Sebestyen (1962) and Macqueen (1967) in the 1960s. Since then, many variants of the k-means algorithm have been developed. In this section, we introduce the traditional k-means algorithm.

The k-means algorithm was developed as a strategy to minimize within-group variation (Thorndike, 1953; Cox, 1957; Fisher, 1958). Given a set of n data points $X = \{\mathbf{x}_1, \mathbf{x}_2, \ldots, \mathbf{x}_n\}$, the k-means algorithm tries to divide the dataset into k clusters by minimizing the following objective function:

$$P(U, Z) = \sum_{l=1}^{k} \sum_{i=1}^{n} u_{il} \|\mathbf{x}_i - \mathbf{z}_l\|^2, \tag{12.7}$$

where k is the desired number of cluster specified by the user, $U = (u_{il})_{n \times k}$ is an $n \times k$ partition matrix, $Z = \{\mathbf{z}_1, \mathbf{z}_2, \ldots, \mathbf{z}_k\}$ is a set of cluster centers, and $\|\cdot\|$ is the

L^2 norm or Euclidean distance, i.e.,

$$\|\mathbf{x} - \mathbf{y}\|^2 = \sum_{j=1}^{d} (x_j - y_j)^2. \tag{12.8}$$

Here d denotes the dimensionality of the dataset.

If the ith data point $\mathbf{x}_i$ belongs to the lth cluster, then $u_{il} = 1$. Otherwise, $u_{il} = 0$. As a result, the partition matrix U satisfies the following conditions:

$$u_{il} \in \{0, 1\}, \quad i = 1, 2, \ldots, n, \, l = 1, 2, \ldots, k, \tag{12.9a}$$

$$\sum_{l=1}^{k} u_{il} = 1, \quad i = 1, 2, \ldots, n. \tag{12.9b}$$

The pseudo-code of the k-means algorithm is shown in Algorithm 12.2. From the pseudo-code, we see that the k-means algorithm consists of two phases: the initialization phase and the iteration phase. In the initialization phase, k initial cluster centers are selected randomly. In the iteration phase, the algorithm repeats updating the cluster memberships and the cluster centers until some criterion is met.

Algorithm 12.2: Pseudo-code of the k-means algorithm.

Input: A dataset X, k
Output: k clusters
1 Initialize $\mathbf{z}_1, \mathbf{z}_2, \ldots, \mathbf{z}_k$ by randomly selecting k points from X;
2 **repeat**
3   Calculate the distance between $\mathbf{x}_i$ and $\mathbf{z}_j$ for all $1 \le i \le n$ and $1 \le j \le k$;
4   Update the partition matrix U according to Equation (12.10);
5   Update cluster centers Z according to Equation (12.11);
6 **until** *No further changes of cluster membership;*
7 Return the partition matrix U and the cluster centers Z;

The partition matrix is updated as follows. Let the cluster centers $Z = \{\mathbf{z}_1, \mathbf{z}_2, \ldots, \mathbf{z}_k\}$ be fixed. Then the objective function given in Equation (12.7) is minimized if and only if

$$u_{il} = \begin{cases} 1, & \text{if } \|\mathbf{x}_i - \mathbf{z}_l\| = \min_{1 \le j \le k} \|\mathbf{x}_i - \mathbf{z}_j\|; \\ 0, & \text{if otherwise,} \end{cases} \tag{12.10}$$

for $i = 1, 2, \ldots, n$ and $l = 1, 2, \ldots, k$.

The cluster centers are updated as follows. Let the partition matrix U be fixed. The objective function given in Equation (12.7) is minimized if and only if

$$z_{lj} = \frac{\sum_{i=1}^{n} u_{il} x_{ij}}{\sum_{i=1}^{n} u_{il}}, \quad l = 1, 2, \ldots, k, \, j = 1, 2, \ldots, d, \tag{12.11}$$

where z_{lj} is the jth component of $\mathbf{z}_l$, x_{ij} is the jth component of $\mathbf{x}_i$, and d is the dimensionality of the dataset.

Exercise 12.6. Let C be a nonempty cluster. Let $\boldsymbol{\mu}_C$ be the center of C, i.e.,

$$\boldsymbol{\mu}_C = \frac{1}{|C|} \sum_{\mathbf{x} \in C} \mathbf{x},$$

where $|C|$ denotes the number of points in C. Show that

$$\sum_{\mathbf{x} \in C} \|\mathbf{x} - \boldsymbol{\mu}_C\|^2 = \frac{1}{2|C|} \sum_{\mathbf{x} \in C} \sum_{\mathbf{y} \in C} \|\mathbf{x} - \mathbf{y}\|^2.$$

12.4 Summary

In this chapter, we introduced basics of data clustering and some clustering algorithms. In particular, we introduced some agglomerative hierarchical clustering algorithms and the traditional k-means algorithms. For more information about data clustering, readers are referred to (Gan et al., 2007) and (Gan, 2011).

12.5 End-of-Chapter Exercises

Exercise 12.7. Consider the following dataset with four points:

	V_1	V_2
A	0	0
B	2	2
C	3	1
D	6	1

(a) Calculate the pairwise Euclidean distances between the points.

(b) Calculate the pairwise Manhattan distances between the points, where the Manhattan distance between two points $\mathbf{x}$ and $\mathbf{y}$ is defined as

$$D(\mathbf{x}, \mathbf{y}) = \sum_{j=1}^{d} |x_j - y_j|.$$

(c) Use the single-linkage algorithm based on the Euclidean distance and the Manhattan distance to cluster the dataset. How are the resulting dendrograms different?

Exercise 12.8. Consider the following dataset:

	V_1	V_2
A	1	1
B	1	2
C	2	1
D	2	3
E	3	1

(a) Let $k = 2$ and initial centers be A and D. What are the partition matrix U and cluster centers Z after the first iteration?

(b) Let $k = 2$ and initial centers be D and E. What are the partition matrix U and cluster centers Z after the first iteration?

Chapter 13

Case Study: Clustering Variable Annuity Policies

In Chapter 5, we used random sampling to select representative variable annuity policies to build a predictive model. In this chapter, we introduce how to use a clustering algorithm to select representative policies. Selecting representative policies is an important step in developing predictive models for the valuation of large portfolios of variable annuities. For our purpose, the hierarchical k-means algorithm is a suitable clustering algorithm for our dataset.

13.1   Hierarchical k-means

The clustering algorithms introduced in the previous chapter focus on dividing a dataset into a small number of clusters. When the clustering results are used as input in subsequent steps to build predictive models, we need a large number of clusters to produce accurate predictions. Most existing clustering algorithms, including k-means and hierarchical algorithms, are not efficient in dividing a large dataset into a large number of clusters. In this section, we introduce the hierarchical k-means algorithm, which combines divisive hierarchical clustering and k-means, for efficiently dividing a large dataset into a large number of clusters.

Algorithm 13.1 shows the pseudo-code of the hierarchical k-means algorithm. In this algorithm, we divide an existing cluster into two at each step. The clustering result is similar to a binary tree.

Algorithm 13.1: Pseudo-code of the hierarchical k-means algorithm.

Input: A dataset X, k

Output: k clusters

1 Apply the k-means algorithm to divide the dataset into two clusters;

2 **repeat**

3 | Apply the k-means algorithm to divide the largest existing cluster into two clusters;

4 **until** *The number of clusters is equal to k*;

5 Return the k clusters;

Exercise 13.1. Let n and k denote the size of the dataset and the desired number of clusters, respectively. Why is the k-means algorithm much slower than the hierarchical k-means algorithm when both n and k are large?

13.2 Preparing Data

To perform data clustering, we first need to load the data into R. We can load the data in the same way as we did in Chapter 5:

```
> inforce <- read.csv("inforce10k.csv")
> fmv <- read.csv("fmv_seriatim.csv")
> names(inforce)
  [1] "recordID"       "survivorShip"      "gender"
  [4] "prodType"       "issueDate"         "matDate"
  [7] "birthDate"      "currentDate"       "age"
 [10] "baseFee"        "riderFee"          "gmdbAmt"
 [13] "dbRollUpRate"   "gmwbAmt"           "gmwbBalance"
 [16] "wbRollUpRate"   "wbWithdrawalRate"  "gmmbAmt"
 [19] "mbRollUpRate"   "withdrawal"        "ttm"
 [22] "FundNum1"       "FundValue1"        "FundFee1"
 [25] "FundNum2"       "FundValue2"        "FundFee2"
 [28] "FundNum3"       "FundValue3"        "FundFee3"
 [31] "FundNum4"       "FundValue4"        "FundFee4"
 [34] "FundNum5"       "FundValue5"        "FundFee5"
 [37] "FundNum6"       "FundValue6"        "FundFee6"
```

```
17 [40]  "FundNum7"              "FundValue7"              "FundFee7"
18 [43]  "FundNum8"              "FundValue8"              "FundFee8"
19 [46]  "FundNum9"              "FundValue9"              "FundFee9"
20 [49]  "FundNum10"             "FundValue10"             "FundFee10"
21 > names(fmv)
22 [1] "RecordID"  "fmv"
```

Since the fair market values and the policies are saved in different data frames, we can merge them as follows:

```
1 > inforce2 <- merge(inforce, fmv, by.x = "recordID", by.y
    = "RecordID")
```

As mentioned in Chapter 5, some variables contained in the data are not needed for building a regression model. We can create a new data frame with the selected variables as follows:

```
1 > vNames <- c("recordID", "gender", "prodType", "
    issueDate", "matDate", "age", "gmdbAmt", "gmwbAmt", "
    gmwbBalance", "gmmbAmt", "withdrawal", paste("
    FundValue", 1:10, sep=""), "fmv")
2 > dat10k <- inforce2[,vNames]
```

Now we can prepare the data for clustering purpose. Since the hierarchical k-means algorithm applies to numerical data only, we need to convert the categorical variables (e.g., gender and prodType) to dummy variables. This can be done as follows:

```
1  > X <- model.matrix(fmv ~ . -1 - recordID, data=dat10k)
2  > summary(X)
3     genderF             genderM             prodTypeDBRU
4   Min.   :0.0000    Min.   :0.0000     Min.   :0.0000
5   1st Qu.:0.0000    1st Qu.:0.0000     1st Qu.:0.0000
6   Median :0.0000    Median :1.0000     Median :0.0000
7   Mean   :0.4071    Mean   :0.5929     Mean   :0.2018
8   3rd Qu.:1.0000    3rd Qu.:1.0000     3rd Qu.:0.0000
9   Max.   :1.0000    Max.   :1.0000     Max.   :1.0000
10    prodTypeMB          prodTypeWB          prodTypeWBSU
11  Min.   :0.0000    Min.   :0.0000     Min.   :0.0000
12  1st Qu.:0.0000    1st Qu.:0.0000     1st Qu.:0.0000
13  Median :0.0000    Median :0.0000     Median :0.0000
14  Mean   :0.1959    Mean   :0.1991     Mean   :0.2004
15  3rd Qu.:0.0000    3rd Qu.:0.0000     3rd Qu.:0.0000
16  Max.   :1.0000    Max.   :1.0000     Max.   :1.0000
17    issueDate           matDate                 age
```

```
18  Min.   :36528      Min.   :42009      Min.   :34.36
19  1st Qu.:37811      1st Qu.:45559      1st Qu.:42.08
20  Median :39077      Median :47084      Median :49.40
21  Mean   :39079      Mean   :47106      Mean   :49.38
22  3rd Qu.:40350      3rd Qu.:48639      3rd Qu.:56.82
23  Max.   :41639      Max.   :52230      Max.   :64.37
24     gmdbAmt            gmwbAmt           gmwbBalance
25  Min.   :     0     Min.   :     0     Min.   :      0
26  1st Qu.:     0     1st Qu.:     0     1st Qu.:      0
27  Median :     0     Median :     0     Median :      0
28  Mean   :135117     Mean   :  7889     Mean   :  94152
29  3rd Qu.:256529     3rd Qu.:15042      3rd Qu.:149781
30  Max.   :986536     Max.   :69404      Max.   :991482
31     gmmbAmt           withdrawal          FundValue1
32  Min.   :     0     Min.   :     0     Min.   :      0
33  1st Qu.:     0     1st Qu.:     0     1st Qu.:      0
34  Median :     0     Median :     0     Median :  12639
35  Mean   : 54715     Mean   : 26349     Mean   :  33325
36  3rd Qu.:     0     3rd Qu.:     0     3rd Qu.:  49292
37  Max.   :499925     Max.   :418565     Max.   :1030517
38    FundValue2         FundValue3          FundValue4
39  Min.   :     0     Min.   :     0     Min.   :      0
40  1st Qu.:     0     1st Qu.:     0     1st Qu.:      0
41  Median : 18844     Median : 12162     Median :  12466
42  Mean   : 43224     Mean   : 28624     Mean   :  27479
43  3rd Qu.: 60463     3rd Qu.: 41359     3rd Qu.:  41114
44  Max.   :1094840    Max.   :672927     Max.   :547874
45    FundValue5         FundValue6          FundValue7
46  Min.   :     0     Min.   :     0     Min.   :      0
47  1st Qu.:     0     1st Qu.:     0     1st Qu.:      0
48  Median : 11326     Median : 14898     Median :  11367
49  Mean   : 24225     Mean   : 35305     Mean   :  28904
50  3rd Qu.: 36498     3rd Qu.: 53520     3rd Qu.:  44194
51  Max.   :477843     Max.   :819144     Max.   :794471
52    FundValue8         FundValue9         FundValue10
53  Min.   :     0     Min.   :     0     Min.   :      0
54  1st Qu.:     0     1st Qu.:     0     1st Qu.:      0
55  Median : 11289     Median :  7591     Median :   6525
56  Mean   : 28745     Mean   : 27191     Mean   :  26666
57  3rd Qu.: 44972     3rd Qu.: 41633     3rd Qu.:  41284
58  Max.   :726032     Max.   :808214     Max.   :709233
```

In the formula used in the model.matrix function, we used "-1" to exclude the intercept because it is not needed in clustering.

Since the hierarchical k-means uses the Euclidean distance to measure the dissimilarity between points, we need to normalize the variables so that no single variable dominates the distance. Since the dummy variables have a range of 1, we use the **minmax normalization** to normalize the variables. Let $X = \{x_1, x_2, \ldots, x_n\}$ denote the dataset after the categorical variables are converted to dummy variables. In the minmax normalization method, the normalized value of x_{ij} is calculated as

$$\frac{x_{ij} - L_j}{H_j - L_j},$$ (13.1)

where L_j and H_j denote the minimum and maximum values of the jth variable, respectively.

We can normalize the dataset as follows:

```
> vMin <- apply(X, 2, min)
> vMax <- apply(X, 2, max)
> X <- (X - matrix(vMin, nrow=nrow(X), ncol= ncol(X),
    byrow=TRUE)) / matrix(vMax-vMin, nrow=nrow(X), ncol=
    ncol(X), byrow=TRUE)
> summary(X)
    genderF              genderM             prodTypeDBRU
 Min.    :0.0000    Min.    :0.0000    Min.    :0.0000
 1st Qu.:0.0000    1st Qu.:0.0000    1st Qu.:0.0000
 Median :0.0000    Median :1.0000    Median :0.0000
 Mean    :0.4071    Mean    :0.5929    Mean    :0.2018
 3rd Qu.:1.0000    3rd Qu.:1.0000    3rd Qu.:0.0000
 Max.    :1.0000    Max.    :1.0000    Max.    :1.0000
    prodTypeMB           prodTypeWB          prodTypeWBSU
 Min.    :0.0000    Min.    :0.0000    Min.    :0.0000
 1st Qu.:0.0000    1st Qu.:0.0000    1st Qu.:0.0000
 Median :0.0000    Median :0.0000    Median :0.0000
 Mean    :0.1959    Mean    :0.1991    Mean    :0.2004
 3rd Qu.:0.0000    3rd Qu.:0.0000    3rd Qu.:0.0000
 Max.    :1.0000    Max.    :1.0000    Max.    :1.0000
    issueDate            matDate              age
 Min.    :0.0000    Min.    :0.0000    Min.    :0.0000
 1st Qu.:0.2510    1st Qu.:0.3473    1st Qu.:0.2572
 Median :0.4987    Median :0.4965    Median :0.5013
 Mean    :0.4990    Mean    :0.4987    Mean    :0.5006
 3rd Qu.:0.7478    3rd Qu.:0.6487    3rd Qu.:0.7484
 Max.    :1.0000    Max.    :1.0000    Max.    :1.0000
    gmdbAmt              gmwbAmt             gmwbBalance
 Min.    :0.000     Min.    :0.0000    Min.    :0.00000
 1st Qu.:0.000     1st Qu.:0.0000    1st Qu.:0.00000
 Median :0.000     Median :0.0000    Median :0.00000
```

```
30   Mean     :0.137      Mean     :0.1137     Mean     :0.09496
31   3rd Qu.:0.260        3rd Qu.:0.2167       3rd Qu.:0.15107
32   Max.     :1.000      Max.     :1.0000     Max.     :1.00000
33        gmmbAmt              withdrawal            FundValue1
34   Min.     :0.0000     Min.     :0.00000    Min.     :0.00000
35   1st Qu.:0.0000       1st Qu.:0.00000      1st Qu.:0.00000
36   Median :0.0000       Median :0.00000      Median :0.01226
37   Mean     :0.1094     Mean     :0.06295    Mean     :0.03234
38   3rd Qu.:0.0000       3rd Qu.:0.00000      3rd Qu.:0.04783
39   Max.     :1.0000     Max.     :1.00000    Max.     :1.00000
40        FundValue2           FundValue3            FundValue4
41   Min.     :0.00000    Min.     :0.00000    Min.     :0.00000
42   1st Qu.:0.00000      1st Qu.:0.00000      1st Qu.:0.00000
43   Median :0.01721      Median :0.01807      Median :0.02275
44   Mean     :0.03948    Mean     :0.04254    Mean     :0.05016
45   3rd Qu.:0.05523      3rd Qu.:0.06146      3rd Qu.:0.07504
46   Max.     :1.00000    Max.     :1.00000    Max.     :1.00000
47        FundValue5           FundValue6            FundValue7
48   Min.     :0.00000    Min.     :0.00000    Min.     :0.00000
49   1st Qu.:0.00000      1st Qu.:0.00000      1st Qu.:0.00000
50   Median :0.02370      Median :0.01819      Median :0.01431
51   Mean     :0.05070    Mean     :0.04310    Mean     :0.03638
52   3rd Qu.:0.07638      3rd Qu.:0.06534      3rd Qu.:0.05563
53   Max.     :1.00000    Max.     :1.00000    Max.     :1.00000
54        FundValue8           FundValue9            FundValue10
55   Min.     :0.00000    Min.     :0.000000   Min.     :0.000000
56   1st Qu.:0.00000      1st Qu.:0.000000     1st Qu.:0.000000
57   Median :0.01555      Median :0.009392     Median :0.009201
58   Mean     :0.03959    Mean     :0.033644   Mean     :0.037599
59   3rd Qu.:0.06194      3rd Qu.:0.051513     3rd Qu.:0.058209
60   Max.     :1.00000    Max.     :1.000000   Max.     :1.000000
```

From the summary, we see that all normalized variables have a range of 1.

13.3 Performing Data Clustering

Once we have the normalized data, we are ready to perform data clustering. Since the hierarchical k-means algorithm produced nested partitions, we need a tree structure to store the clustering results. We use the R package data.tree, which provides a general purpose hierarchical data structure, to create a tree to store the clustering results. After installing this R package, we load the package as follows:

```
1   library(data.tree)
```

We implement the hierarchical *k*-means algorithm as follows:

```
1  hkmean <- function(X, k) {
2    res <- Node$new("Node 0")
3    nCount <- 0
4    tmp <- kmeans(X, 2)
5    for(i in 1:2) {
6        nCount <- nCount + 1
7        nodeA <- res$AddChild(paste("Node", nCount))
8        nodeA$members <- names(which(tmp$cluster==i))
9        nodeA$size <- length(nodeA$members)
10       nodeA$center <- tmp$centers[i,]
11   }
12
13   while(TRUE) {
14     vSize <- res$Get("size", filterFun = isLeaf)
15     if(length(vSize) >= k) {
16        break
17     }
18     maxc <- which(vSize == max(vSize))
19     nodeL <- FindNode(res, names(maxc))
20     tmp <- kmeans(X[nodeL$members,], 2)
21     for(i in 1:2) {
22        nCount <- nCount + 1
23        nodeA <- nodeL$AddChild(paste("Node", nCount))
24        nodeA$members <- names(which(tmp$cluster==i))
25        nodeA$size <- length(nodeA$members)
26        nodeA$center <- tmp$centers[i,]
27     }
28   }
29   return(res)
30 }
```

The function has two arguments: the dataset and the desired number of clusters. At the beginning, we create a root node named "Node 0" with the new method from the R package data.tree. Then we use the R function kmeans to divide the whole dataset into two clusters. We save the results to two child nodes of the root node. We only store the members of the cluster, the cluster size, and the center to a child node. Each node is given a different name created from the number of nodes so far.

In Lines 13-28, we repeatedly apply the *k*-means algorithm to divide the largest leaf node into two clusters until we have *k* leaf nodes. Finally, we return the tree structure to the caller of this function.

Suppose that we want to select 200 representative variable annuity policies.

We use the function hkmean created above to divide the dataset into 200 clusters as follows:

```
1 set.seed(1)
2 res <- hkmean(X, 200)
```

To see the distribution of the cluster sizes, we can create a histogram as follows:

```
1 vSize <- res$Get("size", filterFun = isLeaf)
2 hist(vSize, br=50)
```

In the above code, we get the sizes of all leaf nodes using the function Get from the R package data.tree. The resulting histogram is shown in Figure 13.1. From the histogram, we see that most clusters contain about 50 data points and a few clusters are small.

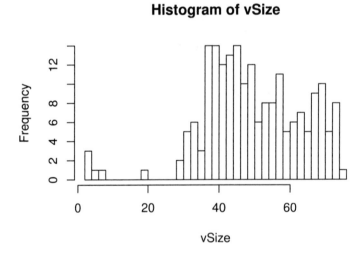

Figure 13.1: *A histogram of the sizes of the 200 clusters.*

The cluster centers in the leaf nodes are not true policies. We need to find the policy in a leaf node that is closest to the center in the leaf node. To do that, we need to use the function Do from the R package data.tree with the following function:

```
1 findPolicy <- function(node, X) {
2   z <- node$center
```

```
3    vD <- apply( (X[node$members,] - matrix(z, nrow=node$
         size, ncol=length(z), byrow=T))^2, 1, sum)
4    iMin <- which(vD == min(vD))
5    node$policy <- node$members[iMin]
6  }
```

The above R function calculates the distances between the center and all policies in a leaf node and saves the policy that is closest to the center to the leaf node.

We use the above function to get the representative policies as follows:

```
1  > res$Do(findPolicy, filterFun = isLeaf, X=X)
2  > vInd <-  res$Get("policy", filterFun = isLeaf)
3  > head(vInd, n=20)
4  Node 317 Node 318 Node 345 Node 346 Node 265 Node 266
5    "7078"   "9309"   "2019"   "9246"   "4569"   "2511"
6  Node 152 Node 249 Node 250 Node 305 Node 306 Node 275
7     "446"   "8933"   "8148"   "3352"    "115"   "8804"
8  Node 276 Node 285 Node 286 Node 251 Node 252 Node 311
9    "6445"   "1088"   "3132"   "3432"   "4064"   "7891"
10 Node 312 Node 253
11   "7630"   "7858"
```

The R variable vInd contains the record identifiers of the representative policies. The name of the leaf node from which the representative policy comes is also shown.

Exercise 13.2. Write a piece of R code to measure the runtime of the hkmean function. How much time did it take to divide the dataset into 200 clusters?

13.4 Predictive Modeling Results

To fit a multiple linear regression model to the selected representative policies, we first create a training dataset with the selected policies:

```
1  > dat10kTrain <- dat10k[vInd,]
2  > summary(dat10kTrain[,c("gender", "prodType")])
3   gender    prodType
4   F: 82     DBRP:41
5   M:118     DBRU:41
```

```
6    MB   :38
7    WB   :40
8    WBSU :40
```

The summary of the categorical variables shows that the proportions of policies in the categories within the training dataset are close to those within the whole dataset.

With the training dataset, we fit a multiple linear regression model as follows:

```
1 > fit1 <- lm(fmv ~ . - recordID, data=dat10kTrain)
2 > summary(fit1)
3
4 Call:
5 lm(formula = fmv ~ . - recordID, data = dat10kTrain)
6
7 Residuals:
8     Min      1Q  Median      3Q     Max
9  -25909   -6186   -1339    4763   73821
10
11 Coefficients:
12                 Estimate Std. Error t value Pr(>|t|)
13 (Intercept)   -1.337e+05  3.268e+04  -4.091 6.54e-05 ***
14 genderM       -8.557e+02  1.863e+03  -0.459 0.646581
15 prodTypeDBRU   1.716e+02  3.866e+03   0.044 0.964638
16 prodTypeMB    -1.061e+03  6.746e+03  -0.157 0.875158
17 prodTypeWB    -9.789e+02  6.406e+03  -0.153 0.878712
18 prodTypeWBSU   3.994e+03  6.145e+03   0.650 0.516612
19 issueDate      2.200e+00  1.362e+00   1.615 0.108023
20 matDate        7.240e-01  9.376e-01   0.772 0.441072
21 age            2.730e+02  1.159e+02   2.356 0.019588 *
22 gmdbAmt        6.969e-02  2.292e-02   3.040 0.002724 **
23 gmwbAmt        9.245e+00  2.434e+00   3.798 0.000200 ***
24 gmwbBalance   -4.444e-01  1.665e-01  -2.668 0.008337 **
25 gmmbAmt        1.916e-01  3.211e-02   5.966 1.31e-08 ***
26 withdrawal    -5.341e-01  1.529e-01  -3.494 0.000602 ***
27 FundValue1    -1.409e-01  6.017e-02  -2.341 0.020342 *
28 FundValue2    -1.213e-02  5.496e-02  -0.221 0.825568
29 FundValue3    -6.989e-02  9.526e-02  -0.734 0.464144
30 FundValue4    -1.659e-02  5.002e-02  -0.332 0.740595
31 FundValue5    -9.090e-02  3.809e-02  -2.387 0.018069 *
32 FundValue6     2.241e-02  5.993e-02   0.374 0.708953
33 FundValue7    -1.541e-01  7.403e-02  -2.082 0.038832 *
34 FundValue8    -7.898e-02  8.260e-02  -0.956 0.340317
35 FundValue9    -1.601e-02  6.974e-02  -0.230 0.818722
36 FundValue10   -1.114e-01  3.232e-02  -3.446 0.000712 ***
```

```
37  ---
38  Signif. codes:
39  0 '***' 0.001 '**' 0.01 '*' 0.05 '.' 0.1 ' ' 1
40
41  Residual standard error: 12680 on 176 degrees of freedom
42  Multiple R-squared:   0.7799,      Adjusted R-squared:
        0.7512
43  F-statistic:  27.12  on  23 and  176 DF,   p-value: < 2.2e-16
```

To see the quality of the representative policies selected by the hierarchical k-means algorithm, we can use the resulting regression model to predict the fair market values for the whole portfolio:

```
1 > yhat <- predict(fit1, dat10k)
2 > dMin <- min(dat10k$fmv)
3 > dMax <- max(dat10k$fmv)
4 > par(mar=c(4,4,1,1))
5 > plot(dat10k$fmv, yhat, xlab="FMV (MC)", ylab="Predicted
      FMV")
6 > lines(c(dMin, dMax), c(dMin, dMax))
```

In the above code, we also plotted the fair market values predicted by the model against those calculated by Monte Carlo. The resulting scatter plot is shown in Figure 13.2. The scatter plot shows that the result looks pretty good even with only 200 representative policies. In fact, the percentage error at the portfolio level is about -4% (see Exercise 13.3).

Exercise 13.3. Let y_i and $\hat{y}_i$ denote the given fair market value and the predicted fair market value of the ith policy in the portfolio, respectively. The percentage error at the portfolio level is defined as

$$\frac{\sum_{i=1}^{n} \hat{y}_i}{\sum_{i=1}^{n} y_i} - 1.$$

Write a piece of R code to calculate the percentage error at the portfolio level for the multiple linear regression model.

Exercise 13.4. Use the following code to select 200 representative policies with random sampling:

```
1 set.seed(1)
2 vInd <- sample(1:nrow(dat10k), 200)
3 dat10kTrain <- dat10k[vInd,]
```

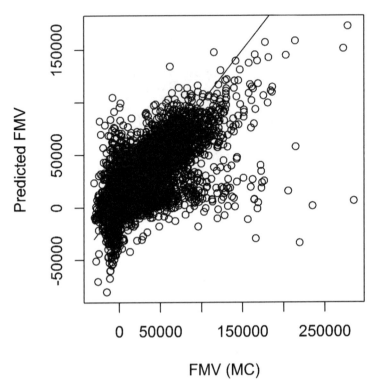

Figure 13.2: *A scatter plot of the fair market values predicted by the model against those calculated by Monte Carlo.*

Then fit a multiple linear regression model using the following code:

```
1 fit1 <- lm(fmv ~ . - recordID, data=dat10kTrain)
```

Calculate the percentage error at the portfolio level based on this model. Between this result and the result based on the representative policies selected by the hierarchical k-means algorithm, which one is better?

13.5 Summary

In this chapter, we illustrated the use of data clustering in life insurance by applying a hierarchical k-means algorithm to select representative variable annuity policies from a large portfolio. We also built a multiple linear regression model based on the clustering result. The result of the regression model shows that the representative policies selected by the clustering algorithm can help the regression model to improve prediction accuracy.

Chapter 14

Principal Component Analysis

Principal component analysis (**PCA**) is a technique for dimension reduction of a high-dimensional dataset. Similar to data clustering, PCA is another popular tool for unsupervised learning. In this chapter, we introduce PCA and, in particular, how to compute principal components.

14.1 Principal Components

Given a multi-dimensional dataset with d variables, PCA finds a low-dimensional representation of the dataset that contains as much as possible of the variation. Each dimension found by PCA is called a **principal component** and is a linear combination of the original d variables.

Let $X_1, X_2, \ldots, X_d$ be a set of variables. The first principal component is a normalized linear combination of the variables that has the largest variance. Mathematically, the first principal component is defined as

$$Z_1 = w_{11} X_1 + w_{12} X_2 + \cdots + w_{1d} X_d, \tag{14.1}$$

where $\mathbf{w}_1 = (w_{11}, w_{12}, \ldots, w_{1d})'$ is a vector of **loadings** such that $\text{Var}(Z_1)$ is maximized subject to the following constraint:

$$\mathbf{w}_1' \mathbf{w}_1 = \sum_{j=1}^{d} w_{1j}^2 = 1. \tag{14.2}$$

The second principal component is defined as

$$Z_2 = w_{21} X_1 + w_{22} X_2 + \cdots + w_{2d} X_d, \tag{14.3}$$

where $\mathbf{w}_2 = (w_{21}, w_{22}, \ldots, w_{2d})'$ is a vector of loadings such that $\mathrm{Var}(Z_2)$ is maximized subject to the following constraints:

$$\mathbf{w}_2'\mathbf{w}_2 = \sum_{j=1}^{d} w_{2j}^2 = 1, \tag{14.4a}$$

$$\mathrm{Cov}(Z_1, Z_2) = 0. \tag{14.4b}$$

For $i = 3, 4, \ldots, d$, the ith principal component is defined as

$$Z_i = w_{i1}X_1 + w_{i2}X_2 + \cdots + w_{id}X_d, \tag{14.5}$$

where $\mathbf{w}_i = (w_{i1}, w_{i2}, \ldots, w_{id})'$ is a vector of loadings such that $\mathrm{Var}(Z_i)$ is maximized subject to the following constraints:

$$\mathbf{w}_i'\mathbf{w}_i = \sum_{j=1}^{d} w_{ij}^2 = 1, \tag{14.6a}$$

$$\mathrm{Cov}(Z_i, Z_j) = 0, \quad j = 1, 2, \ldots, i - 1. \tag{14.6b}$$

The principal components of the variables are related to the **eigenvectors** of the covariance matrix. Since a covariance matrix is nonnegative definite, all its eigenvalues are nonnegative. Let $(\lambda_1, \mathbf{e}_1), (\lambda_2, \mathbf{e}_2), \ldots, (\lambda_d, \mathbf{e}_d)$ be the eigenvalue-eigenvector pairs of the covariance matrix Σ such that $\lambda_1 \geq \lambda_2 \geq \cdots \geq \lambda_d \geq 0$ and the eigenvectors are normalized. Then the ith principal component is given by

$$Z_i = \mathbf{e}_i'\mathbf{X} = \sum_{j=1}^{d} e_{ij}X_j, \tag{14.7}$$

where $\mathbf{X} = (X_1, X_2, \ldots, X_d)'$. In addition, we have

$$\mathrm{Var}(Z_i) = \lambda_i. \tag{14.8}$$

As a result, the proportion of variance explained by the ith principal component can be calculated as

$$\frac{\mathrm{Var}(Z_i)}{\sum_{j=1}^{d} \mathrm{Var}(Z_j)} = \frac{\lambda_i}{\lambda_1 + \lambda_2 + \cdots + \lambda_d}. \tag{14.9}$$

Exercise 14.1. Let $X_1, X_2, \ldots, X_d$ be a set of variables and let Σ be the covariance matrix of these variables, i.e.,

$$\Sigma = \begin{pmatrix} \text{Var}(X_1) & \text{Cov}(X_1, X_2) & \cdots & \text{Cov}(X_1, X_d) \\ \text{Cov}(X_2, X_1) & \text{Var}(X_2) & \cdots & \text{Cov}(X_2, X_d) \\ \vdots & \vdots & \ddots & \vdots \\ \text{Cov}(X_d, X_1) & \text{Cov}(X_d, X_2) & \cdots & \text{Var}(X_d) \end{pmatrix}.$$

For $i = 1, 2, \ldots, d$, let Z_i be a linear combination of $X_1, X_2, \ldots, X_d$ defined as follows:

$$Z_i = w_{i1} X_1 + w_{i2} X_2 + \cdots + w_{id} X_d = \mathbf{w}_i' \mathbf{X}.$$

Show that

$$\text{Cov}(Z_i, Z_j) = \mathbf{w}_i' \Sigma \mathbf{w}_j.$$

Exercise 14.2. Let Z_i be the ith principal component of a set of variables $X_1, X_2, \ldots, X_d$, for $i = 1, 2, \ldots, d$. Show that for any $1 \le i < j \le d$,

$$\text{Var}(Z_i) \ge \text{Var}(Z_j).$$

Exercise 14.3. Let $X_1, X_2, \ldots, X_d$ be a set of variables and let Σ be the covariance matrix of these variables. Let Z_i be the ith principal component of $X_1, X_2, \ldots, X_d$ with loadings $\mathbf{w}_i$, for $i = 1, 2, \ldots, d$. Show that

(a) The covariance matrix of $Z_1, Z_2, \ldots, Z_d$ is given by

$$\Sigma_Z = W' \Sigma W,$$

where $W = (\mathbf{w}_1, \mathbf{w}_2, \ldots, \mathbf{w}_d)$.

(b) The sum of the variances of $Z_1, Z_2, \ldots, Z_d$ is equal to the sum of variances of $X_1, X_2, \ldots, X_d$, i.e.,

$$\sum_{i=1}^{d} \text{Var}(X_i) = \sum_{i=1}^{d} \text{Var}(Z_i).$$

14.2 Empirical Principal Components

Let $\mathbf{x}_i = (x_{i1}, x_{i2}, \ldots, x_{id})'$ be the ith observation of a set of variables $X_1, X_2, \ldots, X_d$ for $i = 1, 2, \ldots, n$, where n is the number of observations. In practice, we usually do not know the covariance matrix Σ of these variables. However, we can estimate the covariance matrix as follows:

$$\hat{\Sigma} = \frac{1}{n-1} \sum_{i=1}^{n} (\mathbf{x}_i - \bar{\mathbf{x}})(\mathbf{x}_i - \bar{\mathbf{x}})', \tag{14.10}$$

where

$$\bar{\mathbf{x}} = \frac{1}{n} \sum_{i=1}^{n} \mathbf{x}_i.$$

Let $(\lambda_1, \mathbf{e}_1)$, $(\lambda_2, \mathbf{e}_2)$, ..., $(\lambda_d, \mathbf{e}_d)$ be the eigenvalue-eigenvector pairs of the covariance matrix $\hat{\Sigma}$ such that $\lambda_1 \geq \lambda_2 \geq \ldots \geq \lambda_d \geq 0$ and the eigenvectors are normalized. Then the ith empirical principal component $\mathbf{z}_i = (z_{1i}, z_{2i}, \ldots, z_{ni})'$ is defined by

$$z_{li} = \mathbf{e}_i' \mathbf{x}_l, \quad l = 1, 2, \ldots, n. \tag{14.11}$$

The numbers $z_{1i}, z_{2i}, \ldots, z_{ni}$ are called **scores** of the ith principal component.

14.3 Computing Principal Components

We can obtain principal components through the **eigenvalue decomposition** and the **singular value decomposition**. Let Σ be the covariance matrix. The eigenvalue decomposition is defined as

$$\Sigma = V \Lambda V', \tag{14.12}$$

where Λ is a diagonal matrix, i.e.,

$$\Lambda = \begin{pmatrix} \lambda_1 & 0 & \cdots & 0 \\ 0 & \lambda_2 & \cdots & 0 \\ \vdots & \vdots & \ddots & \vdots \\ 0 & 0 & \cdots & \lambda_d \end{pmatrix},$$

and $V = (\mathbf{v}_1, \mathbf{v}_2, \ldots, \mathbf{v}_d)$ is a matrix satisfying the following conditions:

$$VV' = V'V = I.$$

The diagonal elements $\lambda_1 \geq \lambda_2 \geq \cdots \geq \lambda_d \geq 0$ are the eigenvalues of Σ. The column vectors $\mathbf{v}_1, \mathbf{v}_2, \ldots, \mathbf{v}_d$ are the eigenvectors of Σ.

The singular value decomposition can also be used to obtain principal components. Let M be an $n \times d$ matrix. The singular value decomposition of M is given by

$$M = USV', \tag{14.13}$$

where U is an $n \times n$ orthonormal matrix (i.e., $UU' = U'U = I$), S is an $n \times d$ rectangular diagonal matrix, and V is a $d \times d$ orthonormal matrix. The columns of U are the eigenvectors of the matrix MM' and the columns of V are the eigenvectors of the matrix $M'M$. The diagonal entries of the matrix S, which are called **singular values**, are all non-negative and equal to the positive square root of the eigenvalues of the matrix $M'M$.

Exercise 14.4. Let $(\lambda_1, \mathbf{e}_1)$, $(\lambda_2, \mathbf{e}_2)$, ..., $(\lambda_d, \mathbf{e}_d)$ be the eigenvalue-eigenvector pairs of the covariance matrix Σ. Based on the eigenvalue decomposition, show that

(a)
$$\Sigma = V\Lambda V',$$

where
$$\Lambda = \begin{pmatrix} \lambda_1 & 0 & \cdots & 0 \\ 0 & \lambda_2 & \cdots & 0 \\ \vdots & \vdots & \ddots & \vdots \\ 0 & 0 & \cdots & \lambda_d \end{pmatrix}$$

and $V = (\mathbf{v}_1, \mathbf{v}_2, \ldots, \mathbf{v}_d)$.

(b)
$$\Sigma = \sum_{i=1}^{d} \lambda_i \mathbf{v}_i \mathbf{v}_i'.$$

Exercise 14.5. Let M be an $n \times d$ matrix such that each column has a mean of zero. Let the singular value decomposition of M be

$$M = USV'.$$

Let Σ be the covariance matrix of M, i.e.,

$$\Sigma = \frac{1}{n-1} M'M.$$

Let the eigenvalue decomposition of Σ be

$$\Sigma = W\Lambda W'.$$

Show that

$$\Lambda = \frac{1}{n-1} S'S.$$

14.4   Other Issues

We now discuss some issues to consider in PCA. The first issue is related to data transformations. If we use the singular value decomposition to obtain principal components from the raw data matrix, then we need to subtract the mean of each column from all elements of that column so that each column has a mean of zero. This transformation is called mean centering and is important when the singular value decomposition is used. If we use the eigenvalue decomposition to obtain principal components, then the mean centering transformation is not necessary.

We may also consider scaling the original data so that each column has a standard deviation of one. Scaling is quite useful if the columns of the data matrix have different orders of magnitudes. If both mean centering and scaling are performed to the data matrix, then the covariance matrix will be the correlation matrix.

Another issue is to decide how many principal components to use. While there is no objective way to decide how many principal components are enough, we can use an ad hoc approach by looking at the scatter plot of the proportion of variance explained against the number of components. We can look for an **elbow**, which is a point at which the proportion of variance explained by each subsequent principal component drops off.

14.5   Summary

In this chapter, we introduced PCA, which is another tool for unsupervised learning. PCA can also be used to visualize high-dimensional data because it can project high-dimensional data into a low-dimensional space. For more information about PCA, readers are referred to (James et al., 2013) and (Tsay, 2005).

14.6   End-of-Chapter Exercises

Exercise 14.6. Use the eigenvalue decomposition to find the principal components of the following correlation matrix

$$\begin{pmatrix} 1 & \rho \\ \rho & 1 \end{pmatrix},$$

where $\rho \in (0, 1)$.

Chapter 15

Case Study: PCA on Interest Rate Swaps

In this chapter, we apply PCA to analyze the changes of swap rates at different tenors. In particular, we will introduce how principal components can be used to explain the changes in the swap rates.

An **interest rate swap** (**IRS**) is an over-the-counter financial derivative in which two parties agree to exchange interest rate cash flows, based on a specified notional amount. A typical interest rate swap consists of two legs of cash flows: a fixed leg and a floating leg. The cash flows of the fixed leg are calculated according to a fixed rate and the cash flows of the floating leg are calculated according to a floating rate. The maturity of an IRS is called the **tenor** of the IRS. Common tenors of interest rate swaps in the market include 2 years, 5 years, 7 years, 10 years, and 30 years.

The swap rate is the discount rate that makes the present value of the fixed cash flows equal to that of the floating cash flows. Given swap rates at different tenors and an interpolation method, we can derive the spot rates at different times (Gan, 2017).

15.1 Loading Swap Rates into R

We obtained the 2-year, 5-year, 7-year, 10-year, and 30-year swap rates from the Federal Reserve Bank of St. Louis[1]. The swap rates are monthly rates and cover the periods from July 1, 2000 to September 1, 2016. These swap rates are saved in the CSV file named swaprates.csv.

---

[1]https://fred.stlouisfed.org

Suppose that the folder of the CSV file is the current working directory. Then we can load the swap rates into R as follows:

```
> swaprates <- read.csv("swaprates.csv", stringsAsFactors
    =F)
> swaprates$Date <- as.Date(swaprates$Date, "%Y-%m-%d")
> summary(swaprates)
      Date                    Y2                   Y5
 Min.   :2000-07-01   Min.   :0.370    Min.   :0.780
 1st Qu.:2004-07-16   1st Qu.:0.785    1st Qu.:1.670
 Median :2008-08-01   Median :1.820    Median :3.160
 Mean   :2008-07-31   Mean   :2.394    Mean   :3.188
 3rd Qu.:2012-08-16   3rd Qu.:3.900    3rd Qu.:4.560
 Max.   :2016-09-01   Max.   :7.120    Max.   :7.170
      Y7                  Y10                  Y30
 Min.   :1.190    Min.   :1.390    Min.   :1.750
 1st Qu.:2.155    1st Qu.:2.610    1st Qu.:3.270
 Median :3.680    Median :4.190    Median :4.650
 Mean   :3.542    Mean   :3.881    Mean   :4.404
 3rd Qu.:4.835    3rd Qu.:5.020    3rd Qu.:5.375
 Max.   :7.200    Max.   :7.240    Max.   :7.200
```

To see the movements of the swap rates during the period, we plot the swap rates against the dates as follows:

```
par(mfrow=c(5,1), mar=c(4,4,1,1))
for(i in 1:5) {
  plot(swaprates[,1], swaprates[,i+1], type="l", xlab="
      Date", ylab=names(swaprates)[i+1], ylim=c(0,8))
}
```

The resulting plots are shown in Figure 15.1. From the plots, we see that the swap rates at various tenors were moving together.

We can also see the changes of the swap rates as follows:

```
datSR <- swaprates[-1,-1] - swaprates[-195,-1]
par(mfrow=c(5,1), mar=c(4,4,1,1))
for(i in 1:5) {
  plot(swaprates[-1,1], datSR[,i], type="l", xlab="Date",
      ylab=names(swaprates)[i+1])
}
```

Executing the above code produces the plot shown in Figure 15.2. We can see that the changes of the swap rates are also highly correlated. To see the pairwise

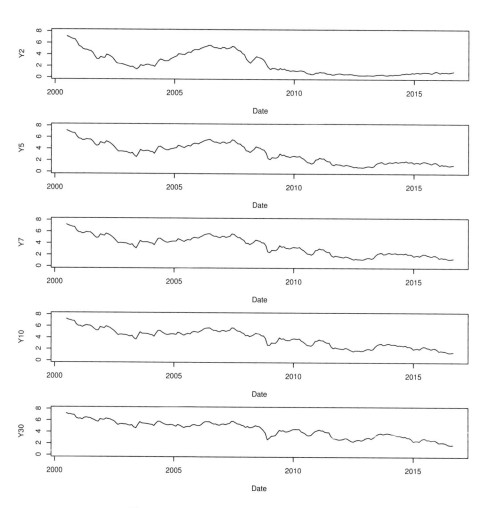

Figure 15.1: *Swap rates at various tenors.*

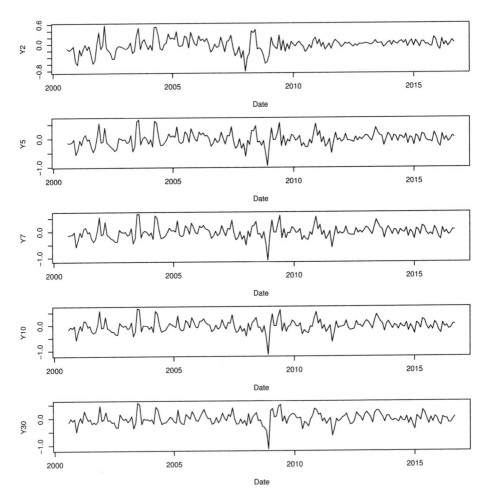

Figure 15.2: *Changes of swap rates at various tenors.*

scatter plots of the changes of the swap rates at different tenors, we use the `pairs` function to create a scatter plot matrix:

```
1 pairs(datSR)
```

The resulting scatter plot matrix is shown in Figure 15.3. The scatter plots show that the changes of the swap rates have a strong linear relationship.

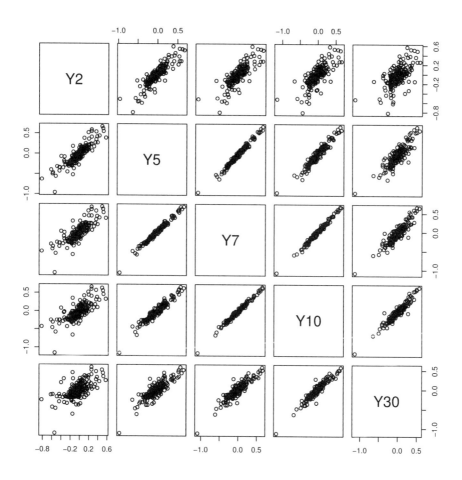

Figure 15.3: *Scatter plots of the changes of the swap rates at various tenors.*

15.2 Principal Component Analysis

As we see from the plots created in the previous section, there are some common factors that drive the changes of the swap rates at different tenors. We can use the PCA tool to figure out the common factors.

To calculate the principal components, we can use the R function prcomp as follows:

```
 1 > datSR2 <- scale(datSR, center=T, scale=F)
 2 > pc <- prcomp(datSR2)
 3 > pc
 4 Standard deviations (1, .., p=5):
 5 [1] 0.474873766 0.136078892 0.053939186 0.014770651
 6 [5] 0.005110728
 7
 8 Rotation (n x k) = (5 x 5):
 9              PC1           PC2          PC3          PC4
10 Y2   0.3692428  -0.78219200   0.4651431   0.18575152
11 Y5   0.4829713  -0.17363417  -0.3856154  -0.66007100
12 Y7   0.4882600   0.06417698  -0.3696844   0.09398443
13 Y10  0.4766118   0.26064358  -0.1737046   0.66590346
14 Y30  0.4060072   0.53476452   0.6841804  -0.27846392
15              PC5
16 Y2   -0.03120389
17 Y5    0.39012423
18 Y7   -0.78229400
19 Y10   0.48094221
20 Y30  -0.05949866
```

Since the prcomp function uses the singular value decomposition to obtain principal components, we used the scale function to perform the mean centering transformation to the changes of the swap rates.

We can plot the loadings of the first three principal components as follows:

```
 1 par(mar=c(4,4,1,1))
 2 plot(pc$rotation[,1], type="b", pch=1, ylim=c(-1, 1),
      xlab="Variable", ylab="Loading")
 3 lines(pc$rotation[,2], type="b", pch=2)
 4 lines(pc$rotation[,3], type="b", pch=3)
 5 legend(4, -0.5, c("PC1", "PC2", "PC3"), pch=c(1,2,3))
```

Figure 15.4 shows the plot of the loadings of the first three principal components. From the figure, we see that the first principal component has positive loadings that are close to each other. The first principal component corresponds to the parallel shift of swap rates. The second and the third principal components correspond to the slope and the curvature of the swap rates.

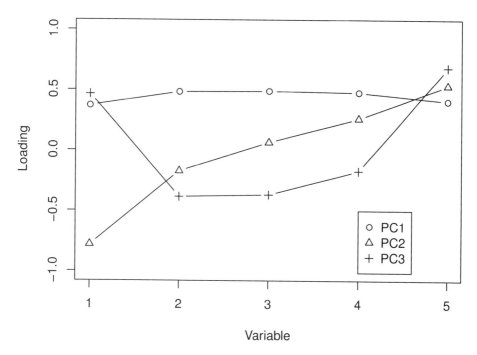

Figure 15.4: *Loadings of the first three principal components.*

To see the cumulative proportions of the variance explained, we can run the following code:

```
> cumsum(pc$sdev^2) / sum(pc$sdev^2)
[1] 0.9123250 0.9872410 0.9990117 0.9998943 1.0000000
```

The result shows that the first three principal components explained about 99.9% of the total variance. The parallel shift and the slope explain about 98.7% of the total variance.

Exercise 15.1. Calculate the covariance matrix of the dataset datSR and apply the eigen function to the covariance matrix to get the eigenvalues and eigenvectors. Do you get the same results as those obtained by applying prcomp to the dataset datSR2?

Exercise 15.2. Write a piece of R code to verify that the sum of the variances of the columns of datSR is equal to the sum of the variances of the principal components.

15.3 Summary

In this chapter, we introduced how to use principal components to explain the changes of swap rates at different tenors. In this example, most of the variation can be explained by the first two or three principal components. For more information about the use of PCA on financial time series, readers are referred to (Tsay, 2005).

15.4 End-of-Chapter Exercises

Exercise 15.3. Consider the dataset of swap rates used in this chapter. Extract the swap rates from year 2015 only and do the following:

(a) Use the singular value decomposition and the eigenvalue decomposition to compute the principal components. You should get equivalent results.

(b) Calculate the cumulative proportions of variance explained by the principal components.

(c) Plot the loadings of the first two principal components.

Part III

Time Series Models

Chapter 16

Time Series Models

In this chapter, we introduce some classical models for time series analysis. In particular, we introduce trend models, random walks, and the general ARIMA (autoregressive integrated moving average) models.

16.1 Introduction

A **time series** is a sequence of data points, which are successive measurements made over a time interval. Examples of time series include the daily closing values of the S&P 500 index and the currency exchange rates at particular times throughout each day. A time series is denoted by $y_1, y_2, \ldots, y_T$, where T is the number of observations available.

Time series analysis is a field of study that focuses on analyzing time-dependent data in order to extract meaningful patterns from the data. One of the goals of time series analysis is forecasting, which refers to the process of using a model to predict future realizations of a time series based on previously observed values of the time series.

A time series can be decomposed into three components: a **trend component**, a **seasonal component**, and a random or irregular component. Mathematically, the decomposition can be written as

$$y_t = T_t + S_t + \epsilon_t, \tag{16.1}$$

where T_t represents the trend, S_t represents the seasonality, and ϵ_t is the random component.

The trend component is the long-term, slow evolution of the time series. The seasonal component of a time series corresponds to the part that repeats itself periodically. The random component corresponds to the short-term fluctuation, which is often difficult to predict. Forecasting a time series can be done by extrapolating each of these three patterns.

16.2   Trend Models

The trend of a time series is important for long-term forecasts. To forecast the trend component, we fit trend models to the time series. If a time series does not have a trend, we can fit an intercept-only model:

$$y_t = \beta_0 + \epsilon_t. \tag{16.2}$$

If we see a time series has a linear trend, we can fit a **linear trend in time model**:

$$y_t = \beta_0 + \beta_1 t + \epsilon_t. \tag{16.3}$$

If a time series has a quadratic trend, we can fit a **quadratic trend in time model**:

$$y_t = \beta_0 + \beta_1 t + \beta_2 t^2 + \epsilon_t. \tag{16.4}$$

Seasonal effects can be incorporated into trend models through the use of categorical variables or the use of trigonometric functions. For example, the January effect can be incorporated into the linear trend in time model as follows:

$$y_t = \beta_0 + \beta_1 t + \beta_2 z_t + \epsilon_t \tag{16.5}$$

where z_t is a binary variable defined as

$$z_t = \begin{cases} 1, & \text{if } t \text{ is in January,} \\ 0, & \text{if } t \text{ is not in January.} \end{cases}$$

16.3   Random Walk Models

A time series $\{y_1, y_2, \ldots, y_T\}$ is said to be **weakly stationary** if

- The mean $E[y_t]$ is independent of t.
- The covariance between y_s and y_t depends only on $|t - s|$.

A **white noise process** is an example of **stationary time series**. A white noise process is a series of independent and identically distributed (i.i.d) random variables. For i.i.d variables, we expect a pattern of uncorrelated random variables with constant mean and constant variance. In time series analysis, the modeling effects are directed toward reducing a time series to a white noise process. The procedure of reducing a time series to a white noise process is called **filtering**.

One common method to reduce a time series to a white noise process is by taking differences. If the first difference of a time series is a white noise process, then the time series is called a **random walk**. In other words, a random walk is a partial sum of a white noise process. Let $\{c_1, c_2, \ldots, c_T\}$ be a white noise process. Then the process $\{y_1, y_2, \ldots, y_T\}$ defined by

$$y_t = y_{t-1} + c_t, \quad t \geq 1, \tag{16.6}$$

is called a random walk, where y_0 is a constant. By repeated substitution, we have

$$y_t = y_{t-1} + c_t = y_{t-2} + c_{t-1} + c_t = \cdots = y_0 + \sum_{i=1}^{t} c_i. \tag{16.7}$$

By taking the expectation and variance of Equation (16.7), we get the mean and the variance of the random walk process:

$$E[y_t] = y_0 + t\mu_c, \quad \text{Var}(y_t) = t\sigma_c^2, \tag{16.8}$$

where μ_c and σ_c are the mean and the standard deviation of the white noise process, respectively. Since the mean and the standard deviation of a random walk are dependent on the time, a random walk is not stationary.

Fitting a random walk model to a time series is straightforward and does not involve the method of least squares, which is used to fit linear regression models. To fit a random walk model to a time series $\{y_1, y_2, \ldots, y_T\}$, we just need to estimate the mean and the standard deviation of the corresponding white noise process defined by

$$c_t = y_t - y_{t-1}, \quad t \geq 2.$$

Since the white noises are independent and identically distributed, we can estimate the mean and the standard deviation as follows:

$$\bar{c} = \frac{1}{T-1} \sum_{t=2}^{T} c_t, \quad s_c = \sqrt{\frac{1}{T-2} \sum_{t=2}^{T} (c_t - \bar{c})^2}. \tag{16.9}$$

Forecasting the future values of a random walk is also straightforward. Let $l \geq 1$ be an integer. Then we can calculate the l-step ahead random variable y_{T+l} as

$$y_{T+l} = y_T + c_{T+1} + \cdots + c_{T+l}.$$

Since the forecast of c_{T+k} is $\bar{c}$ for $k = 1, 2, \ldots, l$, the l-step ahead forecast of a random walk is given by

$$\hat{y}_{T+l} = y_T + l\bar{c}. \tag{16.10}$$

An approximate 95% prediction interval for this l-step ahead forecast is calculated as

$$(y_T + l\bar{c} - 2s_c\sqrt{l},\ y_T + l\bar{c} + 2s_c\sqrt{l}), \tag{16.11}$$

where $\bar{c}$ and s_c are defined in Equation (16.9).

Exercise 16.1. Let $\{y_t : t = 0, 1, \ldots\}$ be a random walk such that $y_t = y_{t-1} + c_t$ for $t \geq 1$, where $\{c_t : t = 1, 2, \ldots\}$ is a white noise process with $E[c_t] = \mu_c$ and $\text{Var}(c_t) = \sigma_c^2$. Show that

$$E[y_t] = y_0 + t\mu_c$$

and

$$\text{Var}(y_t) = t\sigma_c^2.$$

Exercise 16.2. Let $\{y_t : t = 0, 1, \ldots\}$ be a random walk such that $y_t = y_{t-1} + c_t$ for $t \geq 1$, where $\{c_t : t = 1, 2, \ldots\}$ is a white noise process with $\text{Var}(c_t) = \sigma_c^2$. Show that

(a) The l-step forecast error is

$$y_{T+l} - \hat{y}_{T+l} = \sum_{j=1}^{l} (c_{T+j} - \bar{c}),$$

where $\bar{c}$ is the average of the white noise process.

(b) The approximate variance of the l-step forecast error is $l\sigma_c^2$.

16.4   Autoregressive Models

Autoregressive models explore the relationship between y_t and its lagged values. To quantify the linear relationship between $\{y_t\}$ and $\{y_{t-1}\}$, we calculate the lag 1 (sample) **autocorrelation**, which is defined as

$$r_1 = \frac{\sum_{t=2}^{T}(y_{t-1} - \bar{y})(y_t - \bar{y})}{\sum_{t=1}^{T}(y_t - \bar{y})^2}, \tag{16.12}$$

where

$$\bar{y} = \frac{1}{T}\sum_{t=1}^{T} y_t.$$

The autocorrelation is a correlation of a time series with itself. The lag 1 autocorrelation summarizes the linear relationship between observations that are one time unit apart. We can extend this linear relationship to k time units apart, $\{y_t\}$ and $\{y_{t-k}\}$, using the lag k (sample) autocorrelation defined by

$$r_k = \frac{\sum_{t=k+1}^{T}(y_{t-k} - \bar{y})(y_t - \bar{y})}{\sum_{t=1}^{T}(y_t - \bar{y})^2}. \tag{16.13}$$

The linear relationship between $\{y_t\}$ and $\{y_{t-1}\}$ motivates us to build a regression model with $\{y_t\}$ as the dependent variable and $\{y_{t-1}\}$ as the independent variable. For example, we can build the following regression model:

$$y_t = \beta_0 + \beta_1 y_{t-1} + \epsilon_t, \quad t = 2, 3, \ldots, T, \tag{16.14}$$

where β_0 is a constant, β_1 is a parameter, and $\{\epsilon_t\}$ is a white noise process such that $\text{Cov}(\epsilon_{t+k}, y_t) = 0$ for all $k > 0$. The above regression model is called the **autoregressive model** of order 1 and is denoted by $AR(1)$. In general, an autoregressive model of order p, denoted by $AR(p)$, can be written as

$$y_t = \beta_0 + \beta_1 y_{t-1} + \cdots + \beta_p y_{t-p} + \epsilon_t, \quad t = p+1, p+2, \ldots, T. \tag{16.15}$$

The $AR(1)$ model defined in Equation (16.14) is similar to the basic linear regression model introduced in Chapter 2. However, the $AR(1)$ model is different from the basic linear regression model in that the independent variable $\{y_{t-1}\}$ is not deterministic but stochastic. In addition, the parameter β_1 is restricted to be between -1 and 1 inclusive so that the model is stationary. If $\beta_1 = 1$, the model is a random walk and hence is not stationary.

There are several ways to estimate the parameters of the $AR(1)$ model. One of them is the method of conditional least squares, which finds estimates that best fit an observation conditional on the previous observations. Under the method of conditional least squares, the estimates of β_0 and β_1 can be closely approximated by

$$b_1 = \hat{\beta}_1 = r_1, \quad b_0 = \hat{\beta}_0 = \bar{y}(1 - r_1), \tag{16.16}$$

where r_1 is the lag 1 autocorrelation defined in Equation (16.12) and $\bar{y}$ is the mean of $y_1, y_2, \ldots, y_T$.

We can check diagnostically whether an $AR(1)$ model is suitable for a time series as follows. Under the $AR(1)$ model, the lag k autocorrelation can be calculated as

$$\rho_k = \text{Corr}(y_t, y_{t-k}) = \beta_1^k, \quad k \geq 1, \tag{16.17}$$

where $\text{Corr}(\cdot, \cdot)$ is defined in Equation (1.1). Hence if the $AR(1)$ model is an appropriate model for a time series, then ρ_k should approximately match the lag k (sample) autocorrelation r_k.

Exercise 16.3. Calculate lag 2 (sample) autocorrelation for the following time series

$$2.72, 2.5, 2.52, 2.62, 2.72, 2.4$$

Exercise 16.4. Consider the $AR(1)$ model

$$y_t = \beta_0 + \beta_1 y_{t-1} + \epsilon_t, \quad t = 2, 3, \ldots, T.$$

Let $\hat{\beta}_0$ and $\hat{\beta}_1$ be the conditional least squares estimates. Let

$$\bar{y} = \frac{1}{T} \sum_{t=1}^{T} y_t.$$

Show that

(a)
$$\hat{\beta}_1 = \frac{\sum_{t=1}^{T-1} \left(y_t - \frac{T\bar{y} - y_T}{T-1} \right) \left(y_{t+1} - \frac{T\bar{y} - y_1}{T-1} \right)}{\sum_{t=1}^{T-1} \left(y_t - \frac{T\bar{y} - y_T}{T-1} \right)^2}.$$

(b)
$$\hat{\beta}_0 = \frac{T\bar{y} - y_1}{T-1} - \frac{T\bar{y} - y_T}{T-1} \hat{\beta}_1.$$

(c) $\hat{\beta}_1 \approx r_1$, where r_1 is the lag 1 autocorrelation.

(d) $\hat{\beta}_0 \approx \bar{y}(1 - r_1)$, where r_1 is the lag 1 autocorrelation.

Exercise 16.5. Consider the $AR(1)$ model

$$y_t = \beta_0 + \beta_1 y_{t-1} + \epsilon_t, \quad t = 2, 3, \ldots, T$$

with $\text{Var}(y_t) = \sigma_y^2$ and $\text{Var}(\epsilon_t) = \sigma^2$. Show that

(a) $\sigma_y^2 (1 - \beta_1^2) = \sigma^2$.

(b) $\text{Cov}(y_t, y_{t-1}) = \beta_1 \sigma_y^2$.

(c) $\text{Cov}(y_t, y_{t-k}) = \beta_1^k \sigma_y^2$.

16.5   ARIMA Models

The autoregressive integrated moving average (**ARIMA**) model of order (p, d, q), denoted by $ARIMA(p, d, q)$, is defined as

$$w_t = \beta_0 + \beta_1 w_{t-1} + \cdots + \beta_p w_{t-p} + \epsilon_t - \theta_1 \epsilon_{t-1} - \cdots - \theta_q \epsilon_{t-q}, \tag{16.18}$$

where $\{w_t\}$ is the time series obtained by differencing $\{y_t\}$ d times, $\{\epsilon_t\}$ is a white noise process such that $\text{Cov}(\epsilon_{t+k}, y_t) = 0$ for all $k > 0$, and $\beta_0, \ldots, \beta_p, \theta_1, \ldots, \theta_q$ are parameters. The autoregressive models introduced in the previous section are special cases of the ARIMA models. For example, the $ARIMA(p, 0, 0)$ model is just the $AR(p)$ model. One reason we use ARIMA models is that we can achieve a good fit with a small number of parameters.

The $ARIMA(0, 0, q)$ is the **moving average** (MA) model of order q, denoted by $MA(q)$. The model equation of $MA(q)$ is

$$y_t = \beta_0 + \epsilon_t - \theta_1 \epsilon_{t-1} - \cdots - \theta_q \epsilon_{t-q}, \tag{16.19}$$

where $\{\epsilon_t\}$ is a white noise process such that $\text{Cov}(\epsilon_{t+k}, y_t) = 0$ for all $k > 0$ and β_0, $\theta_1, \ldots, \theta_q$ are parameters.

When $d = 0$, then the $ARIMA(p, 0, q)$ is simply called the $ARMA(p, q)$ model, which has the following form:

$$y_t = \beta_0 + \beta_1 y_{t-1} + \cdots + \beta_p y_{t-p} + \epsilon_t - \theta_1 \epsilon_{t-1} - \cdots - \theta_q \epsilon_{t-q}. \tag{16.20}$$

The $ARMA(p, q)$ model can also be written in the following concise form:

$$\phi(B) y_t = \beta_0 + \theta(B) \epsilon_t, \tag{16.21}$$

where B is the **backward shift operator** (i.e., $B^j y_t = y_{t-j}$ and $B^j \epsilon_t = \epsilon_{t-j}$), and $\phi(\cdot)$ and $\theta(\cdot)$ are the pth and qth-degree polynomials defined as

$$\phi(x) = 1 - \beta_1 x - \cdots - \beta_p x^p$$

and

$$\theta(x) = 1 - \theta_1 x - \cdots - \theta_q x^q,$$

respectively.

Since the white noise process $\{\epsilon_t\}$ in the $ARIMA(p, d, q)$ model is not observable, fitting an ARIMA model to a time series is not straightforward. An optimization procedure is generally required to estimate the parameters of an ARIMA model.

Exercise 16.6. Let the **autocovariance function** of a process $\{y_t : t = 0, 1, \ldots\}$ be defined as

$$\gamma_y(h) = \text{Cov}(y_{t+h}, y_t), \quad h = 0, 1, \ldots.$$

Calculate $\gamma_y(0)$ and $\gamma_y(1)$ for the $MA(1)$ process defined as

$$y_t = \epsilon_t - \theta \epsilon_{t-1},$$

where $\{\epsilon_t : t = 0, 1, \ldots\}$ is a white noise process with mean 0 and variance σ^2.

16.6 Smoothing Techniques

Forecasting a time series can also be done by smoothing. The most simple smoothing technique is the **moving average** estimate (also called **running average** estimate), which is defined as

$$\hat{s}_t = \frac{1}{k} \sum_{j=0}^{k-1} y_{t-j}, \tag{16.22}$$

where k is the moving average length. The larger the value of k, the smoother the estimate. When $k = 1$, there is no smoothing.

The moving average technique gives equal weight to observations within k time units of the evaluation time and zero weight to other observations. Intuitively, the more recent observations should be given more weight. This can be achieved by the **exponential smoothing** technique, which is defined as

$$\hat{s}_t = (1 - w) \sum_{j=0}^{t} w^j y_{t-j}, \tag{16.23}$$

where $w \in (0, 1)$ is a weight number.

Forecasting with moving average or exponential smoothing is done as follows:

$$\hat{y}_{T+l} = \hat{s}_T, \quad l \geq 1. \tag{16.24}$$

Exercise 16.7. Let $\{\hat{s}_t : t = k, k+1, \ldots\}$ be the moving average estimates of length k of a time series $\{y_t : t = 0, 1, 2, \ldots, \}$. Show that

$$\hat{s}_t = \hat{s}_{t-1} + \frac{y_t - y_{t-k}}{k}.$$

Exercise 16.8. Let $\{\hat{s}_t : t = 0, 1, \ldots\}$ be the exponential smoothing estimates with weight w of a time series $\{y_t : t = 0, 1, 2, \ldots,\}$. Show that

$$\hat{s}_t = (1 - w)y_t + w\hat{s}_{t-1}.$$

16.7 ARCH

Financial time series often exhibit time-varying volatilities. The autoregressive conditional heteroskedasticity (**ARCH**) model introduced by Engle (1982) can be used to model the changing volatility. Under the ARCH model, the variance of the current error term is a function of the actual sizes of the error terms in previous periods.

To describe the ARCH model, let ϵ_t denote the error terms with respect to a mean process. The ARCH model assumes that (1) the error terms ϵ_t are serially uncorrelated, but dependent; (2) the dependence of ϵ_t can be described by a quadratic function. In particular, the ARCH(q) model assumes that

$$\epsilon_t = \sigma_t z_t, \quad \sigma_t^2 = \alpha_0 + \alpha_1 \epsilon_{t-1}^2 + \cdots + \alpha_q \epsilon_{t-q}^2 \tag{16.25}$$

where z_t is a sequence of independent and identically distributed random variables with mean 0 and variance 1, $\alpha_0 > 0$, and $\alpha_i \geq 0$ for $i = 1, 2, \ldots, q$. To ensure that the unconditional variance of ϵ_t is finite, the coefficients α_i need to satisfy some regularity conditions. The random variable z_t is often assumed to follow the standard normal or a student-t distribution.

The simplest ARCH model is the ARCH(1) model, which has the following form:

$$\epsilon_t^2 = \sigma_t^2 z_t^2 = \alpha_0 z_t^2 + \alpha_1 \epsilon_{t-1}^2 z_t^2. \tag{16.26}$$

From the recursion given above, we can show that under certain conditions, the following relationship holds:

$$\epsilon_t^2 = \alpha_0 \sum_{j=0}^{\infty} \alpha_1^j \prod_{k=0}^{j} z_{t-k}^2. \tag{16.27}$$

The ARCH model has the following advantages:

(a) It can model the **volatility clustering** (i.e., volatility is high for some periods and low for other periods), which is often observed in asset returns. Under the ARCH model, large errors tend to be followed by another large error.

(b) The unconditional mean of ϵ_t remains zero. Let $\mathscr{F}_t$ denote the information up to time t. Then by the tower rule of conditional expectation, we have

$$E[\epsilon_t] = E[E[\epsilon_t | \mathscr{F}_{t-1}]] = 0.$$

(c) The tail distribution of ϵ_t is heavier than that of a normal distribution.

The ARCH model also suffers from the following drawbacks (Pena et al., 2001):

(a) Positive and negative errors are treated in the same manner. This may not be appropriate for financial time series, where prices respond differently to positive and negative returns.

(b) The ARCH model is restrictive. To ensure that the fourth moment of the error terms is finite under the ARCH(1) model, for example, α_1^2 must be between 0 and $\frac{1}{3}$.

(c) The ARCH model responds slowly to isolated large errors. As a result, it often over-predicts the volatility.

(d) The ARCH model does not provide any new insight for understanding the error terms because it only provides a mechanical way to describe the unconditional variance.

16.8   Model Evaluation

In this section, we introduce out-of-sample validation techniques to compare different time series models. One advantage of **out-of-sample validation** is that it can be used to compare the accuracy of forecasts from any forecasting models.

The procedure of out-of-sample validation is given as follows:

(a) Divide the time series with T observations into two subsamples, a model development subsample $(t = 1, \ldots, T_1)$ and a model validation subsample $(t = T_1 + 1, \ldots, T_1 + T_2)$.

(b) Fit a candidate model to the development subsample.

(c) Use the model created in the previous step to forecast the dependent variables, $\hat{y}_t$, in the validation subsample.

(d) Use actual observations and the predicted values to compute forecast residuals, $e_t = y_t - \hat{y}_t$, for the model validation subsample.

(e) Calculate one or more comparison statistics based on the forecast residuals.

(f) Repeat steps (b) through (e) for each of the candidate models.

(g) Choose the model with the smallest set of comparison statistics.

Name	Formula
Mean Error	$ME = \dfrac{1}{T_2} \displaystyle\sum_{t=T_1+1}^{T_1+T_2} e_t$
Mean Percentage Error	$MPE = \dfrac{100}{T_2} \displaystyle\sum_{t=T_1+1}^{T_1+T_2} \dfrac{e_t}{y_t}$
Mean Square Error	$MSE = \dfrac{1}{T_2} \displaystyle\sum_{t=T_1+1}^{T_1+T_2} e_t^2$
Mean Absolute Error	$MAE = \dfrac{1}{T_2} \displaystyle\sum_{t=T_1+1}^{T_1+T_2} |e_t|$
Mean Absolute Percentage Error	$MAPE = \dfrac{100}{T_2} \displaystyle\sum_{t=T_1+1}^{T_1+T_2} \dfrac{|e_t|}{|y_t|}$

Table 16.1: *Some commonly used comparison statistics.*

Table 16.1 gives a list of some commonly used statistics for comparing forecasts. The **mean error** (ME) statistic measures the recent trends that are not anticipated by the forecasting model. Similar to the mean error statistic, the **mean percentage error** (MPE) statistic also measures the recent trends, but examines the error relative to the actual values. The **mean square error** (MSE), the **mean absolute error** (MAE), and the **mean absolute percentage error** ($MAPE$) statistics can capture more patterns than the mean error and the mean percentage error statistics.

Exercise 16.9. There are three pricing models for gold plated widgets of different size, shape, and quality: models A, B, and C. All of the models are fit to most of the data and then they are used to predict the price for the remaining three widgets. The results for three of the predicted observations are given in the following table, where $\hat{y}_A$ is the predicted value from model A.

y	$\hat{y}_A$	$\hat{y}_B$	$\hat{y}_C$
3	4	2	1
4	4	4	4
2	3	3	4

Calculate the Mean Error (ME), Mean Absolute Error (MAE), and Mean Square Error (MSE) for those three models.

Model	ME	MAE	MSE
A			
B			
C			

16.9   Summary

For more information about time series models, readers are referred to Hamilton (1994), Pena et al. (2001), Brockwell and Davis (2002), Tsay (2005), Frees (2009). Brockwell and Davis (2002) discusses different methods for fitting time series models. Tsay (2005) focuses on financial time series analysis and covers a wide range of topics.

16.10   End-of-Chapter Exercises

Exercise 16.10. Describe the linear trend model and the random walk model. What is the difference?

Exercise 16.11. Assume that y_t follows a random walk:

$$y_t = y_{t-1} + c_t, \quad t = 2, 3, \ldots, T$$

(a) How would you estimate $\bar{c}$?

(b) Now assume you know the associated white noise process has a variance of 9. Derive the variance of a four-step ahead forecast (i.e., don't just write down the formula).

(c) Now assume you know the associated white noise process has a mean of 2 and the current value of $\{y_t\}$ is $y_T = 1$. What is the 3-step forecast of the model?

Exercise 16.12. Consider the MA(1) time series model given below:

$$y_t = \epsilon_t - \theta \epsilon_{t-1},$$

where ϵ_t is a white noise process with mean 0 and variance σ^2. Define a new times series by adding a linear in time trend component to the series y_t:

$$x_t = a + bt + y_t,$$

where a and b are fixed constants.

(a) Explain why x_t is not a stationary process.

(b) Let $z_t = x_t - x_{t-1}$. Explain why the time series z_t is stationary.

(c) Show that the autocovariance function of z_t can be expressed as

$$\gamma_z(h) = \text{Cov}(z_{t+h}, z_t) = 2\gamma_y(h) - \gamma_y(h+1) - \gamma_y(h-1), \quad \text{for } h = 0, 1, 2, \ldots$$

where $\gamma_y(h)$ is the autocovariance of y_t.

(d) Use part (c) to show that

$$\text{Var}(z_t) = 2(1 + \theta^2)\sigma^2 + 2\theta\sigma^2.$$

Explain why the variance of z_t is indeed larger than the variance of y_t.

Exercise 16.13. Consider the $AR(2)$ process given below:

$$y_t = \phi_1 y_{t-1} + \phi_2 y_{t-2} + \epsilon_t$$

where ϵ_t is a white noise process with mean 0 and variance σ^2.

(a) Show that

$$\rho_k = \phi_1 \rho_{k-1} + \phi_2 \rho_{k-2},$$

where $\rho_k = \text{Corr}(y_t, y_{t-k})$ is the autocorrelation of lag k. These are called the Yule-Walker equations for the $AR(2)$ model.

(b) For the $AR(2)$ process below:

$$y_t = \frac{1}{4} y_{t-1} + \frac{2}{5} y_{t-2} + \epsilon_t,$$

Calculate ρ_1 and ρ_2.

Chapter 17

Case Study: Forecasting Currency Exchange Rates

In this case study, we introduce several time series models for forecasting the USD/CAD exchange rates. In particular, we introduce trend models, random walk models, and the general ARIMA models. After working through this case study, readers should be able to

- fit trend models
- fit random walk models
- filter a time series to achieve stationarity
- understand and calculate autocorrelations
- fit and perform diagnostic checks for $AR(1)$ models
- fit ARIMA (AutoRegressive Integrated Moving Average) models
- use various time series models to forecast future values
- evaluate forecast accuracy using out-of-sample validation techniques

17.1 Data Desciption

To demonstrate the performance of various time series models for forecasting the USD/CAD exchange rates, we downloaded the daily noon USD/CAD exchange rates from the website of the Bank of Canada[1]. Since we are interested in the exchange rates in recent years, we only downloaded the exchange rates from the recent four years between October 3, 2011 and September 30, 2015. The exchange rates on weekends and Canadian bank holidays are not available.

---

[1]http://www.bankofcanada.ca

The daily noon exchange rates are saved to a CSV file named `usdcad.csv`. The file contains two columns with headers `Date` and `Rate`, respectively. The first column contains the dates and the second column contains the corresponding exchange rates.

17.2   Loading Data into R

Since the exchange rates are saved in a CSV file, we can use the function `read.csv` to load the data into R. Suppose the current working directory contains the file `usdcad.csv`, then we can load the data into R as follows:

```
> rates <- read.csv("usdcad.csv", stringsAsFactors=FALSE)
> summary(rates)
     Date                 Rate
 Length:1000         Min.   :0.9683
 Class :character    1st Qu.:1.0122
 Mode  :character    Median :1.0461
                     Mean   :1.0838
                     3rd Qu.:1.1172
                     Max.   :1.3418
> head(rates)
        Date    Rate
1  10/3/2011  1.0511
2  10/4/2011  1.0549
3  10/5/2011  1.0402
4  10/6/2011  1.0378
5  10/7/2011  1.0383
6 10/11/2011  1.0279
```

In the above code, we assigned the dataset into a variable named `rates`, which is a data frame. The dates are stored in the data frame as characters.

We convert the characters to date objects in R and plot the time series as follows:

```
> rates$Date <- as.Date(rates$Date, "%m/%d/%Y")
> summary(rates)
      Date                   Rate
 Min.   :2011-10-03    Min.   :0.9683
 1st Qu.:2012-09-30    1st Qu.:1.0122
 Median :2013-09-30    Median :1.0461
 Mean   :2013-09-30    Mean   :1.0838
 3rd Qu.:2014-09-30    3rd Qu.:1.1172
 Max.   :2015-09-30    Max.   :1.3418
```

```
10 > head(rates)
11           Date    Rate
12 1 2011-10-03 1.0511
13 2 2011-10-04 1.0549
14 3 2011-10-05 1.0402
15 4 2011-10-06 1.0378
16 5 2011-10-07 1.0383
17 6 2011-10-11 1.0279
18 > dev.new(width=5, height=4)
19 > with(rates, plot(Date, Rate, type="l"))
```

In the above code, we used the function as.Date to convert the date characters to date objects. We plotted the exchange rates against the dates and specified the size of the plot with the function dev.new. The resulting plot is shown in Figure 17.1.

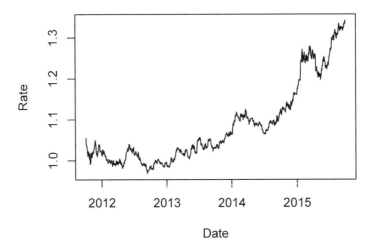

Figure 17.1: *The USD/CAD exchange rates.*

From Figure 17.1, we observe a stable pattern of exchange rates between October 2011 and December 2014. Between December 2014 and September 2015, we notice a rapid weakening of the Canadian dollar against the US dollar.

17.3   Fitting Trend Models

From Figure 17.1, we see that the exchange rates exhibit a linear or quadratic trend. We can fit a linear trend in time model or a quadratic trend in time model to the series. To fit a linear trend in time model, we proceed as follows:

```
 1 > vt <- 1:nrow(rates)
 2 > trend1 <- lm(rates$Rate ~ vt)
 3 > summary(trend1)
 4
 5 Call:
 6 lm(formula = rates$Rate ~ vt)
 7
 8 Residuals:
 9      Min        1Q     Median        3Q        Max
10 -0.07563  -0.03763  -0.01542   0.03295    0.11690
11
12 Coefficients:
13               Estimate  Std. Error  t value  Pr(>|t|)
14 (Intercept) 9.374e-01  2.950e-03   317.73   <2e-16 ***
15 vt          2.924e-04  5.106e-06    57.26   <2e-16 ***
16 ---
17 Signif. codes:  0 '***' 0.001 '**' 0.01 '*' 0.05 '.' 0.1
          ' ' 1
18
19 Residual standard error: 0.04661 on 998 degrees of
       freedom
20 Multiple R-squared:  0.7666,   Adjusted R-squared:  0.7664
21 F-statistic:  3279 on 1 and 998 DF,  p-value: < 2.2e-16
```

In the above code, we first created a new time variable vt, which contains the integers from 1 to the number of observations in the series. From the model summary, we see that the linear trend in time model has a decent R^2 of 0.7666. This implies a strong trend in time for the data. We plot the fitted model and the original time series as follows:

```
 1 > dev.new(width=5, height=4)
 2 > plot(vt, rates$Rate, type="l", ylim=c(0.9, 1.4), xlab="
     Day", ylab="Exchange Rate")
 3 > lines(vt, trend1$fitted.values, type="l")
```

The resulting plot is shown in Figure 17.2.

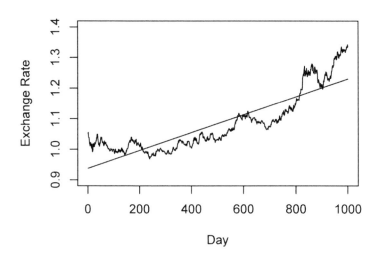

Figure 17.2: *The USD/CAD exchange rates and the fitted linear trend in time model.*

Exercise 17.1. Write R code to fit a quadratic trend in time model to the USD/CAD exchange rates and plot the fitted model and the original series together in one figure. Compare this model with the previously fitted linear trend in time model.

We can add a seasonal component to the linear trend in time model with a categorical variable. If we want to incorporate the January effect into the linear trend in time model, for example, we can create a binary variable that indicates whether the exchange rate is from January or not. We can fit the model with the January effect as follows:

```
 1 > vt <- 1:nrow(rates)
 2 > vm <- format(rates$Date, "%m")
 3 > head(vm)
 4 [1] "10" "10" "10" "10" "10" "10"
 5 > vz <- vm == "01"
 6 > trend1s <- lm(rates$Rate ~ vt + vz)
 7 > summary(trend1s)
 8
 9 Call:
10 lm(formula = rates$Rate ~ vt + vz)
```

```
11
12 Residuals:
13      Min          1Q     Median          3Q        Max
14  -0.07490  -0.03732  -0.01534    0.03323    0.11799
15
16 Coefficients:
17                Estimate  Std. Error  t value  Pr(>|t|)
18 (Intercept)  9.363e-01   3.006e-03  311.444   <2e-16 ***
19 vt           2.929e-04   5.108e-06   57.339   <2e-16 ***
20 vzTRUE       9.605e-03   5.260e-03    1.826   0.0681 .
21 ---
22 Signif. codes:  0 '***' 0.001 '**' 0.01 '*' 0.05 '.' 0.1
       ' ' 1
23
24 Residual standard error: 0.04656 on 997 degrees of
       freedom
25 Multiple R-squared:  0.7674,     Adjusted R-squared:
       0.767
26 F-statistic:  1645 on 2 and 997 DF,  p-value: < 2.2e-16
```

In the above code, we used the function format to convert the dates to strings. Then we created a binary variable to indicate whether the date is in January or not. From the model summary, we see that the p-value of the binary variable is about 0.0681, which shows that the January effect is not significant in the USD/CAD exchange rates at the 5% significance level.

Exercise 17.2. Write R code to fit a quadratic trend in time model by incorporating the January effect to the USD/CAD exchange rates. Does the model indicate that the January effect exists?

17.4   Fitting Random Walk Models

In this section, we introduce how to fit a random walk model to a time series. To do that, we can calculate and plot the first difference and the second difference of the USD/CAD exchange rates as follows:

```
1 > rated1 <- diff(rates$Rate)
2 > rated2 <- diff(rated1)
```

```
3 > par(mfrow=c(1,2))
4 > plot(rates$Date[-1], rated1, type="l", xlab="Date",
    ylab="The First Difference")
5 > plot(rates$Date[-c(1:2)], rated2, type="l", xlab="Date"
    , ylab="The Second Difference")
```

The resulting plot is shown in Figure 17.3. From the figure, we see that the first difference of the exchange rates seems to be a white noise process. However, the volatility (i.e., standard deviation) of the first difference seems to vary over time. We should continue to take the difference of the exchange rates until we get a white noise process.

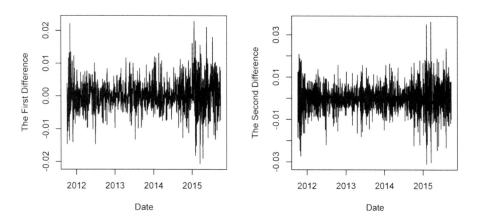

Figure 17.3: *The first difference (Left) and the second difference (Right) of the USD/CAD exchange rates.*

Exercise 17.3. Write R code to calculate and plot the sample mean $\mu_t^{(1)}$ and the sample standard deviation $\sigma_t^{(1)}$ of the first difference of the exchange rates, for $t \geq 23$. Use a moving window of 22 days, that is, $\mu_t^{(1)}$ and $\sigma_t^{(1)}$ are calculated from the points $\Delta y_{t-21}, \Delta y_{t-20}, \ldots, \Delta y_t$, where $\Delta y_t = y_t - y_{t-1}$.

Now let us fit a random walk model to the USD/CAD exchange rates and forecast the future values of the exchange rates. Suppose that we want to forecast the exchange rates in the next 22 days. We can fit the model and plot the forecasts as follows:

```
1 > c <- diff(rates$Rate)
2 > barc <- mean(c)
3 > T <- nrow(rates)
4 > yT <- rates$Rate[T]
5 > yhat <- yT + c(1:22) * barc
6 > dev.new(width=5, height=4)
7 > plot(yhat, type="l", xlab="Day", ylab="Forecast")
```

The resulting forecasts are shown in Figure 17.4. The exchange rates predicted by the random walk model lie in a straight line.

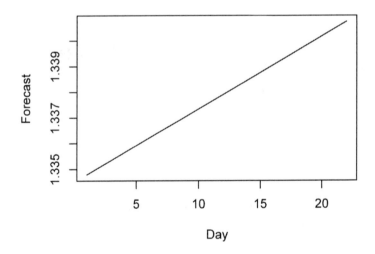

Figure 17.4: *Exchange rates predicted by a random walk model.*

Exercise 17.4. Write R code to calculate the forecasts and the 95% prediction interval of the USD/CAD exchange rates with a random walk model for 22 days. Plot the forecasts and the upper and lower bounds of the prediction interval together in one figure. (Hint: Use a wide range for the y-axis, otherwise, the bounds of the prediction interval are not shown in the figure.)

17.5   Fitting Autoregressive Models

To see the relationship between y_t and y_{t-1}, we can create a scatter plot as follows:

```
> dev.new(width=5, height=4)
> T <- nrow(rates)
> with(rates, plot(Rate[-T], Rate[-1], xlab="Exchange
    Rate", ylab="Lagged Exchange Rate"))
```

The resulting scatter plot is shown in Figure 17.5, which shows a strong linear relationship between y_t and y_{t-1}.

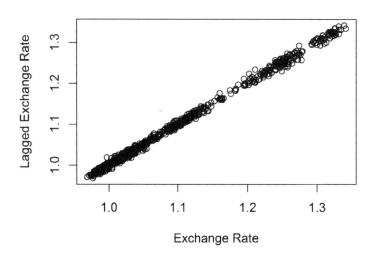

Figure 17.5: *A scatter plot between the USD/CAD exchange rates and the lagged values.*

In R, we can calculate the lag 1 (sample) autocorrelation r_1 as follows:

```
> T <- nrow(rates)
> ybar <- mean(rates$Rate)
> dsum1 <- sum( (rates$Rate[2:T]-ybar) * (rates$Rate[1:(T
    -1)]-ybar) )
```

```
4 > dsum2 <- sum( (rates$Rate - ybar)^2 )
5 > r1 <- dsum1 / dsum2
6 > r1
7 [1] 0.9951107
8 > cor(rates$Rate[2:T], rates$Rate[1:(T-1)])
9 [1] 0.998556
```

From the above output, we see that the lag 1 autocorrelation is about 0.995, which is very close to 1, indicating a very strong positive linear relationship between two successive values of the exchange rates. We also calculated the Pearson correlation coefficient between $\{y_t\}$ and $\{y_{t-1}\}$, using the R function cor. The autocorrelation is a little bit different from the Pearson correlation coefficient because the two numbers have different values in the denominator.

Exercise 17.5. Write an R function named $calAC(y, k)$ to calculate the lag k autocorrelation for a time series y. What is the output of the following function call

```
1 calAC(rates$Rate, 1)
```

To fit an autoregressive model to the USD/CAD exchange rates, we use the R function ar as follows:

```
1 > ar1 <- ar(rates$Rate)
2 > ar1
3
4 Call:
5 ar(x = rates$Rate)
6
7 Coefficients:
8 1
9 0.9951
10
11 Order selected 1  sigma^2 estimated as  9.083e-05
```

The output shows that the estimate of β_1 is 0.9951. The function ar can determine the optimal order k based on some criterion. The above output shows that the optimal order of the autoregressive model is 1 as only one coefficient is shown.

To check whether $AR(1)$ is appropriate for the USD/CAD exchange rates, we compare the autocorrelations $\rho_1, \rho_2, \ldots, \rho_k$ implied by the $AR(1)$ model and the (sample) autocorrelations $r_1, r_2, \ldots, r_k$ as follows:

```
> ar1 <- ar(rates$Rate)
> b1 <- ar1$ar[1]
> k <- 5
> vrho <- vector(mode="numeric",length=k)
> vr <- vector(mode="numeric", length=k)
> for(i in 1:k) {
+       vrho[i] <- b1^i
+       vr[i] <- calAC(rates$Rate, i)
+ }
> vrho
[1] 0.9951107 0.9902453 0.9854037 0.9805858 0.9757914
> vr
[1] 0.9951107 0.9901692 0.9851486 0.9803737 0.9756936
```

In the above code, we used the R function `calAC` from Exercise 17.5 to calculate the autocorrelations of the time series data. The above output shows that ρ_k matches r_k closely for $k = 1, 2, \ldots, 5$. This provides one indication that the $AR(1)$ model is a suitable model for the USD/CAD exchange rates.

17.6 ARIMA Models

We can use the R function `arima` to fit an ARIMA model to a time series. For example, we can fit an $AR(1)$ and an $MA(1)$ to the USD/CAD exchange rates as follows:

```
> ar1 <- arima(rates$Rate, order=c(1,0,0), method="ML",
    optim.control=list(maxit = 1000))
> ma1 <- arima(rates$Rate, order=c(0,0,1), method="ML",
    optim.control=list(maxit = 1000))
> ar1

Call:
arima(x = rates$Rate, order = c(1, 0, 0), method = "ML",
    optim.control = list(maxit = 1000))

Coefficients:
          ar1    intercept
       0.9994       1.0866
s.e.   0.0011       0.1936
```

```
13 sigma^2 estimated as 2.696e-05:   log likelihood =
       3838.38,  aic = -7670.76
14 > ma1
15
16 Call:
17 arima(x = rates$Rate, order = c(0, 0, 1), method = "ML",
       optim.control = list(maxit = 1000))
18
19 Coefficients:
20           ma1   intercept
21        0.9767    1.0838
22 s.e.   0.0080    0.0031
23
24 sigma^2 estimated as 0.002494:   log likelihood = 1576.39,
         aic = -3146.78
```

In the above code, we used the maximum-likelihood method to estimate the parameters by specifying "ML" in the method, and set the maximum number of iterations of the optimization algorithm to be 1000. In the summary of the ARIMA models, we see the estimates of the parameters, the log likelihood, and the **AIC** (Akaike information criterion) values. A lower value of AIC indicates a better model. Hence the $AR(1)$ model is better than the $MA(1)$ model in terms of AIC.

Exercise 17.6. Write R code to fit ARIMA models with parameters (p, d, q) that satisfy the following conditions:

$$p, q \in \{0, 1, 2\}, \quad d \in \{0, 1\}, \quad p + q > 0.$$

Which model is the best in terms of the AIC?

17.7   Forecast Evaluation

Now let us compare the following models with out-of-sample validation: the quadratic trend in time model, the random walk model, the $AR(1)$ model, and the $ARIMA(2, 1, 2)$ model. To do that, we first split the data into two subsamples as follows:

```
1 > T <- nrow(rates)
2 > T1 <- round( 0.9 * T )
3 > rates1 <- rates[1:T1, ]
4 > rates2 <- rates[(T1+1):T, ]
```

The development subsample `rates1` contains about 90% of the data and the validation subsample `rates2` contains the rest of the data
We fit the models as follows:

```
1 > vt <- 1:T1
2 > vt2 <- vt^2
3 > qtrend <- lm(rates1$Rate ~ vt + vt2)
4 > rwcbar <- mean(diff(rates1$Rate))
5 > ar1 <- arima(rates1$Rate, order=c(1,0,0), method="ML",
    optim.control=list(maxit = 1000))
6 > arima2_1_2 <- arima(rates1$Rate, order=c(2,1,2), method
    ="ML", optim.control=list(maxit = 1000))
```

We used the function `lm` to fit the quadratic trend in time model. Fitting a random walk model is even simpler. We only calculated the average, which will be used for forecasting future values. We used the function `arima` to fit the $AR(1)$ and the $ARIMA(2,1,2)$ models.

Once we have these models, we forecast the exchange rates in the validation subsample as follows:

```
1 yhat_qtrend <- predict(qtrend, newdata=data.frame(vt=(T1
    +1):T, vt2=((T1+1):T)^2 ))
2 yhat_rw <- rates1$Rate[T1] + rwcbar * c(1:(T-T1))
3 yhat_ar1 <- predict(ar1, n.ahead=T-T1)
4 yhat_arima2_1_2 <- predict(arima2_1_2, n.ahead=T-T1)
5 listyhat <- list(qtrend=yhat_qtrend, rw=yhat_rw, ar1=yhat
    _ar1$pred, arima2_1_2=yhat_arima2_1_2$pred)
```

We saved the forecasts in a list. Then we calculated the ME statistic and the MAE statistic as follows:

```
1 > me <- function(y, lyhat) {
2 +   res <- list()
3 +   for(i in 1:length(lyhat)) {
4 +     res[[names(lyhat[i])]] <- mean(y - lyhat[[i]])
5 +   }
6 +   return(res)
7 + }
8 >
```

```
 9 > mae <- function(y, lyhat) {
10 +    res <- list()
11 +    for(i in 1:length(lyhat)) {
12 +      res[[names(lyhat[i])]] <- mean( abs(y - lyhat[[i]])
   )
13 +    }
14 +    return(res)
15 +
16 + }
17 >
18 > me(rates2$Rate, listyhat)
19 $qtrend
20 [1] 0.001474548
21
22 $rw
23 [1] 0.05851768
24
25 $ar1
26 [1] 0.07911489
27
28 $arima2_1_2
29 [1] 0.06783632
30
31 > mae(rates2$Rate, listyhat)
32 $qtrend
33 [1] 0.0200835
34
35 $rw
36 [1] 0.05962085
37
38 $ar1
39 [1] 0.08004179
40
41 $arima2_1_2
42 [1] 0.06882862
```

We created two functions to calculate the *ME* and the *MAE* statistics. According to these comparison statistics, we see that the quadratic trend in time model performs the best among the four models.

Exercise 17.7. Write R functions to calculate the *MPE*, the *MSE*, and the *MAPE* statistics. Based on these measures, which one of the following models performs the best: *AR*(1), *AR*(2), *ARIMA*(2,0,2)?

17.8 Summary

In this case study, we implemented several time series models for forecasting the USD/CAD exchange rates. In particular, we implemented the linear trend in time model, the quadratic trend in time model, the random walk model, the autoregressive models, and the general ARIMA models. We also used several out-of-sample validation measures to evaluate time series models.

Part IV

Simulation

Chapter 18

Case Study: Profitability Analysis of Short Term Contracts

In this case study, we examine the profitability of a portfolio of short term insurance contracts using simulation. This is the first of a series of two chapters in this book that applies simulation to illustrate its applicability and importance in insurance company operation and management. After working through this case study, readers will be able to

- Perform simulation

- Understand the applicability and some limitations of simulation

- Understand short-term insurance contracts

- Analyze the profitability of short-term insurance contracts

18.1 Introduction to Simulation

Monte Carlo simulation (or simply simulation) is not a new tool for solving actuarial problems and helping in the decision making process. It has been widely used in the past for solving practical actuarial problems in a variety of situations and it has become increasingly important because of efficiency as a result of computing advances. The speed with which simulation can produce an answer is quite fast these days. However, because actuaries are now more often faced with much more complex issues than in the past, the speed to produce simulation results is still an important aspect of the simulation process (Korn et al., 2010).

Simulation, which involves algorithms using repeated random sampling, is frequently used to solve actuarial problems that involve probability distributions where the expected outcome cannot be explicitly expressed. The principle is based on the strong law of large numbers. Consider the problem of calculating the integral

$$\theta = \int_0^1 g(x)dx \tag{18.1}$$

We can express $\theta = E[g(U)]$ for a uniformly distributed random variable U on $(0,1)$. Exploiting this property, we can generate k independent $U(0,1)$ random variables, $U_1, U_2, \ldots, U_k$ so that $g(U_1), g(U_2), \ldots, g(U_k)$ are identically and independent (i.i.d.) random variables with mean θ.

By the strong law of large numbers, with probability 1, we have

$$\sum_{i=1}^k \frac{g(U_i)}{k} \to E[g(U)] = \theta \text{ as } k \to \infty. \tag{18.2}$$

We can approximate θ by generating a sufficiently large number of random numbers u_i and using the sample average of $g(u_i)$ as the approximation. This is called the Monte Carlo approach of approximating integrals. See Ross (2012b).

As you can see, generating random numbers is the building block of performing simulation. The function `runif` is used in R to generate uniform random numbers as the following illustrates:

```
> set.seed(1)
> n.sim1 <- 100
> n.sim2 <- 5000
> urandom1 <- runif(n.sim1)
> urandom2 <- runif(n.sim2)
> par(mfrow=c(1,2))
> plot(urandom1, typ="p", pch=19, cex=0.5, main="number
    of random values = 100")
> plot(urandom2, typ="p", pch=19, cex=0.5, main="number
    of random values = 5000")
```

In the above code, we generated two sets of uniform random numbers, which are plotted in Figure 18.1. From the figure, we see that generating more values increases the likelihood of covering more possible values.

As a simple illustration, consider approximating the integral $\theta = \int_0^1 (e^{x^2} - 1)dx$ using the Monte Carlo approach. The result of the numerical integration is shown in the following R code:

```
> intex <- function(n.gen){
```

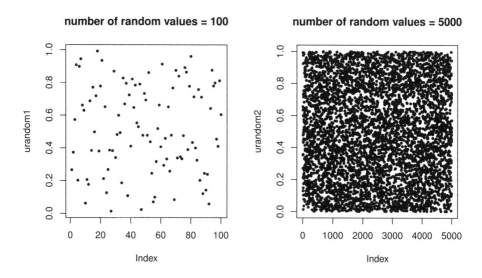

Figure 18.1: *Comparing the random numbers generated.*

```
 2 +         set.seed(1)
 3 +         urandom <- runif(n.gen)
 4 +         g <- exp(urandom^2) -1
 5 +         mean(g)
 6 + }
 7 > intex(10)
 8 [1] 0.5652317
 9 > intex(100)
10 [1] 0.4610446
11 > intex(1000)
12 [1] 0.4633245
13 > intex(10000)
14 [1] 0.46639
15 > intex(100000)
16 [1] 0.4629939
17 > f <- function(x){exp(x^2)-1}
18 > integrate(f,0,1)
19 0.4626517 with absolute error < 5.1e-15
```

In the above code, we also used the R function `integrate` to calculate the true value of the integration. From the output, we see that the true value of the integral is 0.4626517. As we increase the number of simulations, we increase the accuracy of the approximation.

Exercise 18.1. Approximate the integral $\int_0^1 xe^{-x}dx$ using Monte Carlo with 100,000 simulations. Compare the approximate result with the true value of the integral.

18.2 Simulating Discrete Random Variables

Consider a discrete random variable X with probability mass function expressed as

$$P(X = x_j) = q_j, \quad j = 0, 1, \ldots,$$

where $q_j > 0$ for $j = 0, 1, \ldots$ and

$$\sum_j q_j = 1.$$

To generate a value from this distribution, we use the most popular method of simulation called the **inverse transform method**. According to this method, first we generate a random number U and then assign

$$X = \begin{cases} x_0, & \text{if } U < q_0 \\ x_1, & \text{if } q_0 \le U < q_0 + q_1 \\ \vdots \\ x_j, & \text{if } \sum_{i=0}^{j-1} q_i \le U < \sum_{i=0}^{j} q_i \\ \vdots \end{cases}.$$

If the possible values of X's are ordered such as $x_0 < x_1 < x_2 < \cdots$, then the cumulative distribution function can be written as $F(x_k) = \sum_{i=0}^{k} q_i$ and

$$X = x_j \text{ if } F(x_{j-1}) \le U < F(x_j).$$

It follows therefore that after generating the random number U, we determine the value of X by looking for the interval $[F(x_j - 1), F(x_j))$ in which it lies (or equivalently finding the inverse of U). Ordering these possible values can help develop an algorithm that is much more efficient as illustrated below. The reason is that we can reduce the number of comparisons in finding the value of X.

Suppose we are interested in simulating from the discrete distribution with

$$q_1 = 0.30, \quad q_2 = 0.10, \quad q_3 = 0.45, \quad \text{and} \quad q_4 = 0.15,$$

where $q_j = P(X = j)$.

The algorithm can be outlined according to the following steps.

- generate a random number U

- if $U < 0.30$, set $X = 1$ and STOP

- if $U < 0.40$, set $X = 2$ and STOP

- if $U < 0.85$, set $X = 3$ and STOP

- otherwise set $X = 4$.

It is suggested the following could be more efficient:

- generate a random number U

- if $U < 0.45$, set $X = 3$ and STOP

- if $U < 0.75$, set $X = 1$ and STOP

- if $U < 0.90$, set $X = 4$ and STOP

- otherwise set $X = 2$.

Here, the values of the random variable are sorted according to their probabilities, resulting in a more efficient search.

The function simdiscrete below provides an algorithm for generating from a given discrete distribution:

```
simdiscrete <- function(x, probs, n.gen){
  set.seed(1)
  xprobs <- data.frame(x=x,probs=probs)
  xprobs.sorted <- xprobs[order(xprobs["probs"],
    decreasing = T), ]
  cum.probs <- cumsum(xprobs.sorted[,2])
  xprobs.sorted <- cbind(xprobs.sorted,cum.probs)
  urandom <- runif(n.gen)
  sim.vector <- rep(0,n.gen)
  for(i in 1:n.gen) {
    ind <- min(which(cum.probs >= urandom[i]))
    sim.vector[i] <- xprobs.sorted[ind,1]
  }
  sim.vector
}
```

We can simulate a random number from a discrete distribution as follows:

```
1 > x <- c(1,2,3,4)
2 > probs <- c(0.30,0.10,0.45,0.15)
3 > sum(probs)
4 [1] 1
5 > out1 <- simdiscrete(x,probs,100)
6 > out1
7    [1] 3 3 1 2 3 4 2 1 1 3 3 3 1 3 4 1 1 2 3 4 2 3 1 3 3 3
          3 3 4 3 1 1 1 3 4 1 4
8   [38] 3 1 3 4 1 4 1 1 4 3 1 1 1 1 4 3 3 3 3 3 1 1 3 2 3 1
          3 1 3 1 4 3 4 3 4 3 3
9   [75] 1 4 4 3 4 2 3 1 3 3 4 3 1 3 3 3 3 3 1 4 4 4 1 3 4 1
```

To check if the results make sense, we can use the function xtabs to tabulate them as follows:

```
1 > xtabs(~out1)/100
2 out1
3    1     2     3     4
4 0.30  0.06  0.43  0.21
```

It is clear from this tabulated results that we are somewhat close to the actual distribution. However, we can improve on the accuracy of these frequencies by increasing the number of simulations.

———————————————⬮———————————————

Exercise 18.2. Write R code to simulate from the following discrete distribution:

$$P(X = 0) = 0.05, \quad P(X = 2) = 0.15, \quad P(X = 4) = 0.10,$$
$$P(X = 8) = 0.20, \quad \text{and} \quad P(X = 9) = 0.50.$$

Execute this code for 100,000 simulations and tabulate the results by calculating the frequency distribution and comparing it with the actual distribution.

———————————————⬮———————————————

Consider the special case of the discrete uniform distribution where we have equal probabilities for all possible outcomes as

$$P(X = j) = 1/n, \quad \text{for } j = 1, 2, \dots, n.$$

To simulate from this distribution, we generate a random number U and then set

$$X = j \quad \text{if} \quad \frac{j-1}{n} \le U < \frac{j}{n}.$$

This condition is clearly equivalent to $j - 1 \leq nU < j$ so that we can express the generated value as

$$X = \text{Int}(nU) + 1,$$

where $\text{Int}(x)$ is the greatest integer part of x.

Exercise 18.3. Following a similar argument to the discrete uniform distribution, show that under the geometric distribution with

$$P(X = x) = p(1 - p)^{x-1}, \quad \text{for } x = 1, 2, \ldots$$

the generated value can be expressed as

$$X = \text{Int}\left[\frac{\ln(1 - U)}{\ln(1 - p)}\right] + 1.$$

Consider yet another special case where we want to generate from the Poisson distribution with mean parameter λ:

$$P(X = x) = e^{-\lambda}\frac{\lambda^x}{x!}, \quad \text{for } x = 0, 1, 2, \ldots$$

Here, we exploit the recursion property of the Poisson (which is easy to prove):

$$P(X = x + 1) = \frac{\lambda}{x + 1}P(X = x), \quad \text{for } x = 0, 1, 2, \ldots.$$

To generate a value X from a Poisson with parameter λ, we follow the following steps:

Step 1: Generate a random number U.

Step 2: Assign $x = 0$, $p = e^{-\lambda}$, and $F = p$.

Step 3: If $U < F$, assign $X = x$ and STOP.

Step 4: Otherwise, re-assign $p = \lambda p/(x + 1)$, $F = F + p$, and $x = x + 1$.

Step 5: Return to Step 3.

Note that F is indeed the cumulative distribution function $F(x) = P(X \leq x)$. It should be apparent that the average number of iterations in the search grows with the mean parameter λ.

Following these steps outlined above, we can write an R function such as `simPoisson`:

```
1  simPoisson <- function(n.gen,lambda){
2    set.seed(1)
3    urandom <- runif(n.gen)
4    sim.vector <- rep(0,n.gen)
5    for(i in 1:n.gen){
6      x <- 0
7      p <- exp(-lambda)
8      F <- p
9      while(urandom[i] >= F){
10        p <- lambda*p/(x+1)
11        F <- F+p
12        x <- x+1
13      }
14      sim.vector[i] <- x
15    }
16    sim.vector
17  }
```

The following code shows how to use the above function to simulate random numbers from a Poisson distribution:

```
1  > out1 <- simPoisson(1000,5)
2  > mean(out1)
3  [1] 5.027
4  > xtabs(~out1)/1000
5  out1
6       0      1      2      3      4      5      6      7      8
                      9     10     11     12
7  0.004  0.031  0.083  0.141  0.191  0.168  0.149  0.095  0.060
        0.044  0.016  0.013  0.003
8      14     15
9  0.001  0.001
10 > barplot(xtabs(~out1)/1000)
```

In the above code, we used the R function `barplot` to display the frequencies of the simulated values. The resulting **bar plot** is shown in Figure 18.2.

Loops are generally inefficient in R so if at all possible, one should try to avoid writing simulation code that contains loops. For generating discrete random variables, there are built-in functions in R for some known discrete distributions. Most of these functions begin with the letter "r." Some of these functions are shown in Table 18.1. It is advisable to use the 'help' function to figure out how to execute these functions.

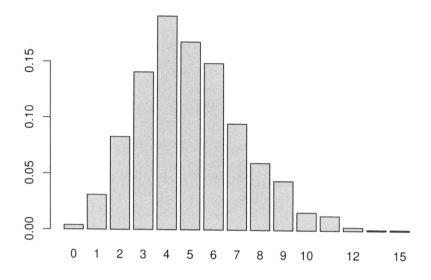

Figure 18.2: *Barplot of the resulting distribution.*

Distribution	R Function
Binomial	rbinom
Negative binomial	rnbinom
Poisson	rpois
Geometric	rgeom
Hypergeometric	rhyper

Table 18.1: *Some R functions for generating discrete random variables.*

Exercise 18.4. Use the built-in function `rbinom` to generate 10,000 values from a binomial distribution with parameters $n = 10$ and $p = 0.15$. Check the mean and draw a bar plot of the resulting simulated distribution. Comment on these results.

18.3 Simulating Continuous Random Variables

We now introduce the concept of inverse transform as an algorithm for generating a continuous random variable X with a cumulative distribution function F. This algorithm is based on the following theory. If F^{-1} is the inverse of F, then the random variable defined by

$$X = F^{-1}(U),$$

where U is a uniform random variable on $(0, 1)$, has distribution function F. The proof of this result is straightforward, can be found in many standard textbooks in introductory mathematical statistics, and is well-known. See Ross (2012b). So long as we can derive the explicit form of F^{-1}, we can use this result to generate from a continuous distribution with cumulative distribution function F.

This procedure is the so-called inverse transform method. According to this method, we generate a random number U and set $X = F^{-1}(U)$.

For a simple illustration, let X come from a distribution with

$$F(x) = x^n, \quad \text{for } 0 < x < 1.$$

We can simulate values from this distribution by setting $X = U^{1/n}$ after generating U.

As yet another example, consider the exponential distribution with mean parameter $1/\lambda$ so that its probability density function is

$$f(x) = \lambda e^{-\lambda x}, \quad \text{for } x > 0.$$

With a random number U, we can generate values from this distribution by setting $X = -\dfrac{1}{\lambda} \ln(U)$.

The following R code simulates values from an exponential distribution with parameter $\lambda = 5$.

```
1 > set.seed(1)
2 > urandom <- runif(10000)
3 > lambda <- 5
4 > x.exp <- -log(urandom)/lambda
5 > summary(x.exp)
6       Min.    1st Qu.    Median      Mean     3rd Qu.
          Max.
7 0.0000139 0.0557100 0.1403000 0.2014000 0.2752000
      1.8300000
8 > hist(x.exp,br=40,xlab="",ylab="",main="10,000
      simulations from exponential",col='grey')
```

The histogram of the simulated values is shown in Figure 18.3.

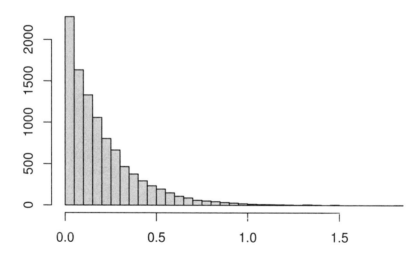

Figure 18.3: *The histogram of random numbers simulated from an exponential distribution.*

One of the widely used distributions in probability and statistics is the normal distribution. It is well-known that the density function of a normal with mean μ

and variance σ^2 can be expressed as

$$f(x) = \frac{1}{\sqrt{2\pi}\sigma} e^{-(x-\mu)^2/2\sigma^2}, \text{ for } -\infty < x < \infty. \tag{18.3}$$

There is no explicit form of the cumulative distribution function for a normal random variable. Hence, the inverse transform method does not work in this case. There are two popular methods of generating from a normal distribution: the **Box-Muller** transformation method and the **polar** method. Both methods are beyond the scope of this book, however, standard textbooks on simulation cover these methods. See Ross (2012b) and Korn et al. (2010).

For our purposes, we will rely on the built-in functions of R for simulating continuous random variables. Some of these are given in Table 18.2.

Distribution	R Function
Exponential	rexp
Gamma	rgamma
Normal	rnorm

Table 18.2: *Some R functions for generating continuous random variables.*

To illustrate, we have the following R code to generate a normal random variable with mean 10 and variance 100.

```
1 > set.seed(1)
2 > x.norm <- rnorm(10000,mean=10,sd=10)
3 > summary(x.norm)
4    Min. 1st Qu.  Median    Mean 3rd Qu.    Max.
5 -26.710   3.266   9.841   9.935  16.780  48.100
6 > hist(x.norm,br=40,xlab="",ylab="",main="10,000
     simulations from normal",col='grey')
```

The histogram of the simulated values is shown in Figure 18.4.

18.4   Problem Description

We now demonstrate the usefulness of simulation by considering the profitability analysis of a portfolio of short term insurance contracts. There are many situations in insurance where the contracts may be issued on a short-term basis, including for example:

- non-life contracts, e.g. automobile, homeowners, renters insurance

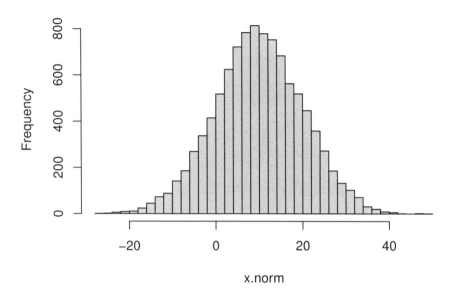

Figure 18.4: *The histogram of random numbers simulated from a normal distribution.*

- professional liability contracts

- workers' compensation

- health insurance

- term life insurance, e.g. one-year

In pricing for these contracts, some important features include:

- Claims consist of two components: frequency (number of claims) and severity (amount, given there is a claim). See Chapters 8 and 9.

- Investment earnings are typically ignored, but are important to consider in an economic environment of high interest rates.

- The obligation may extend beyond the contractual period so it makes it important to look at the tail of the claim distribution.

Let us consider a one-year time horizon and suppose we have been asked to investigate the profitability of a small insurance company's automobile line of business. The company has a portfolio of 100,000 policies all issued at the beginning of the year with the characteristics given in Table 18.3.

Type of Driver	Number of Policies	One-year Premium Per Policy
male, young	10,000	750
male, old	40,000	600
female, young	20,000	650
female, old	30,000	700

Table 18.3: *Characteristics of the portfolio of the policies.*

In addition, the portfolio has an overhead (or fixed) expense of 1,200,000 for the year plus a per policy expense of 4.50 to cover administration and other related expenses.

For certain classes of short-term insurance such as automobile or homeowners, the total (or aggregate) claims for the year, denoted by S, can be modeled with a **collective risk model** where for a given portfolio of policies, both the frequency (or number) and severity (or amount, given a claim) of claims are modeled as random variables. For our portfolio described above, for each class of drivers, say class i, the aggregate claims for the year can be expressed as

$$S_i = X_{i,1} + X_{i,2} + \cdots + X_{i,N_i}$$

where $X_{i,j}$ refers to the j-th claim amount for class i and N_i refers to the number of claims for class i, for $i = 1, 2, 3, 4$.

After reviewing the company's historical claims experience, we have determined that the claim count, N, and the claim size, X, for each type of driver follow the parametric distributions specified in Table 18.4.

In addition, we are given the following simplifying information:

- Premiums are collected at the beginning of the year, and all expenses are incurred at the beginning of the year.

- Claims are paid at the end of the year.

Type of Driver	Frequency (N)	Severity (X)
male, young	Poisson with $\lambda = 2000$	Pareto with $\theta = 1500$, $\alpha = 2$
male, old	Poisson with $\lambda = 4000$	Pareto with $\theta = 1500$, $\alpha = 2$
female, young	Poisson with $\lambda = 2000$	Pareto with $\theta = 1800$, $\alpha = 2.5$
female, old	Poisson with $\lambda = 1500$	Pareto with $\theta = 1800$, $\alpha = 2.5$

Table 18.4: *Frequency and severity distributions by type of driver.*

- Any unused premiums to pay for expenses at the beginning of the year are invested at the risk-free rate of 2.5%.

In reality, at the end of the year, it is possible that there may be claims that have not been reported. Insurance companies typically hold an amount of reserves, funds set aside, to cover for such claims. These reserves could be a substantial amount, however, for our practical purposes, we shall ignore these required reserves.

The claim amount X has a **Pareto distribution** with parameters θ and α if its cumulative distribution function can be expressed as

$$F(x) = 1 - \left(\frac{\theta}{x + \theta} \right)^{\alpha}, \quad \text{for } x > 0.$$

Exercise 18.5. Show that to generate values from a Pareto distribution with parameters θ and α as described above, we can use the inverse transform method with

$$X = \theta \left[(1 - U)^{-1/\alpha} - 1 \right].$$

Use this method to generate 1,000 values from a Pareto distribution with $\theta = 500$ and $\alpha = 2$. Summarize the results with a histogram.

Now to continue with our profitability analysis, we first examine the aggregate claims for the year. To simulate the distribution of these aggregate claims, we need to first simulate the number of claims, N, for each class of driver, and once N is known, we simulate N independent random claim amounts, X. The following R code does this for each class of drivers:

```
1 > # number of policies
2 > n.pol <- c(10000,40000,20000,30000)
3 > tot.pol <- sum(n.pol)
4 > # premium per policy
5 > prem <- c(750,600,650,700)
6 > # allocation of overhead/fixed expense
7 > fexp <- 1200000*(n.pol/tot.pol)
8 > # expense per policy
9 > pexp <- 4.5*n.pol
10 > # distribution parameters
11 > lambda <- c(2000,4000,2000,1500)
12 > theta <- c(1500,1500,1800,1800)
13 > alpha <- c(2,2,2.5,2.5)
14 > # function to simulate the aggregate claims process
15 > simaggclaims <- function(n.gen,ptheta,palpha,nlambda){
16 +   set.seed(1)
17 +   n.claims <- rpois(n.gen,nlambda)
18 +   S.vector <- rep(0,n.gen)
19 +   for (i in 1:n.gen) {
20 +     urandom <- runif(n.claims[i])
21 +     claims <- ptheta * ((1-urandom)^(-1/palpha)-1)
22 +     S.vector[i] <- sum(claims)
23 +   }
24 +   # output
25 +   S.vector
26 + }
27 > # simulate aggregate claims from each type of driver
28 > n.sim <- 10000
29 > aggclms1 <- simaggclaims(n.sim,theta[1],alpha[1],lambda
     [1])
30 > aggclms2 <- simaggclaims(n.sim,theta[2],alpha[2],lambda
     [2])
31 > aggclms3 <- simaggclaims(n.sim,theta[3],alpha[3],lambda
     [3])
32 > aggclms4 <- simaggclaims(n.sim,theta[4],alpha[4],lambda
     [4])
33 > # summary statistics of aggregate claims
34 > summary(aggclms1)
35    Min.  1st Qu.   Median     Mean  3rd Qu.     Max.
36  2409399  2847440  2971543  3005772  3113381 13027321
37 > summary(aggclms2)
```

```
38      Min.   1st Qu.    Median       Mean   3rd Qu.       Max.
39    5141120   5774601   5960032    6003927   6172793  16335192
40  > summary(aggclms3)
41      Min. 1st Qu.   Median       Mean 3rd Qu.     Max.
42   2010436  2314587  2393277    2402369  2478832  4340666
43  > summary(aggclms4)
44      Min. 1st Qu.   Median       Mean 3rd Qu.     Max.
45   1465884  1726346  1793135    1801218  1866865  3491294
46  > # histogram of the aggregate claims
47  > par(mfrow=c(2,2))
48  > hist(aggclms1/1000000,br=40,xlab="in millions",ylab="
        frequency",main="male, young drivers",freq=FALSE)
49  > hist(aggclms2/1000000,br=40,xlab="in millions",ylab="
        frequency",main="male, old drivers",freq=FALSE)
50  > hist(aggclms3/1000000,br=40,xlab="in millions",ylab="
        frequency",main="female, young drivers",freq=FALSE)
51  > hist(aggclms4/1000000,br=40,xlab="in millions",ylab="
        frequency",main="female, old drivers",freq=FALSE)
```

According to the number of policies, 10% are male, young, 40% are male, old, 20% are female, young, and 30% are female, old. Although there is an equal number of male and female drivers, there appears to be a substantial difference in the resulting aggregate claims between them, with the male drivers clearly generating much larger aggregate claims on the average. The male drivers are averaging aggregate claims of about 9 million compared to only 4 million for female drivers, a bit less than a half. What is even more striking is the large skewness in the aggregate claims for male drivers. This is quite evident in the histograms shown in Figure 18.5. Female drivers tend to have smaller skewness while the male, old drivers tend to have highly skewed claims distribution. This is again evident in the maximum aggregate claims of 16 million for male old drivers. This class of drivers should be watched closely.

Exercise 18.6. Approximate 95% confidence intervals of the mean aggregate claims for each class of drivers and comment on these approximations.

In analyzing the profitability, we consider the profit at the end of the year as follows:

$$\text{Profit} = (\text{Premiums} - \text{Expenses}) \times (1 + i) - \text{Aggregate Claims},$$

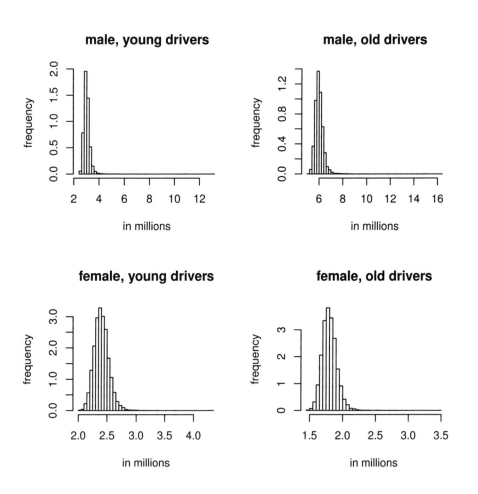

Figure 18.5: *Distribution of the aggregate claims for the various classes of drivers.*

where Premiums, Expenses, and Aggregate Claims are as obviously defined and i is the risk-free rate that is used to accumulate any unused premiums during the calendar year until claims are paid at the end of the year. The only random component in the profit is the aggregate claims which has already been analyzed. The R code for computing profits can be found below:

```
1 > # risk free rate
2 > rf <- .025
3 > # compute profitability for each type of drivers
4 > profit1 <- ((prem[1]*n.pol[1])-fexp[1]-pexp[1])*(1+rf)
      - aggclms1
5 > profit2 <- ((prem[2]*n.pol[2])-fexp[2]-pexp[2])*(1+rf)
      - aggclms2
6 > profit3 <- ((prem[3]*n.pol[3])-fexp[3]-pexp[3])*(1+rf)
      - aggclms3
7 > profit4 <- ((prem[4]*n.pol[4])-fexp[4]-pexp[4])*(1+rf)
      - aggclms4
8 > # summary statistics of aggregate claims
9 > summary(profit1)
      Min.   1st Qu.    Median      Mean   3rd Qu.      Max.
-5508946   4404994   4546832   4512603   4670935   5108976
12 > summary(profit2)
      Min.   1st Qu.    Median      Mean   3rd Qu.      Max.
 7588308  17750707  17963468  17919573  18148899  18782380
15 > summary(profit3)
      Min.   1st Qu.    Median      Mean   3rd Qu.      Max.
 8646084  10507918  10593473  10584381  10672163  10976314
18 > summary(profit4)
      Min.   1st Qu.    Median      Mean   3rd Qu.      Max.
17526331  19150760  19224490  19216407  19291279  19551741
21 > # histogram of the profits
22 > par(mfrow=c(2,2))
23 > hist(profit1/1000000,br=40,xlab="in millions",ylab="
      frequency",main="male, young drivers",freq=FALSE)
24 > hist(profit2/1000000,br=40,xlab="in millions",ylab="
      frequency",main="male, old drivers",freq=FALSE)
25 > hist(profit3/1000000,br=40,xlab="in millions",ylab="
      frequency",main="female, young drivers",freq=FALSE)
26 > hist(profit4/1000000,br=40,xlab="in millions",ylab="
      frequency",main="female, old drivers",freq=FALSE)
```

The statistics above provide for very interesting profit patterns for the various classes of drivers. On average, we see that the old drivers (both male and female) are generating larger profits than the young drivers. We also notice because claims reduce the profits, it has an opposite effect on the profit distributions as seen from the skewness of the profit distributions. They are now all negatively skewed as expected. Notice also that because the only source of randomness is derived from the claims, the variability of profits is exactly that of the aggregate claims. The female, old drivers appear to be the most profitable on the average; even its minimum profit of 17.5 million provides an indication how strong the profits are from this class. The small variation of this profit, as seen in Figure 18.5, provides for an added bonus. On the other hand, the class of male, young drivers provides for the lowest average profit, and its minimum profit in the simulation provides for a loss. The histograms in Figure 18.6 present a graphical representation of the profitability for each class.

Exercise 18.7. Approximate 95% confidence intervals of the mean profit for each class of drivers and comment on these approximations.

It is also useful to examine the overall profitability of the portfolio of policies. Summary statistics are provided below and the histogram of total profit is given in Figure 18.7.

```
1 > tot.profit <- profit1+profit2+profit3+profit4
2 > summary(tot.profit)
3      Min.   1st Qu.    Median      Mean    3rd Qu.      Max.
4 40196654 51952263 52293868 52232964 52594784 53817041
5 > hist(tot.profit/1000000,br=100,xlab="in millions",ylab=
     "frequency",main="Total Profitability",freq=FALSE)
```

According to the summary statistics above, there is not much concern on the average, with the portfolio expected to provide approximately 52 million of profits to the company during the year. There is the concern of the claims made by the class of male, young drivers which could cause negative profits (i.e. losses). However, a closer examination of the data will reveal that this negative profit occurred only twice in the simulation, a very rare event.

Finally, it is an industry practice to examine the **loss (or claims) ratio**, defined by the average amount of claims per dollar of premium, as well as the **profit margin**, defined by the average amount of profit per dollar of premium. These statistics are summarized for each class of drivers in Table 18.5.

These results somehow provide a similar profit picture to what we have already observed. While all classes of drivers are generating positive and large

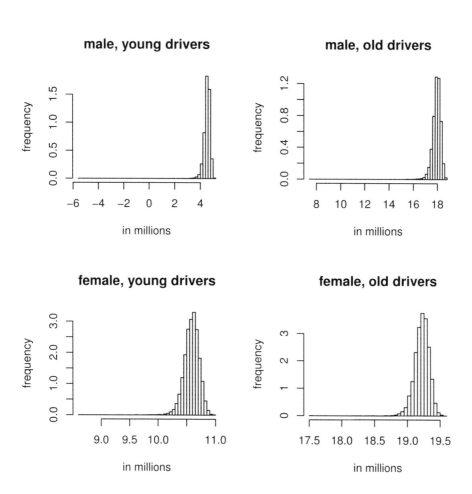

Figure 18.6: *Distribution of the profits for the various classes of drivers.*

Type of Driver	Loss Ratio	Profit Margin
male, young	40%	60%
male, old	25%	75%
female, young	18%	81%
female, old	9%	92%

Table 18.5: *Loss ratios and profit margins by type of driver.*

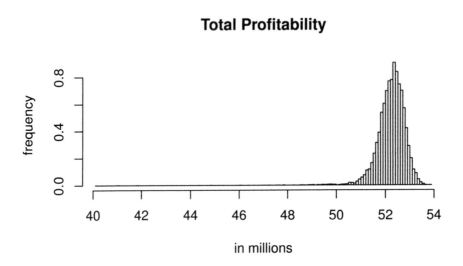

Figure 18.7: *Distribution of the aggregate profits for all classes of drivers combined.*

profit margins, the one class that appears to be least profitable, on a per dollar of premium basis, is the class of male, young drivers. This is generally true for portfolios of automobile insurance policies.

Overall, there appears to be a disparity of profit margins across the different classes of drivers. This may either be driven by competition where the risky classes cannot generate large enough profits because of it, or it could be a result of mispricing by the company. The company should examine this profit margin a bit more carefully because if nothing is done, it could trigger regulators to question the disparity. Furthermore, these levels of profit margins are too high, and usually cannot be sustained for long periods of time particularly in the face of competitiveness in the insurance industry.

18.5 Summary

In this chapter, we provided a short introduction to the concept of simulation. We mainly focused on the inverse transform method for generating random values from either a discrete or continuous distribution. While learning this basic method is useful, R has several built-in functions to simulate from many well-known discrete and continuous distributions. We have referred to them in this chapter as necessary. We also introduced the important concept of Monte Carlo approach for approximating integrals; this is useful in statistical data analysis as a tool for approximating expectations. Mathematical expectations involve integration and hence they can be approximated based on Monte Carlo simulation. We demonstrated how we can use simulation for analyzing the profitability of short-term insurance contracts. The extension to longer term contracts will generally involve stochastic process and hence will be more complicated. However, the extension should come naturally from concepts introduced in this chapter. For more information about simulation, readers are referred to (Korn et al., 2010) and (Ross, 2012a).

18.6 End-of-Chapter Exercises

Exercise 18.8. An alternative to model the total claims is to consider each policy in the portfolio and their likelihood of a claim within a short period, e.g., one year. This is called the **individual risk model** where in a portfolio of n (usually fixed and known) policies, the total claims will equal to

$$S = X_1 \cdot I_1 + X_2 \cdot I_2 + \cdots + X_n \cdot I_n,$$

where I_j for the j-th policy is a Bernoulli random variable with a value of 1 if there is a claim and with probability of a claim q_j, for $j = 1, \ldots, n$. The amount of the claim will be X_j, given there is a claim.

Assume that in an insurance portfolio of 100 policies, the I_j's are Bernoulli distributed with $q_j = 0.10$ and the X_j's are distributed as Pareto with parameters $\theta = 20$ and $\alpha = 3$. The cumulative distribution function of a Pareto with parameters θ and α is given by

$$F(x) = 1 - \left(\frac{\theta}{x + \theta}\right)^\alpha.$$

In addition, the random variables $I_1, I_2, \ldots, I_{100}, X_1, X_2, \ldots, X_{100}$ are independent.

(a) Calculate the true values of the mean and variance of S.

(b) Explain how you would execute a simulation procedure to produce aggregate claims S for this insurance portfolio.

(c) Using the procedure in (b), simulate 100,000 values of S. Provide supporting summary statistics and histogram of these simulated values. Discuss the reasonableness of your simulated values by simply comparing your simulated mean and variance to the true values of the mean and variance of S as calculated in (a).

(Hint: Recall that the Bernoulli is a special case of the Binomial distribution, and hence to simplify your simulation, you are welcome to use the R command `rbinom`.)

Chapter 19

Case Study: Simulating the Future Lifetime of a Person

In this chapter, we focus our attention on long-term insurance contracts that require us to understand the random lifetime of a person. We demonstrate how to simulate the future lifetime of a person and briefly examine how these simulated values can be used in the pricing and reserving of life insurance contracts. After working through this chapter, readers will be able to

- Understand the concept of the future lifetime of a person

- Characterize the distributions of this future lifetime

- Simulate the future lifetime of a person

- Use simulated values for pricing and reserving

19.1 Time-Until-Death Random Variables

Life insurance and annuity contracts are random cash flow contracts for which the cash flows or payments are contingent upon the future lifetime of the insured. In this section, we model and investigate time-until-death random variables, starting with the age-at-death random variable. The age-at-death is essentially the time-until-death for a newborn individual. We introduce survival probabilities and forces of mortality which are ways to characterize the behavior of these random variables. See Bowers et al. (1997).

Let X be the age-at-death random variable assumed to be continuous and non-negative. It is interpreted as the future lifetime of a newborn or an individual from birth. The distribution of X can be described by its survival distribution function defined to be $S(x) = P(X > x)$ and is interpreted as the probability that a newborn will reach age x. This survival function satisfies certain properties:

(a) The probability a newborn survives at least 0 years is 1, that is, $S(0) = 1$.

(b) All newborn individuals will eventually die so that $S(\infty) = \lim_{x \to \infty} S(x) = 0$.

(c) $S(x)$ must be a non-increasing function of x.

The last property is quite obvious because for someone to survive at a later year, say x, he must survive to reach an age earlier than x.

The complement of $S(x)$ is the cumulative distribution function defined by $F(x) = P(X \le x) = 1 - S(x)$. It is interpreted as the probability that the newborn does not reach to age x. The density function is

$$f(x) = \frac{d}{dx} F(x) = -\frac{d}{dx} S(x)$$

Finally, the force of mortality at age x is defined to be

$$\mu_x = -\frac{1}{S(x)} \frac{d}{dx} S(x) = -\frac{d}{dx} \ln S(x). \tag{19.1}$$

The force of mortality is a very important concept in life contingencies. Its interpretation is hardly understood, but by writing the derivative in terms of limit,

$$\mu_x = \frac{1}{S(x)} \lim_{h \to 0} \frac{S(x) - S(x+h)}{h} = \frac{1}{S(x)} \lim_{h \to 0} \frac{P(x \le X < x+h)}{h},$$

we see that for infinitesimally small value of h, we can approximately write $P(x \le X < x + h | X > x) \approx h\mu_x$.

Any one of these four functions, $S(x)$, $F(x)$, $f(x)$ and μ_x characterizes the distribution of X. The knowledge of any one of them allows us to derive the other three functions. This is left as an exercise (See Exercise 19.1.).

Exercise 19.1. Given any one of the functions $S(x)$, $F(x)$, $f(x)$ and μ_x, find expressions for the other three functions in terms of that given function. For example, given the force of mortality μ_x, find expressions for $S(x)$, $F(x)$ and $f(x)$ in terms of μ_x alone.

Example 19.1. You are given: $\mu_x = \dfrac{1}{110-x}$, for $0 \le x < 110$.

(a) Determine $S(x)$ and $f(x)$.

(b) Calculate the probability that a newborn will die between ages 65 and 75.

Solution 19.1.　(a) $S(x) = \exp\left(-\displaystyle\int_0^x \dfrac{1}{110-z}\,dz\right) = \exp\left(\ln(110-z)\Big|_0^x\right) = 1 - \dfrac{x}{110}$

and $f(x) = -\dfrac{d}{dx}S(x) = \dfrac{1}{110}$, for $0 \le x < 110$.

(b) The probability that a newborn will die between ages 65 and 75 is $\displaystyle\int_{65}^{75} f(x)\,dx =$

$\displaystyle\int_{65}^{75} \dfrac{1}{110}\,dx = \dfrac{1}{11}$. It can also be shown that such a probability can be expressed as the difference between survival probabilities as

$$S(65) - S(75) = \left(1 - \dfrac{65}{110}\right) - \left(1 - \dfrac{75}{110}\right) = \dfrac{1}{11}.$$

Consider a person age x observed at time 0. We refer to this person as life (x). The future lifetime of (x), also called the time-until-death, is denoted by T_x. A person of age x will die at the random age of $x + T_x$ years. If no confusion is possible, we will sometimes simply denote T_x by T. For a newborn, $x = 0$, so that we have $T_0 = X$.

The survival function, $S_T(t)$, of T_x will be denoted by $_tp_x$:

$$S_T(t) = P(T_x > t) = P(X > x + t \mid X > x) = \dfrac{P(X > x + t)}{P(X > x)} = \dfrac{S(x+t)}{S(x)} = {}_tp_x. \quad (19.2)$$

This refers to the probability that (x) survives t years. The cumulative distribution function, $F_T(t)$, of T_x is the complement of the survival function and will be denoted by $_tq_x$:

$$F_T(t) = P(T_x \le t) = 1 - S_T(t) = 1 - \dfrac{S(x+t)}{S(x)} = {}_tq_x = 1 - {}_tp_x. \quad (19.3)$$

This refers to the probability that (x) dies within t years. The prefix t is omitted for $t = 1$. We assume that $P(0 < T_x < \infty) = 1$, that T_x has a continuous distribution and that its density function defined by

$$f_T(t) = \dfrac{d}{dt}{}_tq_x = -\dfrac{d}{dt}{}_tp_x \quad (19.4)$$

exists whenever it is used.

It should be obvious that $_0p_x = 1$, $_0q_x = 0$, $\lim_{t\to\infty} {}_tp_x = 0$, and $\lim_{t\to\infty} {}_tq_x = 1$. These equations tell us that at age x, the person is alive, and that all lives eventually die.

For a person age x, its force of mortality at time t can be defined as

$$\mu_{x+t} = -\frac{1}{{}_tp_x}\frac{d}{dt}{}_tp_x = -\frac{d}{dt}\ln {}_tp_x. \qquad (19.5)$$

Using fundamental concepts in differential equations, it can be shown from Equation (19.5) that the following important formula holds:

$$_tp_x = \exp\left(-\int_0^t \mu_{x+s}ds\right) \qquad (19.6)$$

Finally, it follows immediately from Equations (19.4) and (19.5) that

$$f_T(t) = {}_tp_x\mu_{x+t}. \qquad (19.7)$$

Exercise 19.2. Suppose you are given the survival function: $S(x) = \left(1 - \frac{x}{100}\right)^{1/2}$, for $0 \le x < 100$.

(a) Find an expression for μ_{x+t}.

(b) Calculate the probability that a person now age 40 survives to reach age 65.

(c) Calculate the probability that a person now age 40 survives to reach age 65, but dies between ages 65 and 75.

Exercise 19.2 part (c) above illustrates a deferred probability that is quite important in life contingencies. The probability that (x) dies between u and $u + t$ years from now is denoted by $_{u|t}q_x$. This is equivalent to the probability that (x) will die between the ages of $x + u$ and $x + u + t$, and can be computed in several ways:

$$
\begin{aligned}
_{u|t}q_x &= P(u < T_x \le u + t) = P(T_x \le u + t) - P(T_x < u) \\
&= {}_{u+t}q_x - {}_uq_x = {}_up_x - {}_{u+t}p_x \\
&= {}_up_x \times {}_tq_{x+u}.
\end{aligned}
$$

In the case where $t = 1$, the t portion of the prefix is omitted and we simply use the notation $_{u|}q_x$. This symbol then represents the probability that (x) survives for u years, but dies the following year.

The probability of survival satisfies the multiplicative property in the sense that

$$_{s+t}p_x = {_sp_x} \times {_tp_{x+s}} = {_tp_x} \times {_sp_{x+t}}.$$ (19.8)

This does not hold true in the case of probabilities of death. Instead, if we want to decompose the probability of dying within two subsequent intervals, we use the following:

$$_{s+t}q_x = {_sq_x} + {_sp_x} \times {_tp_{x+s}}.$$ (19.9)

The reader can think through the formulas to understand the intuition.

19.2 Curtate Future Lifetime

The curtate future lifetime of (x) is the number of integral years completed by (x) prior to death. This will be denoted by K_x and is defined by $K_x = \lfloor T_x \rfloor$, the greatest integer of T_x. Here, K_x has a discrete distribution with a probability mass function derived as follows

$$
\begin{aligned}
P(K_x = k) &= P(k \le T_x < k+1) = P(k < T_x \le k+1) \\
&= S_T(k) - S_T(k+1) = {_{k+1}q_x} - {_kq_x} = {_{k|}q_x},
\end{aligned}
$$

for $k = 0, 1, 2, \ldots$. Its distribution function is

$$P(K_x \le k) = \sum_{h=0}^{k} {_{h|}q_x} = {_{k+1}q_x}.$$

Note that it can be shown that $\sum_0^\infty P(K_x = k) = \sum_0^\infty {_{k|}q_x} = 1$.

Example 19.2. Suppose we have a constant force of mortality $\mu_x = \mu$. Find expressions for the probability mass function and the distribution function of K_x.

Solution 19.2. It follows that

$$P(K_x = k) = {_{k|}q_x} = {_kp_x} \cdot q_{x+k} = \left(1 - e^{-\mu}\right)e^{-\mu k}$$

and

$$P(K_x \le k) = {_{k+1}q_x} = 1 - {_{k+1}p_x} = 1 - e^{-\mu(k+1)}.$$

The last equation can also be directly shown from the probability mass function as follows:

$$P(K_x \le k) = \sum_{h=0}^{k} {_{h|}q_x} = \left(1 - e^{-\mu}\right)\sum_{h=0}^{k} e^{-\mu h} = \left(1 - e^{-\mu}\right)\frac{1 - e^{-\mu(k+1)}}{(1 - e^{-\mu})} = 1 - e^{-\mu(k+1)}.$$

Exercise 19.3. You are given the following survival function:

$$S(x) = \left(1 - \frac{x}{110}\right)^{2/3}, \qquad \text{for } 0 \le x < 110.$$

Calculate $P(K_{20} = 10)$ where K_{20} is the curtate future lifetime of (20). Interpret this probability.

Exercise 19.4. Suppose you are given that $q_x = 0.001$, for all $x > 0$.

(a) Find an expression for the probability mass function of K_x.

(b) Calculate the probability that a 30 year old will die between the ages of 40 and 45.

19.3   Expectation of Life

The expected value of the time-until-death random variable for (x) refers to the complete expectation of life and is simply interpreted as the average future lifetime of a person now age x. This is denoted by $\mathring{e}_x$ and is equal to

$$\mathring{e}_x = \mathrm{E}(T_x) = \int_0^\infty t f_T(t) \, dt = \int_0^\infty {}_t p_x \mu_{x+t} \, dt. \qquad (19.10)$$

Assuming this expectation exists and using integration by parts, we can show the simplified formula:

$$\mathring{e}_x = \int_0^\infty {}_t p_x \, dt \qquad (19.11)$$

Exercise 19.5. Suppose you are given that $\mu_x = \dfrac{1}{3(110 - x)}$, for $0 \le x < 110$.

(a) Find an expression for $S(x)$.

(b) Find an expression for ${}_t p_x$.

(c) Calculate $\mathring{e}_{50}$.

We have analogous formulas for the case of the **curtate (or discrete) future lifetime**. The expected value of K_x is called the curtate expectation of life and is simply denoted by e_x:

$$e_x = \mathrm{E}(K_x) = \sum_{k=0}^{\infty} k \cdot P(K_x = k) = \sum_{k=0}^{\infty} k \cdot {}_{k|}q_x. \tag{19.12}$$

By noting that ${}_{k|}q_x = {}_kp_x - {}_{k+1}p_x$, we can be shown that

$$e_x = \sum_{k=1}^{\infty} {}_kp_x.$$

For the n-year curtate expectation of life, we have

$$e_{x:\overline{n}|} = \sum_{k=1}^{n} {}_kp_x. \tag{19.13}$$

This refers to the average lifetime of a person (x) within the next n years.

Exercise 19.6. Suppose you are given that $\mu_x = \dfrac{1}{2(x+1)}$, for $x > 0$. Calculate $e_{50:\overline{5}|}$.

19.4 Simulating Gompertz Lifetime Distributions

The **Gompertz lifetime** distribution has widely appeared in actuarial literature. It has the appeal that its distribution is somewhat tractable and, at the same time, it provides the intuitive interpretation that mortality generally increases exponentially with age. It has been demonstrated in the literature how good a Gompertz fits, especially for older ages. See Milevsky (2012) and Bowers et al. (1997).

Mortality is said to follow the Gompertz distribution if we can express its force of mortality as

$$\mu_x = Bc^x,$$

where B and c are constants satisfying $B > 0$ and $c > 1$. It is easy to show that, for an issue age x, its future lifetime T_x follows the survival pattern

$$S_T(t) = P(T_x > t) = \exp\left[\frac{-Bc^x}{\ln(c)}(c^t - 1)\right], \tag{19.14}$$

for $t \geq 0$.

This explicit form of the survival probability allows us to use the inverse transform method to simulate from Gompertz.

Begin with a random number U, generate a Gompertz lifetime, say T, from the following equation:

$$\exp\left[\frac{-Bc^x}{\ln(c)}(c^T - 1)\right] = U,$$

or equivalently, we have

$$T = \frac{1}{\ln(c)}\ln\left[1 - \frac{\ln(c)\cdot\ln(U)}{Bc^x}\right]. \tag{19.15}$$

Running this procedure m (number of simulations) times, we can then have a simulated distribution of the Gompertz lifetime.

19.5   Applications to Life Insurance Pricing and Reserving

In pricing for life insurance contracts, it is widely accepted to use the notion of the **actuarial equivalence principle**. According to this principle, the present value of loss is calculated at issue and the premium is determined by setting its expectation to zero. On average, the insurance company breaks even on a present value basis.

However, the actuarial equivalence principle has one main drawback: it simply looks at the mean or average of the loss-at-issue distribution. An alternative is to examine the variability of this loss, but this does not give the complete picture of the loss distribution. A much better alternative is to examine the (entire) loss distribution itself. In many cases, it is impossible to derive the explicit form of the loss distribution. Simulating the loss distribution is one method to do it; the main drawback is that it requires computationally intensive calculations.

For illustrative purposes, we now demonstrate this for a whole life insurance policy issued to a single person where we consider the case that the benefit is paid immediately upon death and that premiums are continuously paid. In practice, the procedure is much more complicated because the product may not be whole life, premiums may be paid less frequently than continuously, and profit and expenses may be factored in.

With a simulated value of T (which could depend on attained age x), we simulate the present value of the loss-at-issue. For example, in a fully continuous whole life insurance contract as previously explained, the present value of the loss-at-issue can be expressed as

$$L_0 = b_T\, v^T - \pi \cdot \ddot{a}_{\overline{T}|} \tag{19.16}$$

where $v = 1/(1+i)$ is the discount factor, π is the annual premium rate assumed to be payable continuously throughout the year, b_T is the amount of insurance payable immediately at death, and $\ddot{a}_{\overline{T}|}$ is the present value of an annuity (Kellison, 2008). After generating future lifetimes m number of times, we evaluate Equation (19.16) for each simulated value of T to get a simulated distribution of the loss-at-issue.

Reserves are generally funds set aside by the insurer to cover its future financial obligations as promised by the insurance contract. They show up as a liability item in the insurer's balance sheet and increases in reserves are expense items in the income statement. Reserve calculations may vary because of the purpose of the reserve and differences in assumptions and basis. The chief actuary of an insurance company is responsible for preparing an opinion that the company's assets are sufficient to back up each reserve.

When computing reserves prospectively, we need to evaluate the loss at time of valuation. Suppose we are interested in the loss after k years, then it can be shown that the simulated lifetime for the person who is then aged $x + k$ is

$$T = \frac{1}{\ln(c)} \ln\left[1 - \frac{\ln(c) \cdot \ln(U)}{B c^{x+k}}\right],$$

where U is a uniform random number.

For a fully continuous whole life insurance contract, we would have the loss after k years evaluated as

$$L_k = b_T\, v^T - \pi \cdot \ddot{a}_{\overline{T}|},$$

where T is the future lifetime of the person (x) who has now attained age $x + k$.

Now to illustrate, we assume the following Gompertz parameter values:

$$B = 0.0000429 \quad \text{and} \quad c = 1.1070839.$$

Consider a fully continuous whole life insurance contract issued to age 30 and we are interested in both the present value of the loss-at-issue and the reserve distribution after 10 years from issue. In addition, we set the benefit amount to be \$100, premium at \$0.0095 per \$1 of insurance, and $i = 5\%$. We will repeat the simulation 50,000 times.

The following R code shows how to do these calculations:

```
 1 > set.seed(1)
 2 > # set the number of pairs to generate
 3 > n.sim <- 50000
 4 > # enter Gompertz parameters
 5 > B <- 0.0000429
 6 > c <- 1.1070839
 7 > # issue age
 8 > iss.age <- 30
 9 > benefit <- 100
10 > # generate Uniform values
11 > U1 <- runif(n.sim)
12 > U2 <- runif(n.sim)
13 > temp1 <- B*c^iss.age
14 > temp2 <- 1 - (log(c)*log(U1)/temp1)
15 > t.30 <- log(temp2)/log(c)
16 > # set premium
17 > prem <- .0095
18 > interest <- 0.05
19 > v <- 1/(1+interest)
20 > delta <- log(1+interest)
21 > # compute the PV of loss at issue
22 > annuity.t.30 <- (1-v^t.30)/delta
23 > loss.30 <- benefit*(v^t.30 - prem*annuity.t.30)
24 > # now for the reserve (after 10 years)
25 > temp3 <- B*c^(iss.age+10)
26 > temp4 <- 1 - (log(c)*log(U2)/temp3)
27 > t.40 <- log(temp4)/log(c)
28 > # compute the PV of loss after 10 years
29 > annuity.t.40 <- (1-v^t.40)/delta
30 > loss.40 <- benefit*(v^t.40 - prem*annuity.t.40)
31 > summary(t.30)
32     Min.  1st Qu.   Median     Mean  3rd Qu.      Max.
33  0.07618 34.41222 42.90461 41.15446 49.65836 70.56225
34 > summary(loss.30)
35     Min.  1st Qu.   Median     Mean  3rd Qu.      Max.
36 -15.6508  -8.8777  -4.7431  -0.1356   2.8179  99.5567
37 > summary(t.40)
38     Min.  1st Qu.   Median     Mean  3rd Qu.      Max.
39  0.02106 24.90930 33.14562 31.75681 39.89747 61.20332
40 > summary(loss.40)
41   Min. 1st Qu.  Median   Mean 3rd Qu.    Max.
```

```
42  -13.440    -2.416    4.239    10.152    15.965    99.877
43  > par(mfrow=c(2,2))
44  > hist(t.30,cex.lab=1.25,br=40,xlab="t.30",ylab="
       frequency",main="Distribution of T(30)",col='grey',
       freq=FALSE)
45  > lines(density(t.30),col="black",lwd=2)
46  > hist(loss.30,cex.lab=1.25,br=40,ylim=c(0,0.07),xlab="
       loss.30",ylab="frequency",main="Distribution of Loss-
       at-issue",col='grey',freq=FALSE)
47  > lines(density(loss.30),col="black",lwd=2)
48  > hist(t.40,cex.lab=1.25,br=40,xlab="t.40",ylab="
       frequency",main="Distribution of T(40)",col='grey',
       freq=FALSE)
49  > lines(density(t.40),col="black",lwd=2)
50  > hist(loss.40,cex.lab=1.25,br=40,xlab="loss.40",ylab="
       frequency",main="Distribution of Loss at 10 yrs",col=
       'grey',freq=FALSE)
51  > lines(density(loss.40),col="black",lwd=2)
```

We note that a 30 year old has a median lifetime of 43 and a mean lifetime of 41 years. Based on the pricing assumptions outlined above, we note that the average present value of the loss at issue is about -0.14, close enough to zero. For the prospective reserves, the average amount is about 10.15 with a 75th percentile of 15.97. The simulated distributions for the various quantities of interest (future lifetime of (30), future lifetime after 10 years, present values of losses at issue, and at duration 10 years) are displayed in Figure 19.1.

19.6 Simulating Makeham Lifetime Distributions

A variation to the Gompertz is the **Makeham** law of mortality which has an additional constant that is independent of age. The force of mortality in this case is expressed as

$$\mu_x = A + Bc^x$$

See Bowers et al. (1997). Under this mortality law, for an individual currently aged x, the future lifetime T_x has survival distribution

$$S_T(t) = P(T_x > t) = e^{-At - \frac{Bc^x}{\ln(c)}(c^t - 1)} \tag{19.17}$$

and density function

$$f_T(t) = (A + Bc^{x+t}) e^{-At - \frac{Bc^x}{\ln(c)}(c^t - 1)}. \tag{19.18}$$

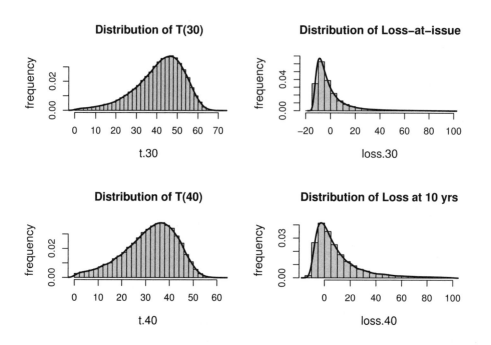

Figure 19.1: *Graphical display of the simulation results.*

The addition of the constant A in the Makeham law makes it difficult to apply the inverse transform method because it is not possible to explicitly solve the inverse of the cumulative distribution function. We use the **rejection method** in this case.

Suppose we wish to generate X from a distribution with density function $f(x)$. Assume that we are able to generate Y from a distribution with density function $g(y)$ and that there is a constant k such that

$$\frac{f(y)}{g(y)} \leq k, \text{ for all } y.$$

According to the rejection method, we can generate X using the following steps:

Step 1: Generate Y from the distribution with density g.

Step 2: Generate a random number U.

Step 3: If $U \leq \dfrac{f(Y)}{kg(Y)}$, set $X = Y$.

Step 4: Otherwise, return to step 1.

We skip the proof of this algorithm but we encourage readers to check out Ross (2012b).

In the case of Makeham, to apply the rejection method, first, we need to determine the constant k by maximizing the ratio of the density of Makeham to that of Gompertz. Note that Gompertz is just a special case of Makeham where $A = 0$ so that the ratio of the two densities can be expressed as

$$\frac{A + Bc^{x+t}}{Bc^{x+t}} e^{-At} \tag{19.19}$$

Note that to maximize Equation (19.19), taking the first derivative will lead us nowhere. However, it can be shown that this function is indeed decreasing from $t = 0$ to ∞ so that the maximum is obtained at $t = 0$.

Now consider the case where we have

$$A = 0.001, \quad B = 0.0000070848535, \quad \text{and } c = 1.1194379.$$

These parameter values have been suggested in (Mereu, 1962). We now demonstrate how to simulate, using the Makeham law, the future lifetime, T_{50}, of a person currently age 50.

In using the rejection method, the value of k chosen in this case is

$$k = \frac{0.001 + (0.0000070848535)(1.1194379)^{50}}{(0.0000070848535)(1.1194379)^{50}}.$$

Thus, according to the rejection method, the following steps will simulate future lifetimes T_{50}^M from the Makeham law. We will use the superscripts M and G to refer to Makeham and Gompertz, respectively.

Step 1: Generate a Gompertz lifetime T_{50}^G.

Step 2: Generate a uniform random number U.

Step 3: If $U \le \dfrac{f^M(T_{50}^G)}{k f^G(T_{50}^G)}$, set $T_{50}^M = T_{50}^G$.

Step 4: Otherwise, return to step 1 and follow the procedure again.

This method has been coded in R as shown below. The results of the simulation are summarized both numerically below and in the form of a histogram displayed in Figure 19.2.

```
 1 > # enter parameter values
 2 > x <- 50
 3 > A <- 0.001
 4 > B <- 0.0000070848535
 5 > c <- 1.1194379
 6 > # t* that maximizes ratio (is zero)
 7 > t.star <- 0
 8 > # function to evaluate density of Gompertz
 9 > d.gompertz <- function(t,x,A,B,c){
10 +    temp1 <- B*c^(x+t)
11 +    temp2 <- B*c^x*(c^t-1)/log(c)
12 +    out <- temp1 * exp(-temp2)
13 +    out
14 + }
15 > # function to evaluate density of Makeham
16 > d.makeham <- function(t,x,A,B,c){
17 +    temp1 <- A+B*c^(x+t)
18 +    temp2 <- B*c^x*(c^t-1)/log(c)
19 +    out <- temp1 * exp(-A*t-temp2)
20 +    out
21 + }
22 > # function to simulate from Gompertz
23 > sim.gompertz <- function(x,A,B,c){
24 +    u.random <- runif(1)
25 +    temp1 <- B*c^x
26 +    temp2 <- 1 - (log(c)*log(u.random)/temp1)
27 +    t.x <- log(temp2)/log(c)
28 +    t.x
29 + }
30 > n.sim <- 10000
31 > sim.vector <- rep(0,n.sim)
32 > # acceptance rejection method
33 > set.seed(1)
34 > for(j in 1:n.sim){
35 +    u.random <- runif(1)
36 +    c.star <- d.makeham(t.star,x,A,B,c)/d.gompertz(t.star
       ,x,A,B,c)
37 +    y <- sim.gompertz(x,A,B,c)
38 +    ratio <- d.makeham(y,x,A,B,c)/(c.star*d.gompertz(y,x,
       A,B,c))
39 +    while(u.random > ratio){
40 +       u.random <- runif(1)
41 +       y <- sim.gompertz(x,A,B,c)
42 +       ratio <- d.makeham(y,x,A,B,c)/(c.star*d.gompertz(y,
```

```
        x,A,B,c))
43 +    }
44 +    sim.vector[j] <- y
45 + }
46 > summary(sim.vector)
47     Min.   1st Qu.   Median    Mean   3rd Qu.    Max.
48   0.08959 24.27501 32.27345 30.72140 38.51720 55.39276
49 > hist(sim.vector,br=50,xlab="T50",main="Future Lifetime
       of 50 year old",freq=FALSE)
```

The histogram of the simulated values is shown in Figure 19.2.

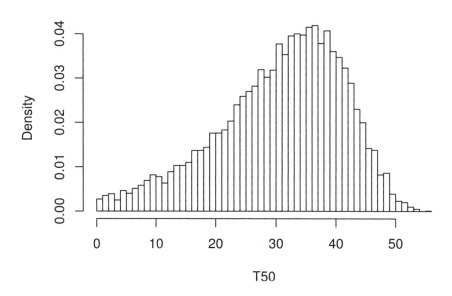

Figure 19.2: *Histogram of the simulated future lifetime of a 50-year-old.*

19.7 Simulating from a Mortality Table

This is useful in practice because valuation may be based on a prescribed mortality table and pricing may be based on the insurance company's mortality experience.

A mortality table provides the evolution of the death (or survival) of a cohort of lives in a tabular format, usually with:

- age x

- number of survivors, ℓ_x, at age x

- number of deaths, d_x, between ages x and $x+1$

Given a person has reached a fixed age x, the probability of surviving the following year is

$$p_x = \frac{\ell_{x+1}}{\ell_x}$$

and the probability of dying during the following year is

$$q_x = 1 - p_x = \frac{d_x}{\ell_x}.$$

Given a mortality table, we can reproduce (or simulate) the (discrete) age at which a newborn will die in the future. Starting with a cohort of ℓ_0 lives at birth, a newborn has a probability of dying between ages x and $x+1$ equal to

$$\frac{d_x}{\ell_0}.$$

Thus, the simulation procedure is that applicable to a discrete distribution.

To illustrate, we use the synthetic mortality table saved in the file `2013ABVT.csv`. The table consists of three columns: age x, number of survivors ℓ_x, and number of deaths d_x. The annual probability of dying from the mortality table is graphically displayed in Figure 19.3.

We now illustrate how to simulate the curtate future lifetime of a person now age 40. The following R code provides the simulation from this mortality table.

```
 1 > # required inputs: x, probabilities, number to generate
 2 > simdiscrete <- function(x, probs, n.gen){
 3 +     set.seed(1)
 4 +     xprobs <- data.frame(x=x,probs=probs)
 5 +     xprobs.sorted <- xprobs[order(xprobs["probs"],
         decreasing = T), ]
 6 +     cum.probs <- cumsum(xprobs.sorted[,2])
 7 +     xprobs.sorted <- cbind(xprobs.sorted,cum.probs)
 8 +     urandom <- runif(n.gen)
 9 +     sim.vector <- rep(0,n.gen)
10 +     for(i in 1:n.gen) {
11 +         ind <- min(which(cum.probs >= urandom[i]))
```

Annual Probability of Dying

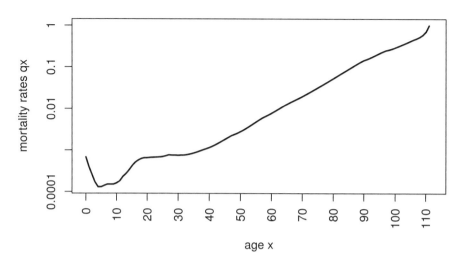

Figure 19.3: *Annual mortality rates from the mortality table 2013ABVT.csv.*

```
12 +       sim.vector[i] <- xprobs.sorted[ind,1]
13 +    }
14 +    sim.vector
15 + }
16 >
17 > ABVT2013 <- read.csv("2013ABVT.csv")
18 > attach(ABVT2013)
19 > names(ABVT2013)
20 [1] "x"   "lx" "dx"
21 >
22 > dprob <- dx/lx[1]
23 > X0 <- simdiscrete(x,dprob,50000)
24 > # consider only those who have reached 40
25 > K40 <- X0[which(X0>39)] - 40
26 > summary(K40)
27    Min. 1st Qu.  Median    Mean 3rd Qu.    Max.
28    0.00   34.00   43.00   40.69   49.00   70.00
29 > hist(K40,br=40,xlab="(discrete) time until death from
      age 40",ylab="frequency",main="50,000 simulations",
      col='grey',freq=FALSE)
30 > lines(density(K40),col="black",lwd=2)
```

The histogram of the simulated values of K_{40} is shown in Figure 19.4.

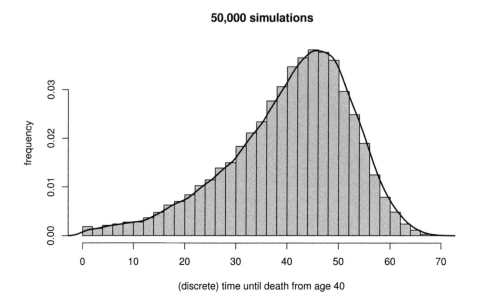

50,000 simulations

Figure 19.4: *Histogram of the simulated values of K_{40}.*

Consider a whole life insurance policy that pays a death benefit of 1,000 at the moment of death but premiums of 6.8 are payable once at the beginning of each year. Assume that the interest rate is 5%. The present value of the loss-at-issue in this case is

$$L_0 = b_T \, v^T - \pi \cdot \ddot{a}_{\overline{K+1}|},$$

where T is the exact time of death, K is the (discrete) time of death, and $\ddot{a}_{\overline{K+1}|}$ is the annuity-due. With a simulated value of K from the mortality table, we can adjust this with the addition of a Uniform random variable as

$$T = K + U.$$

Such is equivalent to assuming a so-called **uniform distribution of death (UDD)** over each year of age. See Bowers et al. (1997).

The following R code provides the simulation results of the present value of loss-at-issue.

```
1 > set.seed(1)
2 > ben <- 1000
3 > ann.prem <- 6.8
```

```
 4 > i <- 0.05
 5 > v <- 1/(1+i)
 6 > ann <- function(k){(1-v^(k+1))/(1-v)}
 7 > urandom <- runif(length(K40))
 8 > T40 <- K40 + urandom
 9 > pvloss <- 1000*v^T40 - ann.prem*ann(K40+1)
10 > summary(pvloss)
11      Min.    1st Qu.    Median      Mean    3rd Qu.      Max.
12  -107.228    -42.361    -4.282    41.465    68.647    986.542
13 > hist(pvloss,br=40,ylim=c(0,0.007),xlab="present value
       of loss",ylab="frequency",main="Present Value of Loss
       at Issue",col='grey',freq=FALSE)
14 > lines(density(pvloss),lwd=2)
```

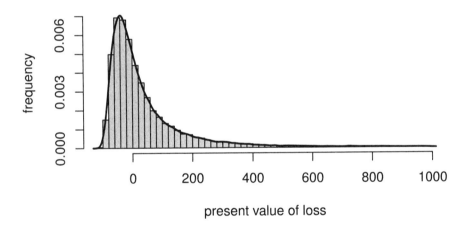

Figure 19.5: *Histogram of the simulated values of present value of loss at issue.*

Exercise 19.7. For a whole life insurance policy issued to a person aged 40, a death benefit of 1,000 is payable at the moment of death, premiums of 6.8 are payable once at the beginning of each year, and the interest rate is 5%. Use the mortality table in the file 2013ABVT.csv to simulate the future lifetime of the person after 10 years and the corresponding loss after 10 years.

19.8 Summary

In this chapter, we introduced the concept of simulating the future lifetime of a person. In order to be self-contained, we provided brief introductions to survival models and mortality tables. These models are useful for life insurance contracts that have longer than one year of maturity period. We examined two widely known parametric mortality models: the Gompertz and Makeham laws of mortality. We illustrated how to simulate future lifetimes from these mortality models and demonstrated the use of the results in pricing and reserving. Finally, for practical reasons, we also added the idea of how to simulate from a mortality table. For additional information, readers are referred to (Bowers et al., 1997) and Korn et al. (2010).

19.9 End-of-Chapter Exercises

Exercise 19.8. In this chapter, we learned about simulating the loss resulting from a life insurance policy. The counterpart of a life insurance policy is a life annuity, which pays a benefit so long as you are alive, and this type of policy is useful for retirement. Indeed, when we studied life insurance, we considered life annuities because premiums were paid so long as the insured was alive.

Consider pricing a life annuity issued to a person aged 65 with a single premium, say π, and the policy pays a benefit of 20,000 so long as the annuitant (here the buyer of the policy) is alive. Consider only the case where the payment is made at the beginning of each year that the annuitant is alive. Therefore, the present value of the loss-at-issue to the insurer is expressed as

$$L_0 = \pi - 20000 \times \ddot{a}_{\overline{K+1}|},$$

where K is the discrete time of death, for a person aged 65. Assume that mortality follows the life table in the file 2013ABVT.csv and the interest rate is 5%. However, this table is applicable for life insurance policies, and buyers of life annuities often have what is called the selection effect: that the survival of those policyholders buying life annuities is generally better than those buying life insurance. To account for this effect, you adjust the age 65 to the age 60 for pricing purposes; here, you are saying that the survival pattern of an annuitant aged 65 is similar to a buyer of life insurance aged 60.

Whenever you are asked to simulate, do it at least 10,000 times.

(a) Use simulation to approximate the premium π so that your average loss-at-issue is zero.

(b) Use simulation to approximate the premium π so that you are 75% certain you will have a positive gain. (Remark: Here you may have to do a trial-and-error, but you can also code this in R using a loop by incrementally changing the single premium until you get the desired result within a small difference.)

(c) Suppose you were told that for this cohort of age 65 annuitants, there is a yearly improvement rate in mortality by 0.5%. Explain how you would reflect this in your calculation for the premium π. Then, use simulation to approximate this premium so that your average loss-at-issue is zero. Explain why mortality improvement will increase or decrease the cost of life annuities.

Appendix A

Introduction to R

R is a programming language and an open source software environment for statistical computing and graphics. As a popular statistical software, R has the following features (Matloff, 2011):

- R is an open source implementation of the S statistical computing language developed at Bell Laboratories in the 1970s.
- R is a general-purpose programming language with many statistical operations.
- R is platform independent and can be used in Windows, Mac, and Linux.

In addition, R supports the development, testing, and distribution of user-created packages, thereby allowing implementation of advanced statistical techniques. It has the superb capability of and flexible tools for creating high quality graphics for data visualization.

In this chapter, we give a short introduction to R. After reading this chapter, readers should be able to

- install and invoke R
- create and run R scripts
- create and manipulate vectors, matrices, lists, data frames, factors, and tables
- read and write files
- write simple R functions and R programs using flow controls and loops
- produce graphics

311

A.1 How to Run R

If your computer does not have R, you can download R from the R project web-site http://www.r-project.org/ and install it. The Comprehensive R Archive Network (CRAN) has many mirrors or replicas around the world. You can choose a mirror that is close to you and download the precompiled binary distributions of the base system and contributed packages.

Once R is installed in your computer, you can start the R environment. On a Windows machine, for example, you will see something like this:

```
 1  R version 3.4.0 (2017-04-21) -- "You Stupid Darkness"
 2  Copyright (C) 2017 The R Foundation for Statistical
        Computing
 3  Platform: i386-w64-mingw32/i386 (32-bit)
 4
 5  R is free software and comes with ABSOLUTELY NO WARRANTY.
 6  You are welcome to redistribute it under certain
        conditions.
 7  Type 'license()' or 'licence()' for distribution details.
 8
 9    Natural language support but running in an English
          locale
10
11  R is a collaborative project with many contributors.
12  Type 'contributors()' for more information and
13  'citation()' on how to cite R or R packages in
        publications.
14
15  Type 'demo()' for some demos, 'help()' for on-line help,
        or
16  'help.start()' for an HTML browser interface to help.
17  Type 'q()' to quit R.
18
19  >
```

The window showing the above message is called the R **Console**.

The > sign is the R prompt. You execute R commands by typing the commands after this prompt and hitting the enter key. For example, if you type pi after the > sign and hit the enter key, you get:

```
 1  > pi
 2  [1] 3.141593
 3  >
```

In R, `pi` represents the mathematical constant π, which is the ratio of a circle's circumference to its diameter. To see where your current working directory is, you type `getwd()` after the prompt and hit the enter key. For example, my current working directory is:

```
1 > getwd()
2 [1] "C:/Users/Guojun Gan/Documents"
3 >
```

Unlike the command `pi`, the command `getwd()` is a function without any arguments. To call the function, you have to include the brackets `()` in the command. If you just type `getwd` and hit the enter key, you get

```
1 > getwd
2 function ()
3 .Internal(getwd())
4 <bytecode: 0x0000000010820ca0>
5 <environment: namespace:base>
```

The R output shows that `getwd` is a built-in function of the base system.

You can also type R commands in a text file, referred to as a script file, and execute all the commands in the script file by calling the function `source()`. For example, we can type the previous commands into a text file and save the text file as `sample.R` to the current working directory. Listing A.1 shows the content of the script file. In lines 1, 2, 3, and 5, the texts following the symbol # are considered comments, which are not executable.

```
1 # a sample R script
2 pi # show the mathematical constant pi
3 # get the current working directory
4 getwd()
5 # see what happens if we call getwd without brackets
6 getwd
```

Listing A.1: *A sample R script.*

To execute the script, we type `source("sample.R")` after the prompt and hit the enter key. After executing the command, you get

```
1 > source("sample.R")
2 >
```

If you call the `source` function to execute these commands, you will not see the intermediate outputs. To see the intermediate outputs of commands in a script file, you can open the script file in the R environment and execute the selected commands in the script file.

In a Windows machine, you open the script file and run all the commands by clicking "Run all" from the "Edit" menu[1]. For example, if we open the "sample.R" file and click "Run all" from the "Edit" menu, we see the following output:

```
 1  > # a sample R script
 2  > pi # show the mathematical constant pi
 3  [1] 3.141593
 4  > # get the current working directory
 5  > getwd()
 6  [1] "C:/Users/Guojun Gan/Documents"
 7  > # see what happens if we call getwd without brackets
 8  > getwd
 9  function ()
10  .Internal(getwd())
11  <bytecode: 0x0000000010820ca0>
12  <environment: namespace:base>
13  >
```

If you do not want to run all the commands, you can run the commands in a single line or multiple lines by clicking "Run line or selection" from the "Edit" menu or hitting the key combination "Ctrl+R." In a Mac computer, the key combination to run a single line or multiple liners of R code is "Command+Enter."

Usually you type one command in a line. However, you can type multiple commands in a line and separate them by semicolons. For example, if we type the following commands in the R Console:

```
 1  getwd();setwd("C:\\Users\\Guojun Gan\\Documents\\Code");
      getwd()
```

we see the following output:

```
 1  > getwd();setwd("C:\\Users\\Guojun Gan\\Documents\\Code")
      ;getwd()
 2  [1] "C:/Users/Guojun Gan/Documents"
 3  [1] "C:/Users/Guojun Gan/Documents/Code"
 4  >
```

In this single line, we type three commands: get the current working directory, set the working directory to a specified one, and get the current working directory.

---

[1]To see the "Run all" item from the "Edit" menu, make sure the script window is the current active window. Otherwise, the "Run all" item is not shown in the "Edit" menu.

The R function setwd allows you to change the working directory to a specified directory. In R, you specify a directory using double backslashes (\\) or a single forward slash (/). For example, we can call the setwd function using

```
setwd("C:/Users/Guojun Gan/Documents/Code")
```

To exit the R environment, you can type the function q() in the R Console. In a Windows machine, you can click the "Exit" in the "File" menu to exit R. In a Mac computer, you can click "Quit R" in the "R" menu to exit R. In a Windows machine, R will pop up a dialog and ask you whether you want to save the workspace image. If you click the "Yes" button, all the objects in the current session will be saved and loaded automatically the next time you start R. This feature is useful if you work with lots of data.

A.2 Variables

Variables allow us to store results for reuse. In R, we use the operator <- to assign a value to a variable. There are several assignment operators in R: <-, ->, and =. If you type help(assignOps) in the R Console, you will be directed to the description of these assignment operators.

Variable names can contain letters, numbers, dots, and underscores. However, variable names cannot start with a number or a dot followed by a number. The following example shows how we can assign a value to a variable and illustrates what variable names are illegal.

```
> x <- 5 # assign 5 to the variable x
> x + 6 # x plus 6
[1] 11
> x < -5 # notice the space between < and -
[1] FALSE
> 3x <- 5
Error: unexpected symbol in "3x"
> .x <- 5
> .x
[1] 5
> .3x <- 5
Error: unexpected symbol in ".3x"
```

Note that there are no spaces in the assignment operator <-. If you insert a space between < and -, the statement becomes a logical statement.

Exercise A.1. Examine the following R code and answer the question:

```
x <- 1
y <- x+10
x <- x+y
z <- y - x
```

What are the values of x, y, and z after the code is executed?

A.3 Vectors

The **vector** is a fundamental data type in R. Unlike in other programming languages such as C, individual numbers (i.e., scalars) in R are special cases of vectors. In this section, we introduce vectors in R and vector operations such as **recycling**, **filtering**, and **vectorization**.

There are several ways to create a vector: use the c function, use the `vector` function, use the `seq` function, and use the colon operator `:`. In the following example, we illustrate how to use these approaches to create vectors:

```
 1 > v1<-c()
 2 > v1
 3 NULL
 4 > v2<-c(1,2,3)
 5 > v2
 6 [1] 1 2 3
 7 > v3<-vector(length=4)
 8 > v3
 9 [1] FALSE FALSE FALSE FALSE
10 > v3[2]<-2
11 > v3
12 [1] 0 2 0 0
13 > v3[3:4]<-c(3,4)
14 > v3
15 [1] 0 2 3 4
16 > v4<-seq(from=0,to=6,by=2)
17 > v4
18 [1] 0 2 4 6
19 > v5<-2:5
20 > v5
21 [1] 2 3 4 5
22 > v6<-1.2:4.5
```

```
23 > v6
24 [1]  1.2  2.2  3.2  4.2
```

The first vector v1 is an empty vector, which does not contain any elements. The second vector v2 contains three elements specified in the c function. The third vector v3 is created by the vector function with four elements. The default mode of the elements of the vectors created by the vector function is logical. A logical variable has two possible values: FALSE and TRUE. The fourth vector v4 is created by the seq function, and finally, the last two vectors are created by the colon operator.

The above example also shows how we can change one or more elements of a vector. For example, we first change the second element of v3 to 2. The mode of the vector is changed to numeric automatically with the unspecified elements defaulting to zero. Then we change the third and the fourth elements to 3 and 4, respectively. Note that unlike in other programming languages such as C and Java, vector indices in R begin at 1.

Exercise A.2. Use one of the three functions c, vector, and seq to create the following vectors:

(a) $(1, 2, \ldots, 100)$

(b) $(2, 4, 6, \ldots, 200)$

(c) $(10, 12, 14, \ldots, 200)$

Exercise A.3. Use the functions c and seq to create the following vector:

$$(1, 4, 7, 7, 6, 5, 6, 10, 14).$$

Exercise A.4. Use the functions vector and seq and the assignment operator <- to create the vector $(x_1, x_2, \ldots, x_{100})$ such that $x_{2i-1} = 1$ and $x_{2i} = 0$ for $i = 1, 2, \ldots, 50$, i.e.,

$$(1, 0, 1, 0, \ldots, 1, 0).$$

Exercise A.5. Use the functions c and seq to create the following vector:

$$(1, 2, \ldots, 10, 11, 10, 9, \ldots, 1).$$

In addition to the aforementioned functions for creating vectors, the functions rep and paste can also be used to create vectors as shown in the following example:

```
1 > x <- c(1:3)
2 > x
3 [1] 1 2 3
4 > rep(x,3)
5 [1] 1 2 3 1 2 3 1 2 3
6 > paste("str",x)
7 [1] "str 1" "str 2" "str 3"
8 > paste("str",x, sep="")
9 [1] "str1" "str2" "str3"
```

The function rep produces a vector by repeating another vector. The function paste is very useful to convert a vector of numbers to a vector of characters.

Exercise A.6. Use the functions c and rep to create the vector in Exercise A.4.

Exercise A.7. Use the function help to find the usage of the function rep and then use the function rep to create the following vector:

$$(1,1,1,2,2,2,3,3,3)$$

Exercise A.8. Use the function help to find the usage of the function paste and then use the function paste to create the following string:

"1, 2, ..., 100"

which contains 100 numbers separated by commas.

To get the number of elements in a vector, we use the length function. To get the sum of the elements of a numeric vector, we use the sum function.

```
1 > x<-c(1,2,3)
2 > length(x)
3 [1] 3
4 > sum(x)
5 [1] 6
```

Exercise A.9. Use vectors and the function sum to calculate the following sum:

$$\sum_{i=1}^{100}(i+i^2).$$

We can insert an element to a vector easily by using the c function. For example, we insert 4 to the vector x after the first element:

```
1 > x<-c(1,2,3)
2 > x<-c(x[1],4,x[2:3])
3 > length(x)
4 [1] 4
5 > x
6 [1] 1 4 2 3
```

We can get a subvector of a vector by specifying the indices of the elements in square brackets. In the following example, we first get a subvector containing the first and third elements of x and a subvector containing the fourth and second elements of x. Then we concatenate the two subvectors into a new vector and assign the new vector to x.

```
1 > x<-c(1,4,2,3)
2 > x<-c(x[c(1,3)],x[c(4,2)])
3 > x
4 [1] 1 2 3 4
```

We can apply four basic arithmetic operations (i.e., +, -, *, /) to vectors:

```
1 > x<-c(1,2,3)
2 > x
3 [1] 1 2 3
4 > y<-1:6
5 > y
6 [1] 1 2 3 4 5 6
7 > x+y
8 [1] 2 4 6 5 7 9
9 > x-y
10 [1]  0  0  0 -3 -3 -3
11 > x*y
12 [1]  1  4  9  4 10 18
13 > x/y
14 [1] 1.00 1.00 1.00 0.25 0.40 0.50
```

In the above example, we apply the four basic operations to the vectors x and y. Note that x is a three-element vector and y is a six-element vector. From the results, we see that R automatically repeats the elements of the shorter vector to match the longer vector. This is the **recycling** feature of R.

When the length of the longer vector is not a multiple of that of the shorter vector, R will issue a warning if you apply the basic operations to the vectors:

```
1 > x<-c(1,2,3)
2 > y<-1:5
3 > x-y
4 [1]   0   0   0  -3  -3
5 Warning message:
6 In x  -  y :  longer  object  length  is  not  a  multiple  of
       shorter  object  length
```

Exercise A.10. Examine the following R code and answer the question:

```
1 x <- 1:3
2 y <- rep(c(0,1,2,3),  times=1,  each=3)
3 z <- x + y
```

What are the elements of the vector z?

Filtering is another feature of the R programming language. Filtering allows us to extract the elements of a vector that satisfy certain conditions. Filtering indices can be generated in two ways. One way is to specify the indices manually; another is to use expressions containing logical operators. Once the filtering indices are generated, we use the square bracket [] operator or the subset function to extract the elements.

In the following example, we first create a vector with eight elements. Then we extract the four elements with odd indices by specifying the filtering indices manually in the vector c(1,3,5,7). We also use an expression with the logical operator == to generate the filtering indices. Both ways produce the same results as shown below:

```
1 > x<-1:8
2 > x[c(1,3,5,7)]
3 [1] 1 3 5 7
4 > x[x%%2==1]
5 [1] 1 3 5 7
```

In the above example, the symbol %% is the **modulus** operator, which calculates the remainder of dividing one number by another.

The following example shows how we can use the subset function to extract elements of a vector.

```
> x<-1:8
> subset(x,x%%2==1)
[1] 1 3 5 7
> subset(x,x>3)
[1] 4 5 6 7 8
> ind<-x>4
> ind
[1] FALSE FALSE FALSE FALSE  TRUE  TRUE  TRUE  TRUE
> subset(x,ind)
[1] 5 6 7 8
```

We can also use filtering to assign a value to the selected elements of a vector. In the following example, we first create a vector containing eight integers. Then we change the elements with odd values to zero. Then we replace the elements with zero values with either 1 or 2. Since there are four elements with zero values, the elements in the vector c(1,2) are repeated.

```
> x<-1:8
> x
[1] 1 2 3 4 5 6 7 8
> x[x%%2==1]<-0
> x
[1] 0 2 0 4 0 6 0 8
> x[x==0]<-c(1,2)
> x
[1] 1 2 2 4 1 6 2 8
> x[c(1,3,5,7)]<-c(-1,-3,-5,-7)
> x
[1] -1 2 -3 4 -5 6 -7 8
```

To see which elements of a vector are selected, we can use the which function. The following example shows the result of applying the which function.

```
> x
[1] 1 2 3 4 5 6 7 8
> which(x%%2==1)
[1] 1 3 5 7
```

Vectorization is an important feature of R that helps simplify our code and dramatically increases the performance of the code. If we want to apply a function to all elements of a vector, we use vectorized operations to call the function on the vector.

The following example illustrates how we use vectorized operations to simplify R code and achieve better performance. In this example, we first create a vector with 100,000 elements. Then we use a for loop (See Section A.10) to calculate the square roots of all the elements. It took about 0.21 seconds to finish the for loop calculation. Then we use a vectorized operation by calling the sqrt function on the vector. It took about 0 seconds to finish the vectorized calculation.

```
> x<-1:100000
> t<-proc.time(); for(i in 1:length(x)) x[i]<-sqrt(x[i]);
    proc.time()-t
   user   system elapsed
   0.21    0.00    0.21
> t<-proc.time(); x<-sqrt(x); proc.time()-t
   user   system elapsed
      0       0       0
```

In the above example, the proc.time function reports the accumulated values of the user CPU, system CPU, and elapsed time. Consider the following output of the function. The user CPU time (3.24 seconds) gives the CPU time spent by the current R session. The system CPU time (11.01 seconds) is the CPU time spent by the operating system on behalf of the R session. The elapsed time (72077.45 seconds) is the time spent by the current R session.

```
> proc.time()
   user   system elapsed
   3.24   11.01 72077.45
```

In R, we assign names to elements of a vector using the names function. We can also extract elements by their names. In the following example, we first create a three-element vector. By default, the names of the elements are NULL, which is a special value of R. Then we assign names to all the elements. Once the elements have names, we can extract elements by names. We remove the names by assigning NULL to the names.

```
> x<-1:3
> names(x)
NULL
> names(x)<-c("a","b","c")
> x
```

```
 6 a  b  c
 7 1  2  3
 8 > x[c("a","c")]
 9 a  c
10 1  3
11 > names(x)<-NULL
12 > x
13 [1]  1  2  3
```

Exercise A.11. Let $x = (x_1, x_2, \ldots, x_{300})$ and $y = (y_1, y_2, \ldots, y_{300})$ be two R vectors created as follows:

```
set.seed(1)
x <- sample(1:1000,300,replace=T)
y <- sample(1:1000,300,replace=T)
```

(a) Calculate the inner product of x and y:

$$\sum_{i=1}^{300} x_i y_i.$$

(b) Create a subvector of x by selecting elements that are larger than 500.

(c) How many elements of y are divisible by 2?

A.4 Matrices

In R, a matrix is a special vector with two attributes: rows and columns. In this section, we introduce how to create matrices, subsetting, and matrix operations.

To create a **matrix**, we use the `matrix` function. This function has several named parameters such as `nrow`, `ncol`, and `byrow`. In the following example, we create four matrices using the `matrix` function. The first matrix contains six `NA`s, which are a special value in R. The second matrix contains six integers given in the parameter. The third matrix is created by arranging the numbers in row-major order. The last matrix is created by arranging the numbers in the default order, which is the column-major order.

```
 1 > m1<-matrix(nrow=2,ncol=3)
 2 > m1
 3        [,1] [,2] [,3]
 4 [1,]    NA   NA   NA
 5 [2,]    NA   NA   NA
 6 > m2<-matrix(1:6,nrow=2,ncol=3)
 7 > m2
 8        [,1] [,2] [,3]
 9 [1,]     1    3    5
10 [2,]     2    4    6
11 > m3<-matrix(1:6,nrow=2,byrow=TRUE)
12 > m3
13        [,1] [,2] [,3]
14 [1,]     1    2    3
15 [2,]     4    5    6
16 > m4<-matrix(1:6,nrow=2)
17 > m4
18        [,1] [,2] [,3]
19 [1,]     1    3    5
20 [2,]     2    4    6
```

Exercise A.12. Use the functions c and matrix to create the following matrix:

$$A = \begin{pmatrix} 1 & -1 & -2 \\ 2 & 0 & 3 \\ -1 & 4 & 0 \end{pmatrix}$$

Exercise A.13. Use the function matrix to convert the following vector

$$(1, -1, -2, 2, 0, 3, -1, 4, 0)$$

to the matrix in Exercise A.12.

If two matrices have the same size, we can apply the four basic arithmetic operations (e.g. +, -, *, /) to the two matrices. The result is a matrix of the same size and each element is the result of applying the operation on an element-wise basis. These matrix operations are illustrated in the following example.

```
 1 > m1<-matrix(data=1:4,nrow=2)
 2 > m1
 3       [,1] [,2]
 4 [1,]    1    3
 5 [2,]    2    4
 6 > m2<-matrix(data=5:8,nrow=2)
 7 > m2
 8       [,1] [,2]
 9 [1,]    5    7
10 [2,]    6    8
11 > m1+m2
12       [,1] [,2]
13 [1,]    6   10
14 [2,]    8   12
15 > m1-m2
16       [,1] [,2]
17 [1,]   -4   -4
18 [2,]   -4   -4
19 > m1*m2
20       [,1] [,2]
21 [1,]    5   21
22 [2,]   12   32
23 > m1/m2
24               [,1]         [,2]
25 [1,]  0.2000000  0.4285714
26 [2,]  0.3333333  0.5000000
```

To perform mathematical matrix multiplication, we need to use the %*% operator. The following example illustrates how to perform mathematical matrix multiplication and the difference between the * operator and the %*% operator. In order to perform mathematical matrix multiplication, the number of columns of the first matrix must be equal to the number of rows of the second matrix. Otherwise, R will issue an error. The size of the resulting matrix is the number of rows of the first matrix by the number of columns of the second matrix.

```
 1 > m1<-matrix(data=1:4,nrow=2)
 2 > m1
 3       [,1] [,2]
 4 [1,]    1    3
 5 [2,]    2    4
 6 > m2<-matrix(data=1:2,nrow=2)
 7 > m2
 8       [,1]
```

```
 9 [1,]    1
10 [2,]    2
11 > m1*m2
12 Error in m1 * m2 : non-conformable arrays
13 > m1%*%m2
14        [,1]
15 [1,]    7
16 [2,]   10
17 > m1*2
18       [,1] [,2]
19 [1,]    2    6
20 [2,]    4    8
21 > m1%*%2
22 Error in m1 %*% 2 : non-conformable arguments
```

Exercise A.14. Let A be the matrix in Exercise A.12. Use the operator $*$ to obtain the following matrices:

$$A2 = \begin{pmatrix} a_{11}^2 & a_{12}^2 & a_{13}^2 \\ a_{21}^2 & a_{22}^2 & a_{23}^2 \\ a_{31}^2 & a_{32}^2 & a_{33}^2 \end{pmatrix}, \quad A5 = \begin{pmatrix} a_{11}^5 & a_{12}^5 & a_{13}^5 \\ a_{21}^5 & a_{22}^5 & a_{23}^5 \\ a_{31}^5 & a_{32}^5 & a_{33}^5 \end{pmatrix},$$

where a_{ij} is the element of A in the ith row and jth column.

Exercise A.15. Let A be the matrix in Exercise A.12. Use the operator $\%*\%$ to calculate A^2 and A^5.

To get the transpose and the inverse of a matrix, we use the t function and the solve function, respectively. In the following example, we create a 3×3 matrix named x by generating 9 random numbers from the standard normal distribution. Then we transpose the matrix x by calling t(x). The matrix y is the inverse of the matrix x as we checked that the product of them is equal to the identity matrix.

```
1 > set.seed(1)
2 > x<-matrix(rnorm(9),nrow=3)
3 > x
4            [,1]        [,2]        [,3]
5 [1,] -0.6264538  1.5952808  0.4874291
6 [2,]  0.1836433  0.3295078  0.7383247
7 [3,] -0.8356286 -0.8204684  0.5757814
```

```
 8 > t(x)
 9                [,1]        [,2]         [,3]
10  [1,]  -0.6264538 0.1836433  -0.8356286
11  [2,]   1.5952808 0.3295078  -0.8204684
12  [3,]   0.4874291 0.7383247   0.5757814
13 > y<-solve(x)
14 > y
15                [,1]         [,2]         [,3]
16  [1,]  -0.50015875   0.82896132  -0.6395669
17  [2,]   0.45439113  -0.02930499  -0.3470881
18  [3,]  -0.07838637   1.16130885   0.3139817
19 > x%*%y
20                [,1]           [,2]            [,3]
21  [1,]  1.000000e+00  1.110223e-16  -1.942890e-16
22  [2,]  0.000000e+00  1.000000e+00   2.775558e-17
23  [3,]  2.081668e-17  0.000000e+00   1.000000e+00
24 > round(x%*%y,0)
25         [,1] [,2] [,3]
26  [1,]     1    0    0
27  [2,]     0    1    0
28  [3,]     0    0    1
```

Exercise A.16. Use the functions `rep` and `matrix` to create the following matrix B with 10 rows and 3 columns:

$$B = \begin{pmatrix} 1 & -1 & 2 \\ 1 & -1 & 2 \\ \vdots & \vdots & \vdots \\ 1 & -1 & 2 \end{pmatrix}$$

and then calculate $B^T B$, where B^T is the transpose of B.

Exercise A.17. Use the function `solve` to solve the following system of linear equations

$$\begin{aligned} x - 2y + 3z &= 7 \\ 2x + y + z &= 4 \\ -3x + 2y - 2z &= -10 \end{aligned}$$

To apply a function to individual rows or columns of a matrix, we use the `apply` function. The following example shows how we use the `apply` function to calculate the sums of all rows and the sums of all columns. The `apply` function has three arguments. The first argument is the underlying matrix. The second argument tells how the function is applied. If 1 is specified for the second argument, then the function is applied row by row. If 2 is specified, the function is applied column by column. The third argument is the function to be applied.

```
 1  > x<-matrix(c(1:9),nrow=3)
 2  > x
 3       [,1] [,2] [,3]
 4  [1,]    1    4    7
 5  [2,]    2    5    8
 6  [3,]    3    6    9
 7  > apply(x,1,sum)
 8  [1]  12 15 18
 9  > apply(x,2,sum)
10  [1]   6 15 24
```

Exercise A.18. Examine the following R code and answer the question:

```
A <- matrix(c(1:6),nrow=3)
B <- apply(A,1,sum)
C <- apply(A,2,sum)
```

What are the values of B and C?

In R, extracting a submatrix from a matrix and assigning values to a submatrix of a matrix can be done easily. To extract a submatrix, we just need to specify the row indices and the column indices of the submatrix. If we want all the rows or all the columns, we do not need to specify the indices. The following example shows how to extract a submatrix and assign values to a submatrix.

```
 1  > m1<-matrix(1:8,nrow=2)
 2  > m1
 3       [,1] [,2] [,3] [,4]
 4  [1,]    1    3    5    7
 5  [2,]    2    4    6    8
 6  > m1[1,c(2,4)]
 7  [1]  3 7
```

```
 8 > m1[,c(2,4)]
 9       [,1] [,2]
10 [1,]    3    7
11 [2,]    4    8
12 > m1[,c(1,3)]<-matrix(0,nrow=2)
13 > m1
14       [,1] [,2] [,3] [,4]
15 [1,]    0    3    0    7
16 [2,]    0    4    0    8
```

Exercise A.19. Use the matrix function and matrix indexing to create the following matrix:

$$\begin{pmatrix} 0 & 1 & 0 & 0 & 0 \\ 1 & 0 & 1 & 0 & 0 \\ 0 & 1 & 0 & 1 & 0 \\ 0 & 0 & 1 & 0 & 1 \\ 0 & 0 & 0 & 1 & 0 \end{pmatrix}$$

Exercise A.20. Use the matrix function and matrix indexing to create the following 100×100 matrix

$$\begin{pmatrix} 0 & 1 & 0 & 0 & \cdots & 0 \\ 1 & 0 & 1 & 0 & \cdots & 0 \\ 0 & 1 & 0 & 1 & \cdots & 0 \\ 0 & 0 & 1 & 0 & \cdots & 0 \\ \vdots & \vdots & \vdots & \vdots & \ddots & 1 \\ 0 & 0 & 0 & 0 & \cdots & 0 \end{pmatrix}$$

In R, we can use negative indices to exclude certain columns or rows of a matrix:

```
1 > m1<-matrix(1:6,nrow=2)
2 > m1
3       [,1] [,2] [,3]
4 [1,]    1    3    5
5 [2,]    2    4    6
6 > m1[,-c(1,3)]
7 [1] 3 4
8 > m1[-1,-2]
9 [1] 2 6
```

In the above example, we see that R changes a matrix to a vector when the matrix has only one row or one column. To prevent dimension reduction, we use the parameter drop=FALSE inside the square bracket operator. The following example shows how we preserve the dimension of the submatrix.

```
 1  > m1<-matrix(1:6,nrow=2)
 2  > m1
 3         [,1] [,2] [,3]
 4  [1,]    1    3    5
 5  [2,]    2    4    6
 6  > m1[,-c(1,3),drop=FALSE]
 7         [,1]
 8  [1,]    3
 9  [2,]    4
10  > m1[-1,-2,drop=FALSE]
11         [,1] [,2]
12  [1,]    2    6
```

To get the number of rows and the number of columns of a matrix, we can use the dim function, which reports the dimensions of a matrix in a vector. The following example shows how we can get the number of rows and the number of columns of a matrix.

```
 1  > m1<-matrix(1:6,nrow=2)
 2  > m1
 3         [,1] [,2] [,3]
 4  [1,]    1    3    5
 5  [2,]    2    4    6
 6  > dim(m1)
 7  [1] 2 3
 8  > dim(m1)[1]
 9  [1] 2
10  > dim(m1)[2]
11  [1] 3
```

To add rows or columns to a matrix, we use the rbind function and the cbind function. The following example illustrates how to add rows and columns to a matrix. Note that the two functions will repeat the rows or columns if the sizes do not match.

```
 1  > m1<-matrix(1,nrow=1)
 2  > m1
 3         [,1]
 4  [1,]    1
 5  > m2<-rbind(m1,2)
```

```
 6 > m2
 7       [,1]
 8 [1;]    1
 9 [2,]    2
10 > m3<-cbind(m2,c(3,4))
11 > m3
12       [,1] [,2]
13 [1,]    1    3
14 [2,]    2    4
15 > m4<-cbind(m3[,1],5:8,m3[,2])
16 > m4
17       [,1] [,2] [,3]
18 [1,]    1    5    3
19 [2,]    2    6    4
20 [3,]    1    7    3
21 [4,]    2    8    4
22 > m5<-cbind(m3[,1],matrix(5:8,nrow=2),m3[,2])
23 > m5
24       [,1] [,2] [,3] [,4]
25 [1,]    1    5    7    3
26 [2,]    2    6    8    4
```

We can also assign names to columns and rows of a matrix. To do that, we use the rownames function and the colnames function as shown in the following example.

```
 1 > m1<-matrix(1:4,nrow=2)
 2 > m1
 3       [,1] [,2]
 4 [1,]    1    3
 5 [2,]    2    4
 6 > rownames(m1)
 7 NULL
 8 > colnames(m1)
 9 NULL
10 > rownames(m1)<-c("r1","r2")
11 > colnames(m1)<-c("c1","c2")
12 > m1
13     c1 c2
14 r1   1  3
15 r2   2  4
```

Exercise A.21. Examine the following R code and answer the question:

```
A <- matrix(1:8, nrow=2)
B <- rbind(A[-1,-c(1,3)],c(dim(A)[2],dim(A)[1]))
C <- cbind(B[,c(2,1)], A[,2])
```

What are the values of *B* and *C*?

_____●_____

A.5   Lists

In R, there are several basic data types: numeric, character, and logical. Numeric is the default computational data type that contains decimal values. Character is the data type used to represent text values. Logical is the data type used to represent binary values. All elements of a vector must have the same data type. However, a **list** can contain data of different types. In this section, we introduce how to create lists and some list operations.

To create a list, we use the `list` function as shown in the following example. In this example, we create a list of three elements, each of which has a different data type. Each element has a name and elements can be extracted by the $ operator. The data type of an element can be determined by the `mode` function.

```
 1 > s1<-list(a=c(1,3,5),b="str",c=TRUE)
 2 > s1
 3 $a
 4 [1]  1  3  5
 5
 6 $b
 7 [1]  "str"
 8
 9 $c
10 [1]  TRUE
11
12 > names(s1)
13 [1]  "a"  "b"  "c"
14 > s1$a
15 [1]  1  3  5
16 > mode(s1$a)
17 [1]  "numeric"
18 > mode(s1$b)
19 [1]  "character"
20 > mode(s1$c)
```

```
21 [1]  "logical"
```

Exercise A.22. Use the function `list` to create a list with two elements: the first element is a vector with name `v` and value $(2,4,6)$; the second element is a matrix with name `m` and value
$$\begin{pmatrix} 1,2 \\ 3,4 \end{pmatrix}.$$

Since a list is a special vector, we can use the `vector` function to create a list. In the following example, we use the `vector` function with the parameter `mode="list"` to create an empty list. Then we add two elements to the list.

```
1  > s2<-vector(mode="list")
2  > s2$a<-c(1,3,5)
3  > s2["b"]<-"str"
4  > s2[["c"]]<-TRUE
5  > s2
6  $a
7  [1]  1 3 5
8
9  $b
10 [1]  "str"
11
12 $c
13 [1]  TRUE
```

In the above example, we see that if we use the $ operator, then we do not need to put the name in quotation marks. If we use the square bracket operator, we need to put the name in quotation marks.

In addition to the $ operator, we can use the single-bracket [] operator and the double-bracket [[]] operator to access elements of a list. In fact, the two operators are different. The single-bracket operator returns a sublist; while the double-bracket operator returns the element. The following example shows the difference between the two square bracket operators.

```
1  > s2<-list(a=c(1,3,5),b="str",c=TRUE)
2  > s2
3  $a
4  [1]  1 3 5
```

```
 5
 6  $b
 7  [1]  "str"
 8
 9  $c
10  [1]  TRUE
11
12  > mode(s2["a"])
13  [1]  "list"
14  > mode(s2[1])
15  [1]  "list"
16  > mode(s2[["a"]])
17  [1]  "numeric"
18  > mode(s2[[2]])
19  [1]  "character"
```

Exercise A.23. Let s2 be a list created by the following code

```
s2<-list(a=c(1,3,5),b="str",c=TRUE)
```

Use two different commands to display the second element.

Exercise A.24. Examine the following R code and answer the question:

```
s <- list(a=c(2,3,5),b="str",c=TRUE)
a <- s[1][1]
b <- s[[1]][1]
```

What are the values of a and b?

To get the size of a list, we use the `length` function:

```
1  > s2<-list(a=c(1,3,5),b="str",c=TRUE)
2  > length(s2)
3  [1]  3
```

To get the names of the elements in a list, we use the `names` function:

```
1  > s2<-list(a=c(1,3,5),b="str",c=TRUE)
2  > names(s2)
3  [1]  "a"  "b"  "c"
```

Since a list can contain different types of data, lists can be nested. In the following example, we create two lists. The first list is an element of the second list.

```
> s1<-list(a=c(1,3),b="str")
> s1
$a
[1] 1 3

$b
[1] "str"

> s2<-list(a=s1,b=TRUE)
> s2
$a
$a$a
[1] 1 3

$a$b
[1] "str"

$b
[1] TRUE

> s2$a$b
[1] "str"
```

To apply a function to all components of a list, we use the `lapply` and `sapply` functions. In the following example, we first create a list of two components. Then we use the `lapply` function to apply the `mode` function to each component. Then we use the same method to get the length of each component.

```
> x <- list(a=1:5,b=c("a","b","a"))
> x
$a
[1] 1 2 3 4 5

$b
[1] "a" "b" "a"

> lapply(x,mode)
$a
[1] "numeric"

$b
```

```
14 [1] "character"
15
16 > lapply(x,length)
17 $a
18 [1] 5
19
20 $b
21 [1] 3
```

The sapply function is similar to the lapply function in that both are used to apply a function to all components of a list. However, the sapply function converts the results into a vector. If we use the sapply function in the previous example, we get

```
1 > sapply(x,length)
2 a b
3 5 3
4 > sapply(x,mode)
5           a           b
6    "numeric"  "character"
```

Exercise A.25. Examine the following R code and answer the question:

```
s <- list(a=c(1,3,5),b=c(2,4))
x <- sapply(s,sum)
y <- x[2]
```

What is the value of y?

Exercise A.26. Examine the following R code and answer the question:

```
s <- list(s=list(a=1,b=c(2,3)), x=c("s","x","y"))
y <- lapply(s,length)
```

What is the value of y?

A.6   Data Frames

A **data frame** is similar to a matrix just as a list is similar to a vector. A matrix contains elements of the same data type, but a data frame can contain columns of different data types. In this section, we introduce how to create data frames and how to work with them.

To create a data frame, we use the data.frame function as shown in the following example. In this example, we create a data frame from two vectors, which contain different types of data. In this data frame, we treat strings as strings not factors, which will be introduced later.

```
> v1<-c(1,2,3)
> v2<-c("a","b","c")
> df<-data.frame(v1,v2,stringsAsFactors=FALSE)
> df
  v1 v2
1  1  a
2  2  b
3  3  c
```

Exercise A.27. Convert the following table of data into a data frame:

First Name	Last Name	Age	Gender
Millicent	Woodrow	25	M
Zella	Vine	25	F
Lenora	Fedler	30	F
Earlie	Costigan	30	F
Suanne	Maisonet	20	F

Because a data frame is similar to a matrix, we use the dim, nrow, and ncol functions to obtain the column and row sizes of the data frame. Continuing with the previous example, we have

```
> dim(df)
[1] 3 2
> nrow(df)
[1] 3
> ncol(df)
[1] 2
```

Technically, a data frame is a special list whose components are vectors of equal length. Accessing elements of a data frame is similar to accessing those of a list as shown in the following example. As we mentioned in Section A.5, the single brackets [] operator returns a sublist; while the double brackets [[]] operator returns an individual component.

```
> v1<-c(1,3,5)
> v2<-c("a","b","c")
> df<-data.frame(v1,v2,stringsAsFactors=FALSE)
> df[1]
  v1
1  1
2  3
3  5
> df[1][1]
  v1
1  1
2  3
3  5
> df[[1]]
[1] 1 3 5
> df[[1]][1]
[1] 1
> df$v2
[1] "a" "b" "c"
> df$v2[2]
[1] "b"
```

Furthermore, we can use a matrix-style method to access elements of a data frame. Continuing with the previous example, we have

```
> df[1,]
  v1 v2
1  1  a
> df[,2]
[1] "a" "b" "c"
> df[1,2]
[1] "a"
```

Exercise A.28. Suppose that person is the data frame created in Exercise A.27. Provide three different ways to extract the last name "Vine."

Exercise A.29. Suppose that person is the data frame created in Exercise A.27. Write R code to extract all females and put them into a new data frame.

Exercise A.30. Suppose that person is the data frame created in Exercise A.27. Use the function subset to extract persons who are 25 years old.

We can expand a data frame by adding more rows or columns. To do so, we use the rbind and cbind functions. In the following example, we first create a data frame with one row and two columns. Then we expand the data frame by adding a row and a column to the data frame.

```
 1 > df <-data.frame(v1=1,v2="a",stringsAsFactors=FALSE)
 2 > df
 3   v1 v2
 4 1  1  a
 5 > df <-rbind(df, list(2,"b"))
 6 > df
 7   v1 v2
 8 1  1  a
 9 2  2  b
10 > df <-cbind(df,v3=c(TRUE,FALSE))
11 > df
12   v1 v2      v3
13 1  1  a    TRUE
14 2  2  b   FALSE
```

To combine two data frames according to the values of a common variable, we use the merge function. In the following example, we create two data frames that have a common variable named student. Applying the merge function to the two data frames results in a combined data frame.

```
 1 > student <-c("Albert","Brian","Cara","David")
 2 > age <-c(19,22,20,21)
 3 > df1 <-data.frame(student,age)
 4 > df1
 5   student age
 6 1  Albert  19
 7 2   Brian  22
 8 3    Cara  20
 9 4   David  21
10 > df2 <-data.frame(student=c("Brian", "Cara", "John"),
        grade=c(88,90,85))
11 > df2
```

```
12    student grade
13 1    Brian     88
14 2     Cara     90
15 3     John     85
16 > merge(df1,df2)
17    student age grade
18 1    Brian  22    88
19 2     Cara  20    90
```

In the above example, the two data frames have a column (variable) with the same name. If two data frames have a column that contains the same information but have different names, we can still merge the two data frames by specifying the column names. Continuing with the previous example, we change the column names of the second data frame and then merge the two data frames by specifying the parameters by.x and by.y.

```
 1 > names(df2)<-c("person","grade")
 2 > df2
 3    person grade
 4 1   Brian     88
 5 2    Cara     90
 6 3    John     85
 7 > merge(df1,df2, by.x="student", by.y="person")
 8    student age grade
 9 1    Brian  22    88
10 2     Cara  20    90
11 > merge(df2,df1, by.y="student", by.x="person")
12    person grade age
13 1   Brian     88  22
14 2    Cara     90  20
```

A.7   Factors and Tables

Factors are similar to vectors but different from vectors. Each element of a factor is a category, which is one of a fixed number of possibilities called **levels**. Factors are used to store categorical data. **Tables** are also used to organize information related to categorical data. In this section, we introduce how to create factors and tables in R.

To create a factor, we use the `factor` function. In the following example, we create three factors using the `factor` function. The levels are the distinct values in the corresponding vectors.

```
1 > f1<-factor()
2 > f1
3 factor(0)
4 Levels:
5 > f2<-factor(c(1,2,1,3,1))
6 > f2
7 [1] 1 2 1 3 1
8 Levels: 1 2 3
9 > f3<-factor(c("a","b","a","c","b"))
10 > f3
11 [1] a b a c b
12 Levels: a b c
13 > mode(f3)
14 [1] "numeric"
```

From the above example, we see that the data type of a factor is numeric. To get
the levels of a factor, we use the levels function:

```
1 > levels(f1)
2 character(0)
3 > levels(f2)
4 [1] "1" "2" "3"
5 > levels(f3)
6 [1] "a" "b" "c"
```

In R, we use the table function to create one-way or multi-way tables. In
the following example, we illustrate how to use the table function to create a
one-way table and a two-way table. A one-way table is a frequency table and a
two-way table is a contingency table.

```
1 > v1<-c(10,11,10,12,10)
2 > f1<-factor(c("a","b","c","b","c"))
3 > t1<-table(v1)
4 > t1
5 v1
6 10 11 12
7  3  1  1
8 > t2<-table(v1,f1)
9 > t2
10     f1
11 v1    a b c
12    10 1 0 2
13    11 0 1 0
14    12 0 1 0
```

Exercise A.31. The following table shows the grades of eight students on two exams:

Student ID	Exam 1	Exam 2
1	A	A
2	B	A
3	B	C
4	A	C
5	C	D
6	B	A
7	D	C
8	A	A
9	B	B
10	A	B

(a) Convert the above table of data into a data frame by treating grades as factors.

(b) Use the function `table` to obtain how many students got an A in Exam 1 and a B in Exam 2.

The elements of a table can be accessed via matrix operations. The following example shows how to access elements in a one-way table. We can use level names or indices to access the elements of a table.

```
> t1<-table(v1=c(10,20,10,30,20))
> t1
v1
10 20 30
 2  2  1
> t1["10"]
10
 2
> t1[1]
10
 2
> t1[1:2]
v1
10 20
 2  2
```

Accessing elements in a two-way table is similar:

```
> t2<-table(v1=c(10,20,10,30,20),v2=c("a","a","b","c","b"
   ))
> t2
      v2
v1    a  b  c
   10 1  1  0
   20 1  1  0
   30 0  0  1
> t2["20","b"]
[1] 1
> t2[,c(1,3)]
       v2
v1    a  c
   10 1  0
   20 1  0
   30 0  1
```

R has several functions for working with tables: `tapply`, `aggregate`, and `cut`. The `tapply` function allows us to apply a function to each of the groups specified by certain factors. The following example illustrates how the `tapply` function is applied. In this example, we first create a list with two components, which are vectors of equal length. We also create a vector of the same length as the list components. Then we use the `tapply` function to apply the function `sum` to all the groups of the vector y that are specified by the two components of the list x. There are 9 groups in total and some groups are empty. For empty groups, the function `sum` returns `NA`, which is a special value in R. We also apply the function `tapply` with groups specified by one component of the list x.

```
> x <- list(a=c(1,3,5,3),b=c("a","b","c","b"))
> y <- c(1, 10, 100, 1000)
> tapply(y, x, sum)
     b
a     a     b     c
  1   1    NA    NA
  3  NA  1010    NA
  5  NA    NA   100
> tapply(y, x$a, sum)
     1     3     5
     1  1010   100
> tapply(y, x$b, sum)
     a     b     c
     1  1010   100
```

```
15 > tapply(y, x$b, length)
16 a b c
17 1 2 1
```

The aggregate function can be used to produce similar results. This function calls the tapply function once for each variable in a group. Continuing with the previous example, we have

```
 1 > aggregate(y, x, sum)
 2     a b   x
 3 1 1 a    1
 4 2 3 b 1010
 5 3 5 c  100
 6 > aggregate(list(c1=y,c2=y), x, sum)
 7     a b   c1    c2
 8 1 1 a    1    1
 9 2 3 b 1010 1010
10 3 5 c  100  100
```

From the output, we see that the aggregate function does not give results for empty groups and can be used for a list of vectors.

Finally, the function cut is used to convert numeric values into factors. In the following example, we convert a vector of numeric values to a vector of integers, which are the indices of the intervals the numeric values belong to.

```
 1 > x <- rnorm(10)
 2 > x
 3  [1] -1.44668175  0.92742073 -0.80807203 -0.57570398
 4  [5] -0.63944691 -0.62282741  1.94055824 -1.50700091
 5  [9] -1.26702989 -0.02886806
 6 > bins <- seq(from=-2,to=2,by=0.5)
 7 > bins
 8 [1] -2.0 -1.5 -1.0 -0.5  0.0  0.5  1.0  1.5  2.0
 9 > cut(x,bins,labels=F)
10  [1] 2 6 3 3 3 3 8 1 2 4
```

A.8   File IO

In this section, we discuss several R functions for reading and writing files. In particular, we discuss how to use the following functions: scan, read.table, read.csv, write.table, and write.csv.

The function scan is used to read data of the same mode (e.g., numeric, character) from a text file. Listing A.2 shows a text file with several numbers and Listing A.3 shows a text file containing several strings. We use the scan function to read the data from these text files.

```
 1 > scan("real.txt")
 2 Read 6 items
 3 [1]  1.2  3.0  4.0  2.0  0.1  1.0
 4 > scan("char.txt")
 5 Error in scan(file, what, nmax, sep, dec, quote, skip,
 6 nlines, na.strings,   :
 7   scan() expected 'a real', got 'a'
 8 > scan("char.txt",what="")
 9 Read 6 items
10 [1]  "a"   "bc"  "aa"  "ab"  "ac"  "d"
```

The scan function has several arguments. If we want to read a text file with numeric data, we use the default values for all the arguments except for the file name. If we want to read a text file with character data, then we need to specify a value for the what argument. Here we just use an empty string to tell the function that the file contains character data.

```
 1 1.2 3 4
 2 2 0.1
 3 1
```

Listing A.2: *Content of the file real.txt.*

```
 1 a bc
 2 aa ab ac
 3 d
```

Listing A.3: *Content of the file char.txt.*

The scan function cannot be used to read files containing mixed data. Listing A.4 shows a text file that contains characters and numbers. If we use the scan function to read this file, we get the following output:

```
 1 > scan("grade.txt")
 2 Error in scan(file, what, nmax, sep, dec, quote, skip,
 3 nlines, na.strings,   :
 4   scan() expected 'a real', got 'Name'
 5 > scan("grade.txt",what="")
 6 Read 8 items
 7 [1] "Name"   "Grade"  "John"    "95"     "Dan"    "85"      "Abel
      "   "100"
```

From the output, we see that the scan function cannot be used to read characters
and numbers from the same file.

```
1 Name Grade
2 John 95
3 Dan 85
4 Abel 100
```

Listing A.4: *Content of the file grade.txt.*

To read a file that contains a table of data, we use the read.table function
as shown in the following example:

```
1 > x <- read.table("grade.txt", header=TRUE)
2 > x
3   Name Grade
4 1 John    95
5 2  Dan    85
6 3 Abel   100
7 > mode(x$Name)
8 [1] "numeric"
9 > mode(x$Grade)
10 [1] "numeric"
11 > x$Name <- as.character(x$Name)
12 > x
13   Name Grade
14 1 John    95
15 2  Dan    85
16 3 Abel   100
17 > mode(x$Name)
18 [1] "character"
```

From the above output, we see that the read.table function automatically reads
the table of data into a data frame. The contents of the first row are used as
column names. The function automatically converts character data into factors.
To change the factors back to characters, we used the as.character function.

The function read.csv can also be used to read tabular data. In fact, this
function calls the read.table function with a different set of default values for
the arguments. To read the grade.txt shown in Listing A.4, we use the read.csv
function as follows:

```
1 > x <- read.csv("grade.txt", sep=" ")
2 > x
```

```
3     Name  Grade
4  1  John     95
5  2   Dan     85
6  3  Abel    100
```

For the `read.csv` function, we do not need to specify a value for the `header` argument. However, we need to specify a value for the `sep` argument as the default value for this argument is a comma.

---◆---

Exercise A.32. Suppose that the file "grade2.txt" contains the following data:

```
John 95
Dan 85
Abel 100
```

Use the function `read.csv` to read all the data into a data frame.

---◆---

To write tabular data (e.g., matrices and data frames) to a file, we use the functions `write.table` and `write.csv`. The function `write.csv` calls the function `write.table` and is used to write CSV (comma-separated values) files. The following example shows how to use the function `write.csv` to save a data frame into a CSV file. In this example, we first read the data from the file `grade.txt` and then save the data to a CSV file called `grade.csv`. The content of the file `grade.csv` is shown in Listing A.5.

```
1  x <- read.csv("grade.txt", sep=" ")
2  write.csv(x,"grade.csv")
```

```
1  "","Name","Grade"
2  "1","John",95
3  "2","Dan",85
4  "3","Abel",100
```

Listing A.5: *Content of the file grade.csv.*

---◆---

Exercise A.33. The file shown in Listing A.5 contains many double quotes. Check the usage of the function `write.csv` by typing `?write.csv` in the R Console and then use the function to write a new CSV file named `grade2.csv` with the following content:

```
,Name,Grade
1,John,95
2,Dan,85
3,Abel,100
```

A.9   Functions

R provides many built-in functions such as vector and list, which we encoun-
tered in previous sections. R also allows us to define our own functions. In this
section, we introduce how to create functions.

To introduce how to define a function in R, we look at the following example:

```
1  add <- function(x, y) {
2       tmp <- x + y
3       return(tmp)
4  }
```

In the above example, we created a function with two arguments x and y. The
name of the function is add. Inside the function, we add the two numbers, assign
the sum to a variable called tmp, and return the value to the caller. As we can
see from this example, defining a function involves two keywords: function and
return.

Once we define a function, we can use the function just like using built-in
functions. For example, we can use the function as follows:

```
1  > add <- function(x, y) {
2  +       tmp <- x + y
3  +       return(tmp)
4  + }
5  > add(1,3)
6  [1] 4
7  > add(c(1,2),c(4,5))
8  [1] 5 7
9  > add(c(1,2),c(1:4))
10 [1] 2 4 4 6
```

In the above R output, the code in Lines 1-4 was used to create the function in R
so that we can use the function later.

Sometime it is convenient to organize the results of a function into a list and
return the list to the caller. In the following example, we modify the function

add by creating a list to store the result as well as the inputs used to generate the results.

```
1  add <- function(x, y) {
2      tmp <- x+y
3      return(list(x=x,y=y,sum=tmp))
4  }
```

If we call the modified function add, we get the following results:

```
1  > add <- function(x, y) {
2  +      tmp <- x+y
3  +      return(list(x=x,y=y,sum=tmp))
4  + }
5  > add(1,3)
6  $x
7  [1] 1
8
9  $y
10 [1] 3
11
12 $sum
13 [1] 4
14
15 > add(c(1,2),c(4,5))
16 $x
17 [1] 1 2
18
19 $y
20 [1] 4 5
21
22 $sum
23 [1] 5 7
```

Exercise A.34. Write an R function named `calStat` to calculate the minimum, maximum, mean, and standard deviation of a vector and return the results in a list. You can use the functions `min`, `max`, `mean`, and `sd` in your function.

Exercise A.35. In Exercise A.19 and Exercise A.20, you were asked to create two similar matrices with different dimensions. Write a function called `makeMatrix` to create such a matrix with the dimension as an argument. When you call makeMatrix(n), the function should return the following $n \times n$ matrix

$$\begin{pmatrix} 0 & 1 & 0 & 0 & \cdots & 0 \\ 1 & 0 & 1 & 0 & \cdots & 0 \\ 0 & 1 & 0 & 1 & \cdots & 0 \\ 0 & 0 & 1 & 0 & \cdots & 0 \\ \vdots & \vdots & \vdots & \vdots & \ddots & 1 \\ 0 & 0 & 0 & 0 & \cdots & 0 \end{pmatrix},$$

where n is a positive integer.

A.10   Flow Control and Loops

In this section, we introduce some flow control statements and loops that allow us to execute code conditionally or to execute some piece of code repeatedly. In particular, we introduce the following statements: if-else, for, while, and repeat.

The if statement can be used when we want to execute some code if a condition is met. The syntax of the if statement is illustrated by the following example:

```
1  > x <- 3
2  > if(x >= 0) {
3  +        sqrt(x)
4  + }
5  [1] 1.732051
6  > x <- -3
7  > if (x >= 0) {
8  +        sqrt(x)
9  + }
10 >
```

In the above example, we calculated the square root of a number if the number is positive. If the number is negative, the code inside the if statement is not executed.

Since <- is a special symbol in R, care must be taken when writing a logical statement to test whether a value is less than another value. In the following example, we first assign -5 to x. Then we want to test whether x is less than 0 and show the value of x if it is less than 0. Then we want to test whether x is less than

-2 and show the value of x if it is less than -2. However, x<-2 is interpreted by R as assigning 2 to x. In order to express the logical statement correctly, we need to put brackets around -2 or put a space between < and -.

```
1 > x<--5
2 > x
3 [1] -5
4 > if(x<0)
5 + x
6 [1] -5
7 > if(x<-2)
8 + x
9 [1] 2
10 > x<--5
11 > x
12 [1] -5
13 > if(x<(-2))
14 + x
15 [1] -5
16 > if(x< -2)
17 + x
18 [1] -5
```

The + sign in the above R output means R expects additional commands to finish the command from the previous line.

Exercise A.36. What is wrong with the following piece of R code?

```
1 x <- 3
2 if {x>=0} {
3     sqrt(x)
4 }
```

Exercise A.37. What is the output of the following piece of R code?

```
1 x <- -10
2 if( x<-5 ) {
3     print(x)
4 }
```

Exercise A.38. The Fibonacci numbers or Fibonacci sequence $\{F_n : n = 1, 2, \ldots\}$ are defined as follows:

$$F_n = \begin{cases} 1, & \text{if } n = 1 \text{ or } 2; \\ F_{n-1} + F_{n-2}, & \text{if } n \geq 3. \end{cases}$$

Write an R function `fibo(n)` with one parameter such that `fibo(n)` returns F_n, for all $n \geq 1$.

Sometimes we want to execute a piece of code when a condition is met and execute a different piece of code when the condition is not met. In such cases, we add an `else` statement to the `if` statement. In the following example, we create a function called `mysqrt` to calculate the square root of a number. If the number is non-negative, the function returns the square root of the number. If the number is negative, the function returns a message.

```
 1 > mysqrt <- function(x) {
 2 +       if(x>=0) {
 3 +             return(sqrt(x))
 4 +       } else {
 5 +             return(paste(x, "is negative"))
 6 +       }
 7 + }
 8 > mysqrt(3)
 9 [1] 1.732051
10 > mysqrt(-1)
11 [1] "-1 is negative"
```

In the above example, `sqrt` and `paste` are built-in functions of R.

If we want to execute a piece of code repeatedly, we can use `for`, `while`, or `repeat` statements. If we know how many times the code should be executed, we can use a `for` loop. The usage of the `for` loop is illustrated in the following example:

```
1 > dsum <- 0
2 > for(i in 1:10) {
3 +       dsum <- dsum + i
4 + }
5 > dsum
6 [1] 55
```

In the above example, we used a `for` loop to add numbers from 1 to 10. In the `for` loop, `i` is an iterator variable that takes values in the vector `c(1:10)`. At each iteration, the iterator variable i takes a value from the vector and the value of i is added to the variable dsum. The loop ends when all values in the vector are taken.

Exercise A.39. Write a for loop to calculate the following sum

$$\sum_{i=1}^{100} i^2.$$

Exercise A.40. For loops can be nested. Write nested for loops to calculate the following sum

$$\sum_{i=1}^{100} \sum_{j=1}^{i} j.$$

Exercise A.41. Let S_n be defined as

$$S_n = \sum_{i=1}^{n} \frac{1}{\sqrt{i}}.$$

Use the function proc.time to measure the runtime of the following two approaches to calculate $S_{1000000}$:

(a) (vectorization) the function sum is applied to the vector $(1, \frac{1}{\sqrt{2}}, \ldots, \frac{1}{\sqrt{n}})$;

(b) (for loop) a for loop is used to calculate the sum.

Which approach is faster?

Sometimes we want to execute a piece of code repeatedly but do not know the number of iterations in advance. In such cases, we use the while loop or the repeat loop. For example, suppose that we want to find the smallest integer n such that

$$\sum_{i=1}^{n} i^3 > 100,000.$$

We can use a while loop to do that as follows:

```
1 > dsum <- 0
2 > n <- 0
3 > while (TRUE) {
4 +     n <- n+1
5 +     dsum <- dsum + n^3
```

```
 6 +          if(dsum > 100000) {
 7 +                break
 8 +          }
 9 + }
10 > n
11 [1]  25
```

In the above code, we first initialized two variables dsum and n to zeros. Inside the while loop, the variable n increases by 1 and the variable dsum increases by n^3. Then we used an if statement to test whether the sum is larger than 100,000. If the sum is larger than 100,000, we terminate the loop using the break statement. It is important to terminate the while loop at some point of the iterative process. Otherwise, R will keep running the code indefinitely.

We can also put the condition in the parenthesis after the keyword while as shown below:

```
1 > dsum <- 0
2 > n <- 0
3 > while(dsum <= 100000) {
4 +        n <- n+1
5 +        dsum <- dsum + n^3
6 + }
7 > n
8 [1]  25
```

The code inside the loop will be executed if the condition is evaluated to be true.

─────────────────────────●─────────────────────────

Exercise A.42. Use the while loop to find the smallest integer n such that

$$\sum_{i=1}^{n} \sqrt{i} > 100,000.$$

Exercise A.43. Consider the following R code:

```
1 n1 <- 1
2 dSum <- 0
3 while(dSum < 10) {
4      n1 <- n1 + 1
5      dSum <- dSum + 1
6 }
7 n1
```

After executing the above code, what is the value of n1?

Exercise A.44. Write a `while` loop to calculate the sum $1 + 2 + \cdots + 100000$ and use an `if` statement and the function `print` to display the total after every 1000 terms.

The `repeat` statement is similar to the `while` statement. In the previous example, we can also use the `repeat` loop to find out the integer:

```
 1 > dsum <- 0
 2 > n <- 0
 3 > repeat {
 4 +       n <- n+1
 5 +       dsum <- dsum + n^3
 6 +       if(dsum > 100000) {
 7 +            break
 8 +       }
 9 + }
10 > n
11 [1]  25
```

Exercise A.45. Write a `repeat` loop to do the same calculation as in Exercise A.44.

A.11 Graphics

One major feature of R is that it provides a rich set of functions for creating graphics. In this section, we introduce how to create some commonly used graphics. In particular, we introduce how to create scatter plots, histograms, and q-q plots. We also introduce how to combine multiple plots into a single graph and how to customize graphs.

A scatter plot between two variables is used to visualize the relationship between the two variables. The following piece of code produces a scatter plot of two vectors. The resulting scatter plot is shown in Figure A.1(a).

```
1 v1 <- c(1:6)
2 v2 <- c(1,3,2,5,4,5)
3 plot(v1,v2)
```

We can also add a caption to the figure by calling `plot` as follows:

```
plot(v1,v2,main="Scatter Plot of v1 and v2")
```

The resulting scatter plot with a caption is shown in Figure A.1(b).

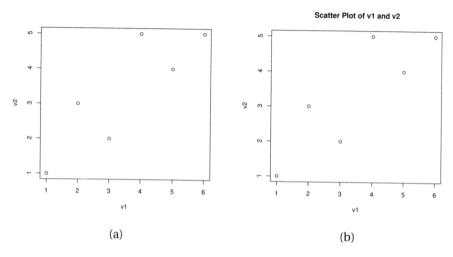

(a)   (b)

Figure A.1: *Scatter plots.*

To further customize a plot, you can use the `help` function by typing `help(plot)` in the R Console.

Exercise A.46. Let x and y be two vectors created by the following code:

```
x <- seq(from=20,to=40,by=1)
y <- x*1.8 + 32
```

The vectors x and y contain measurements of temperature on the Celsius scale and the Fahrenheit scale, respectively. Check the help of the `plot` function to produce a scatter plot of x and y with the x-axis labeled Celsius and the y-axis labeled Fahrenheit.

Histograms are used to visualize the distributions of numerical data. In R, we can create histograms easily using the function `hist`. The following piece of code shows how to create a histogram. In this example, we use the function `rnorm` to generate 1000 random numbers from the standard normal distribution. We also use the function set.seed to fix the seed so that we can replicate the random numbers.

```
1 > set.seed(1)
2 > x <- rnorm(1000)
3 > hist(x)
```

The resulting histogram is shown in Figure A.2(a). From the histogram, we see that the range of the data is divided into bins and the number of points in each bin is plotted as a bar. We can specify the number of bins in a histogram by using the option breaks. For example, we can divide the range of the data into 50 bins as follows:

```
1 > hist(x, breaks=50)
```

The resulting histogram is shown in Figure A.2(b).

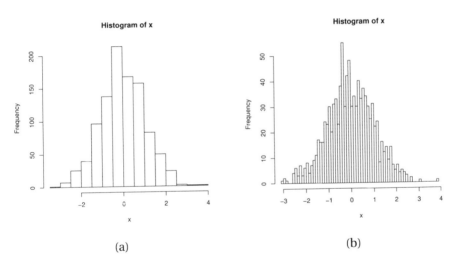

(a)   (b)

Figure A.2: *Histograms.*

A q-q (quantile-quantile) plot is a scatter plot of the quantiles of a dataset against those of another dataset. Here a quantile (or percentile) is a value taken from the inverse of the cumulative distribution function (CDF) of a random variable. Mathematically, there are several ways to define a quantile (Hyndman and Fan, 1996). In general, the pth ($p \in [0, 100]$) quantile is the value at which p percent of the data fall below and $100 - p$ percent fall above that value.

To create a q-q plot of two datasets, we can use the function qqplot as shown in the following example. In this example, we use the functions `rnorm` and `runif` to generate 1000 samples from the standard normal distribution and the uniform distribution, respectively. Then we create a q-q plot of the two datasets. The resulting q-q plot is shown in Figure A.3(a). Since the two datasets are generated from different distributions, we see that the points do not fall in a straight line.

```
1 > x <- rnorm(1000)
2 > y <- runif(1000)
3 > qqplot(x,y)
```

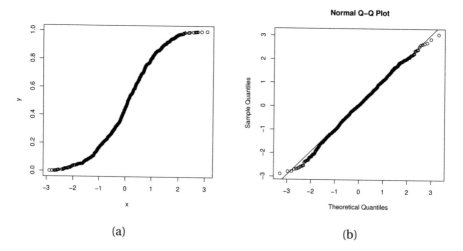

(a)   (b)

Figure A.3: *Two q-q plots.*

To compare the distribution of a dataset with a normal distribution, we can use the function qqnorm. Continuing with the previous example, we can compare the distribution of x to the normal distribution as follows:

```
1 > qqnorm(x)
2 > qqline(x)
```

The resulting q-q plot is shown in Figure A.3(b). We also used the function qqline to add a benchmark straight line to the plot. In this example, since the points are near the straight line, the distribution of x closely matches the normal distribution.

In R, we can combine multiple plots into one graph easily. To do that, we use the function par to specify the layout of the graph. The following piece of code shows how to plot four figures in one graph. The resulting graph is shown in

Figure A.4.

```
1 >  par(mfrow=c(2,2))
2 >  plot(x,y)
3 >  qqplot(x,y)
4 >  qqnorm(x)
5 >  hist(x,breaks=50)
```

The layout of the four plots is a 2 × 2 matrix and is specified by the code in line 1.

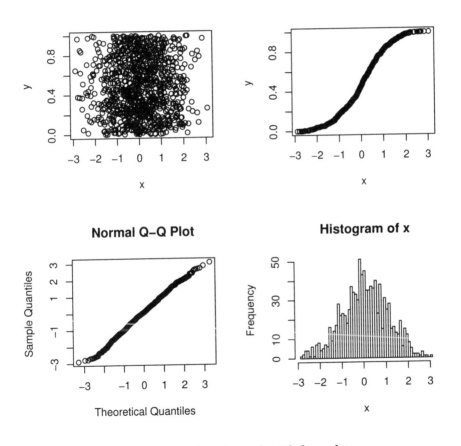

Figure A.4: *A graph with four plots.*

Exercise A.47. Let x and y be two vectors created by the following code:

```
set.seed(1)
x <- rnorm(1000, mean=1, sd=4)
y <- runif(1000, min=-1, max=2)
```

Create a figure with three subfigures in one row such that the subfigure in the left is a scatter plot of x and y, the subfigure in the center is a histogram of y with 50 bins, and the subfigure in the right is a q-q plot of x and a normal distribution.

A.12   Packages

In R, a package consists of a collection of reusable functions, the documentation that describes how to use them, and sample data (if any). R packages generally fall into the following two categories: packages that come with the base installation of R and packages that you have to manually download and install.

To see the packages that have been installed, we can use the following command:

```
 1 > a<-installed.packages()
 2 > a[1:10,c(1,4)]
 3                Package          Priority
 4 base           "base"           "base"
 5 boot           "boot"           "recommended"
 6 class          "class"          "recommended"
 7 clhs           "clhs"           NA
 8 cluster        "cluster"        "recommended"
 9 codetools      "codetools"      "recommended"
10 colorspace     "colorspace"     NA
11 compiler       "compiler"       "base"
12 datasets       "datasets"       "base"
13 DiceKriging    "DiceKriging"    NA
```

The function installed.packages returns a matrix with a row for each package. In the above R output, we can see the names and the priorities of the first ten packages. The priority of a package indicates what is needed in order to use the functions from the package. There are three levels of priorities:

- If the priority of a package is "base," then the package is already installed and loaded. The functions from the package are available upon opening R.
- If the priority of a package is "recommended," then the package was installed with the base R, but not loaded. To use the functions from the

package, users have to load the package by calling the command `library`. To use the functions from the `boot` package, for example, we need to issue the following command in R:

```
1 library(boot)
```

- If the priority of a package is "NA," then the package was installed by the user, but not loaded. To use the functions from the package, we also need to use the command `library` to load the package first.

To see the number of available R packages, we can use the following command:

```
1 > p <- available.packages()
2 > dim(p)
3 [1] 6706      17
```

The function `available.packages` returns a matrix with a row for each package. The above output shows that there are 6,706 packages that are available. Since the community of R users constantly creates new packages, the list of available R packages keeps growing. You may see a different number when executing the above command.

Exercise A.48. The `insuranceData` package contains several insurance data sets.

(a) Install this package within R and then issue the following commands in R:

```
1 library(insuranceData)
2 data(AutoBi)
3 head(AutoBi)
```

What is the output of the above code?

(b) What is the output of the following command?

```
1 data(package = "insuranceData")$results[,3:4]
```

A.13   Summary

In this chapter, we provided a brief introduction to the R programming language and some of its capabilities. In particular, we introduced common data structures such as vectors, matrices, lists, and data frames. We also demonstrated the use of flow control, loops, and some commands for producing graphics. For a more comprehensive introduction to the R programming language, readers are referred to Matloff (2011), Albert and Rizzo (2011), and Cotton (2013). For R code style guide, readers can look at Google's R style guide, which is available at `https://google-styleguide.googlecode.com/svn/trunk/Rguide.xml`[2].

---

[2]This page was accessed when this book was written. If the web page is not available, readers can do a search to find it.

References

Albert, J. and Rizzo, M. (2011). *R by Example.* Springer, New York, NY.

Antonio, K. and Valdez, E. A. (2012). Statistical concepts of a priori and a posteriori risk classification in insurance. *AStA Advances in Statistical Analysis*, 96(2):187–224.

Barkley, E. F., Major, C. H., and Cross, K. P. (2014). *Collaborative Learning Techniques: A Handbook for College Faculty.* Jossey-Bass.

Bingham, N. H. and Fry, J. M. (2010). *Regression: Linear Models in Statistics.* Springer, New York, NY.

Bock, H. (1989). Probabilistic aspects in cluster analysis. In Opitz, O., editor, *Conceptual and Numerical Analysis of Data*, pages 12–44, Augsburg, FRG. Springer-Verlag.

Bowers, N. L., Gerber, H. U., Hickman, J. C., Jones, D. A., and Nesbitt, C. J. (1997). *Actuarial Mathematics.* Society of Actuaries.

Breiman, L., Friedman, J., Stone, C. J., and Olshen, R. (1984). *Classification and Regression Trees.* Chapman and Hall/CRC, Raton Boca, FL.

Brockwell, P. J. and Davis, R. A. (2002). *Introduction to time series and forecasting.* Springer, New York, NY, 2nd edition.

Campbell, J., Lo, A., and MacKinlay, A. (1996). *The Econometrics of Financial Markets.* Princeton University Press.

Chen, M., Mao, S., Zhang, Y., and Leung, V. C. (2014). *Big Data: Related Technologies, Challenges and Future Prospects.* Springer, New York, NY.

Cochrane, J. (2001). *Asset Pricing.* Princeton University Press.

Cotton, R. (2013). *Learning R: A Step-by-Step Function Guide to Data Analysis.* O'Reilly Media, Sebastopol, CA.

Cox, D. R. (1957). Note on grouping. *Journal of the American Statistical Association*, 52(280):543–547.

de Jong, P. and Heller, G. Z. (2008). *Generalized linear models for insurance data.* Cambridge University Press.

Dobson, A. J. and Barnett, A. (2008a). *An Introduction to Generalized Linear Models.* CRC Press, Boca Raton, FL, 3rd edition.

Dobson, A. J. and Barnett, A. (2008b). *An Introduction to Generalized Linear Models.* Chapman and Hall/CRC, Boca Raton, FL, 3rd edition.

Engle, R. F. (1982). Autoregressive conditional heteroscedasticity with estimates of variance of united kingdom inflation. *Econometrica*, 50(4):987–1008.

Everitt, B. S., Landau, S., Leese, M., and Stahl, D. (2011). *Cluster Analysis.* Wiley, Hoboken, NJ.

Faraway, J. (2005). *Extending the Linear Model with R: Generalized Linear, Mixed Effects and Nonparametric Regression Models.* Chapman & Hall/CRC, Boca Raton, FL.

Faraway, J. J. (2014). *Linear Models with R.* Taylor & Francis, Boca Raton.

Ferris, A., Moore, D., Pohle, N., and Srivastava, P. (2014). Big data: What is it, how is it collected and how might life insurers use it? *The Actuary Magazine*, 10(6):28–32.

Fisher, W. D. (1958). On grouping for maximum homogeneity. *Journal of the American Statistical Association*, 53(284):789–798.

Freedman, D. A. (2009). *Statistical Models: Theory and Practice.* Cambridge University Press, Cambridge, UK.

Frees, E. W. (2009). *Regression Modeling with Actuarial and Financial Applications.* Cambridge University Press, Cambridge, UK.

Frees, E. W. and Valdez, E. A. (2008). Hierarchical insurance claims modeling. *Journal of the American Statistical Association*, 103(484):1457 – 1469.

Friedman, L. W. (2013). Simulation metamodeling. In Gass, S. and Fu, M., editors, *Encyclopedia of Operations Research and Management Science*, pages 1404–1410. Springer US.

Gan, G. (2011). *Data Clustering in C++: An Object-Oriented Approach.* Data Mining and Knowledge Discovery Series. Chapman & Hall/CRC Press, Boca Raton, FL, USA.

Gan, G. (2013). Application of data clustering and machine learning in variable annuity valuation. *Insurance: Mathematics and Economics*, 53(3):795–801.

Gan, G. (2015a). Application of metamodeling to the valuation of large variablbe annuity portfolios. In *Proceedings of the 2015 Winter Simulation Conference*, pages 1103–1114.

Gan, G. (2015b). A multi-asset Monte Carlo simulation model for the valuation of variable annuities. In *Proceedings of the Winter Simulation Conference*, pages 3162–3163.

Gan, G. (2017). *An Introduction to Excel VBA Programming: With Application in Finance and Insurance.* Chapman & Hall/CRC Press, Boca Raton, FL, USA.

Gan, G. (2018). Valuation of large variable annuity portfolios using linear models with interactions. *Risks*, 6(3):71.

Gan, G. and Lin, X. S. (2015). Valuation of large variable annuity portfolios under nested simulation: A functional data approach. *Insurance: Mathematics and Economics*, 62:138–150.

Gan, G. and Lin, X. S. (2017). Efficient greek calculation of variable annuity portfolios for dynamic hedging: A two-level metamodeling approach. *North American Actuarial Journal*, 21(2):161–177.

Gan, G., Ma, C., and Wu, J. (2007). *Data Clustering: Theory, Algorithms, and Applications.* SIAM Press, Philadelphia, PA.

Gan, G. and Valdez, E. A. (2018). Regression modeling for the valuation of large variable annuity portfolios. *North American Actuarial Journal*, 22(1):40–54.

Hamilton, J. D. (1994). *Time Series Analysis.* Princeton University Press.

Hardy, M. (2003). *Investment Guarantees: Modeling and Risk Management for Equity-Linked Life Insurance.* John Wiley & Sons, Inc., Hoboken, New Jersey.

Hungelmann, J. (2009). *Insurance for Dummies.* For Dummies, 2nd edition.

Hyndman, R. J. and Fan, Y. (1996). Sample quantiles in statistical packages. *The American Statistician*, 50(4):361–365.

IRI (2011). The 2011 IRI fact book. Insured Retirement Institute.

James, G., Witten, D., Hastie, T., and Tibshirani, R. (2013). *An Introduction to Statistical Learning: with Applications in R.* Springer, New York, NY.

Kellison, S. (2008). *Theory of Interest.* McGraw-Hill/Irwin, 3rd edition.

Korn, R., Korn, E., and Kroisandt, G. (2010). *Monte Carlo Methods and Models in Finance and Insurance.* Chapman & Hall/CRC, Boca Raton, FL.

Lance, G. and Williams, W. (1967). A general theory of classificatory sorting strategies I. Hierarchical systems. *The Computer Journal,* 9(4):373–380.

Lintner, J. (1965). The valuation of risk assets and the selection of risky investments in stock portfolios and capital budgets. *The Review of Economics and Statistics,* 47(1):13–37.

Macqueen, J. (1967). Some methods for classification and analysis of multivariate observations. In LeCam, L. and Neyman, J., editors, *Proceedings of the 5th Berkeley Symposium on Mathematical Statistics andProbability,* volume 1, pages 281–297, Berkely, CA, USA. University of California Press.

Manyika, J., Chui, M., Brown, B., Bughin, J., Dobbs, R., Roxburgh, C., and Byers, A. H. (2011). *Big data: The next frontier for innovation, competition, and productivity.* McKinsey Global Institute.

Matloff, N. (2011). *The Art of R Programming: A Tour of Statistical Software Design.* No Starch Press, San Francisco, CA.

McCullagh, P. and Nelder, J. A. (1989). *Generalized linear models.* Chapman and Hall/CRC, Boca Raton, FL, 2nd edition.

Mereu, J. (1962). Annuity values directly from makeham constants. *Transactions of the Society of Actuaries,* XIV:269–286.

Milevsky, M. A. (2012). *The 7 Most Important Equations for Your Retirement: The Fascinating People and Ideas Behind Planning Your Retirement Income.* Wiley.

Miller, R. and Wichern, D. (1977). *Intermediate Business Statistics: Analysis of Variance, Regression, and Time Series.* Holt Rinehart & Winston, New York, NY.

Olive, D. (2017). *Linear Regression.* Springer, New York, NY.

Pena, D., Tiao, G. C., and Tsay, R. S., editors (2001). *A course in time series analysis.* Wiley, Hoboken, NJ.

Powers, D. M. W. (2011). Evaluation: From precision, recall and f-measure to ROC, informedness, markedness & correlation. *Journal of Machine Learning Technologies*, 2(1):37Ű63.

Ross, S. (2012a). *A First Course in Probability.* Pearson, 9th edition.

Ross, S. M. (2012b). *Simulation.* Academic Press, 5th edition.

Sebestyen, G. S. (1962). Pattern recognition by an adaptive process of sample set construction. *IRE Transactions on Information Theory*, 8(5):82–91.

Sharpe, W. F. (1964). Capital asset prices: A theory of market equilibrium under conditions of risk. *The Journal of Finance*, 19(3):425–442.

Thorndike, R. L. (1953). Who belongs in the family? *Psychometrika*, 18(4):267–276.

Tsay, R. (2005). *Analysis of Financial Time Series.* Wiley, Hoboken, NJ, 2nd edition.

Venables, W. and Ripley, B. (2002). *Modern Applied Statistics with S.* Springer, New York, NY, 4th edition.

Weisberg, S. (2013). *Applied Linear Regression.* Wiley, Hoboken, NJ, 4th edition.

Werner, G. and Modlin, C. (2010). Basic ratemaking. Casualty Actuarial Society.

Index

Index of R Functions